Presidential Leadership and Civil Rights Policy

Recent Titles in
Contributions in Political Science

PRESIDENTIAL LEADERSHIP AND CIVIL RIGHTS POLICY

EDITED BY
James W. Riddlesperger, Jr.
and Donald W. Jackson

Prepared under the auspices of the Policy Studies Organization
Stuart S. Nagel, Publications Coordinator

Contributions in Political Science, Number 356

Greenwood Press
Westport, Connecticut • London

Library of Congress Cataloging-in-Publication Data

Presidential leadership and civil rights policy / edited by James W.
    Riddlesperger, Jr. and Donald W. Jackson.
        p.   cm.—(Contributions in political science, ISSN 0147–1066 ; no. 356)
    "Prepared under the auspices of the Policy Studies Organization."
    Includes bibliographical references and index.
    ISBN 0–313–29624–3 (alk. paper)
        1. Civil rights—United States.   2. Executive power—United
    States.   I. Riddlesperger, James W.   II. Jackson, Donald Wilson.
    III. Policy Studies Organization.   IV. Series.
    JC599.U5P74   1995
    323'.0973—dc20   95–5268

British Library Cataloguing in Publication Data is available.

Library of Congress Catalog Card Number: 95–5268
ISBN: 0–313–29624–3
ISSN: 0147–1066

First published in 1995

Greenwood Press, 88 Post Road West, Westport, CT 06881
An imprint of Greenwood Publishing Group, Inc.

Printed in the United States of America

The paper used in this book complies with the
Permanent Paper Standard issued by the National
Information Standards Organization (Z39.48–1984).

10   9   8   7   6   5   4   3   2   1

Contents

Figures and Tables

FIGURES

TABLES

Introductory Comments

—————————————— JAMES W. RIDDLESPERGER, JR. AND
DONALD W. JACKSON

With *Brown v. Board of Education of Topeka* as the symbolic starting point, forty years have passed since the modern Civil Rights Era began. Most scholars of that era would not focus on the American presidency as the crucial institutional arena for fighting civil rights battles. Instead, they would give equal billing to federal courts and to leaders of the Civil Rights Movement who first sought the courts as their chosen arenas. From the mid-1960s, the analysis would include Congress as well, but, to a large extent, the presidency would be considered only sporadically for its institutional contribution to civil rights policy accomplishments. In fact, some might argue that it was only between 1964 and 1968 that presidential leadership made key contributions to progress in civil rights.

However, the relation between the American presidency and civil rights policy needs study as much for contributions presidents have *not* made (or sometimes for presidential opposition to pro–civil rights initiatives) as for what presidents have done to further civil rights. With the presidency at the center of policymaking during modern times, and civil rights as a perennial domestic policy issue during that time, studying the presidential role is important.

The chapters presented here represent a range of views of the organizing theme of the book—the role presidents have played in civil rights policy in the last five decades. The Brown, Stern, and Jackson and Riddlesperger chapters take the traditional view that presidents have been relatively passive and reactive with respect to civil rights policy. The Shull and Ringelstein, Cohen, and Lamb and Twombly chapters suggest a more active presidential leadership role. Detlefsen and King, Riddlesperger, and Wasby take a middle position in arguing that while presidents may sometimes play an active role, much of what happens remains beyond their control. Shull and Gleiber show a more complex view of presidential leadership across stages of the policy process.

The chapters also vary in their conclusions about the various presidents' interest in and positive or negative orientations toward civil rights issues. Presidents Johnson and Reagan are usually characterized, respectively, as liberal and conservative activists, while portraits of Eisenhower, Kennedy, and Nixon are not so consistent. Stern paints Ike as lukewarm toward civil rights, while a more positive commitment is portrayed by King and Riddlesperger. Likewise, Nixon emerges as a president with little commitment to civil rights in Shull and Ringelstein's chapter while he is depicted as somewhat more favorable to civil rights initiatives by Detlefsen. Jackson and Riddlesperger demonstrate that Kennedy's commitment seems to have changed even during his presidency. But as King and Riddlesperger suggest, such apparent differences may simply reflect the different policy contexts on which the various authors focus.

Most of the chapters suggest that similarities and differences among presidents often transcend partisan political identities. For example, both moderate Republican Eisenhower and liberal Democrat Kennedy were forced by events to uphold the rule of law in much the same manner, while Lyndon Johnson supported civil rights initiatives more aggressively than other Democratic presidents. Of course, context may once again be a key factor.

The chapters also differ in methods and in sources of data. The contributions of Brown, Detlefsen, Wasby, Stern, and Jackson and Riddlesperger represent qualitative, historical, and conceptual analysis, while the rest utilize a quantitative approach. Sources include presidential library and agency archives, State of the Union Addresses, other public statements, survey data, and congressional voting records. Finally, the chapters are grouped according to their treatment of relationships among institutions and among various political actors—all the way from individual presidents to ordinary citizens.

THE PUBLIC, THE PRESIDENT, AND CIVIL RIGHTS

The three studies presented here assess the relationship between the president and mass publics relative to civil rights. Jeffrey Cohen's chapter examines the policy agendas of both the public and presidents on civil rights, evaluating the conventional wisdom that has argued that most presidents have had only a limited and reactive role in civil rights. His data suggest, in contrast, that recent presidents have been important in altering the public's agenda relative to civil rights, but that these presidents have not responded strongly to public opinion on civil rights. One important point is that Cohen (and others) cast civil rights policy as a "discretionary" subject for presidential attention, while "required" policies such as the state of the economy always appear on presidential address agendas.

To test these hypotheses Cohen examines presidents' State of the Union Addresses from 1953 to 1989. His measure is the percentages of sentences in such addresses devoted to civil rights policy. Not surprisingly, he finds that President Johnson's references to civil rights were well above the average. Unexpectedly, however, President Bush's 1989 Address contained almost twice as many references as Johnson's average over the course of his presidency. However, Cohen finds that civil rights only achieved notable significance three times in the thirty-seven State of the Union Addresses covered by the study—a conclusion that is consistent with the special concern about presidential indifference to civil rights raised in Ronald Brown's study.

Accepting the point that presidents may affect public interest and influence public opinion on civil rights issues, Steven Shull and Albert Ringelstein assess the differences in presidential communications between actual civil rights policy-relevant content, on the one hand, and symbolic rhetoric, on the other. Their data come from communications contained in the Public Papers of the Presidents of the United States from Eisenhower through Bush.

The authors show that Presidents Johnson, Carter, Bush, and Reagan were highly attentive to civil rights, but with significant distinctions among them. Reagan showed a surprisingly high level of rhetorical support for civil rights, but his support was largely symbolic, for he was lowest of all on policy-specific references. And consistent with Cohen's finding, Bush was the president most attentive to civil rights, but his attentiveness was that of a conservative activist, particularly in his opposition to "quotas." Johnson and Carter, in contrast, expressed policy-specific positive support for civil rights initiatives. Democratic presidents displayed more attentiveness to civil rights than Republicans, and Democrats were more policy-specific, while Republicans used more symbolism. So Cohen's overall conclusion that presidents do have an impact on civil rights public opinion is here further enhanced by the showing that individual presidents and their partisan and policy orientations sometimes are issue specific.

Ronald Brown's essay places the preceding two chapters in their proper historical context and suggests that in the long run the external course of events has done far more to command presidential attention to civil rights (and sometimes even to produce strong action) than would have come from the presidents' own personal inclinations. Excepting Lincoln, and possibly some rather tentative steps taken by FDR and Truman, any serious study of presidents and civil rights policy usually begins with Eisenhower. Brown argues that in the post–Civil War era, presidential leadership has been the story of avoidance, whenever possible, and reluctant and timid progress, when necessary. Brown shows that Eisenhower's attention to civil rights was stimulated by events largely beyond his control and suggests that even Kennedy and Johnson favored civil rights only to the extent that those issues could be pursued consistent with their own political interests. And taking the points made by Cohen and by Shull and Ringelstein, both Presidents Reagan and Bush were prone to symbolic rhetoric, which sometimes involved responding to white backlash against civil rights policies.

INSTITUTIONS, THE PRESIDENT, AND CIVIL RIGHTS

The next three chapters focus on policy-relevant presidential relationships with other governmental institutions: with Congress, with two executive agencies (the Departments of Justice and Labor) and promulgation of executive orders, and with the "triangle" composed of the presidency, Congress, and the federal courts.

James King and James Riddlesperger contrast the efforts of Presidents Eisenhower and Johnson, through Eisenhower's efforts to secure passage of the Civil Rights Act of 1957 and through Johnson's efforts in favor of the Voting Rights Act of 1965. Their method is to examine the differences between the expected level of overall support for presidents and the actual levels of support by Congressmen on civil rights roll call votes. One notable finding is that, relative to the different content of their proposals and to the changed nature of the times in which they served, Eisenhower and Johnson were similarly successful, despite their quite distinctive leadership styles. Their conclusion—contrary to much of the literature on the presidency—is that presidential legislative leadership must be highly contextual, rather than involving a single fixed model for success.

The enforcement of affirmative action policies through presidential executive orders is the subject of Robert Detlefsen's chapter. Originating during the Kennedy years, but significantly expanded by President Johnson, Executive Order No. 11246 directed the Department of Labor to implement an equal opportunity mandate, which it eventually did through its Office of Federal Contract Compliance Programs (OFCCP). However, according to Detlefsen, the Nixon administration amended OFCCP guidelines to suggest that equal employment opportunity required group parity or proportionality within particular job lines of federal contractors. The balance of Detlefsen's chapter analyzes the ways that partisans within the Reagan administration attempted to revise federal guidelines on Executive Order No. 11246.

Reagan typically delegated responsibility to Attorney General Edwin Meese and his assistants within the Department of Justice. They wanted to remove any suggestion of numerical goals, "quotas," or timetables from the guidelines used to implement 11246, but their efforts were opposed by the then-Secretary of Labor, William Brock, and by the OFCCP. Detlefsen's most interesting point is not that Labor eventually prevailed (though it did). Instead, he suggests that it was the converging interests of equal employment personnel professionals within affected potential large contractors and the interests of large contractors themselves (in avoiding both uncertainty and competition from smaller rivals, who might not be covered by the guidelines) that determined the Reagan administration's defeat. His key finding is that presidential leadership (or even leadership delegated to cabinet-level officials) may not prevail in the hurly-burly politics that often occur at the final stages of detailed policy implementation.

The point that bureaucracies sometimes prevail, even against change-oriented presidential administrations, or against entrenched interests, leads us proximately to the third chapter in this section, Stephen Wasby's reformulation of imagery of "iron triangles."[1] Wasby's chapter discusses first a policy triangle formed by the Supreme Court, Congress, and the president; and second, a policy "diamond" with interest groups as the fourth participant. He argues that as the purposes of each corner of the governmental triangle change, the relationships between them change as well, with the consequence that strategies of interest groups must be adjusted to the transformations of purposes and relationships to succeed within the triangle. One problem is that extant triangles become so familiar—and observers become so accustomed to them—that it can be difficult for us to perceive the transformations that have already occurred and to apply that thinking accordingly.

Wasby proceeds to demonstrate the transformations that have occurred in civil rights since the 1960s and 1970s. He also focuses on the "flip-flops" on civil rights that have happened as one administration has been succeeded by another. His conclusion: neither statics nor constancy should be the normal expectations for civil rights policy.

POLICY ARENAS, THE PRESIDENT, AND CIVIL RIGHTS

The remaining chapters address the changing policy arenas within civil rights. Mark Stern reviews civil rights confrontations that Presidents Eisenhower and Kennedy were forced to confront during their presidencies and federalism issues that were associated with them. His beginning point is that crises often propel public policy in a quite unforeseen and nonincremental manner. He suggests that both the integration of Little Rock Central High School and the admission of James Meredith to the University of Mississippi were such crises. Toward the end of his chapter he reflects on Burke Marshall's 1964 lectures on federalism and civil rights and suggests that the Second "Reconstruction"[2] occurred when Eisenhower and Kennedy were forced, within a span of less than five years, to demonstrate that federal troops would be used to overcome Southern resistance to integration. Some scholars might suggest that federalism had become only an excuse for federal inaction on civil rights, rather than a limitation on federal power since 1937 (when a majority of the Supreme Court rejected dual federalism), but whenever the transformation occurred, the result was predictably the same.

Donald Jackson and James Riddlesperger begin by reviewing the literature on the presidency of John F. Kennedy. Taking a fresh look at the archival material available in the Kennedy library, they argue that a careful assessment of Kennedy can conclude that in balancing civil rights with other arenas, Kennedy wished to pursue a "go slow" approach to civil rights. In that context, the limits on national government power associated with federalism became a convenient crutch. Kennedy's commitment to civil rights was initially quite pro forma, taking on a greater intensity only after the Birmingham riots of 1963.

Charles Lamb and Jim Twombly show that the "Second Reconstruction" itself could be reconstructed, although, to be sure, only for certain limited purposes. They analyze the Reagan administration's success in employing the "New Federalism" to shift fair housing complaints from the federal to state and local agencies for disposition.

They examine the impact of the Reagan administration's implementation of its Fair Housing Assistance Program on housing complaints filed under Title VII. For the first ten years under the 1968 Fair Housing Act, Title VII was not implemented so as to diminish the federal role in processing fair housing complaints. However, after the Carter administration's 1978 Fair Housing Assistance Program, the Reagan administration accomplished a significant shift of cases from HUD to state and local agencies for disposition. Whether that transfer resulted in less stringent enforcement remains to be determined by future research, but Lamb and Twombly's suggestion that some states may have been less aggressive in fair housing enforcement than the federal government raises an interesting question. Have the policy triangles been so transformed that several states may now be more aggressive in fair housing enforcement than the federal government was under Reagan and Bush? Wasby's chapter suggests the possibility of such a transformation, and we must be alert to such changes.

Finally, Steven Shull and Dennis Gleiber show that presidential performance in civil rights can vary from one stage of the policy process to the next. Their analysis focuses on two concepts: policy process and presidential influence. Dividing policy into four stages—agenda setting, formulation-modification, adoption, and implementation—and analyzing sources of presidential influence, they show the complexity of the relationship between the president and civil rights policy. Presidential involvement in civil rights varies from stage to stage in the process, and in its influence. They conclude that persuasion and partisan strength of presidents are important throughout the policy process, and that popular prestige is a conditional variable.

The contributors to this book show the complexity of assessing the role of the presidency in civil rights policymaking, requiring the consideration of the context of leadership rather than a static analysis of the presidential role. Presidents react to public opinion realities, shaping their leadership not primarily by their personal commitments but rather according to their perception of political realities. Thus, the understanding of presidential leadership in civil rights—and perhaps all policy arenas—is dependent on their understandings of public moods, institutional arrangements, and policy environments.

Civil rights policy itself is also fluid. The history of civil rights since *Brown v. Board* encompasses the professional lives of many of the scholars who currently follow civil rights policy. One consequence is that what once were striking initiatives are now familiar—and sometimes viewed as part of the normal and expected order. The collapse of the Soviet Union and the renewal of ethnic nationalism should caution us against blithely confusing the familiar with the inevitable. The chapters in this book, taken together, teach that progress can be slow, and that accomplishments depend on the constant reassessment of changing political environments.

NOTES

1. The traditional "iron triangle" consists of the alliance forged by the persistent contacts among particular governmental agencies, specialized legislative subcommittees, and affected interest groups.

2. A phrase most prominently associated with Carl Brauer's 1977 book, *John F. Kennedy and the Second Reconstruction.* (New York: Columbia University Press).

PART I

The Public, the President, and Civil Rights

1

Presidents, Public Opinion, and Civil Rights: An Agenda-Setting Perspective

JEFFREY E. COHEN

Other than Lyndon Johnson, presidents have been characterized as minor and reactive players in civil rights policy (Shull, 1989). Both Eisenhower and Kennedy were slow to take action on civil rights until events forced them to do so (Stern, 1989a, 1989b, 1992). All of the post-Johnson presidents, save Carter, are commonly described either as having neglected civil rights or as having pursued policies that reversed the direction of the Johnson civil rights policies (Jones, 1992; Shull, 1993). And Carter, who ran on a promise to elevate civil rights' place on the nation's policy agenda, was later criticized for ignoring civil rights, as the economy and the energy crisis pushed civil rights into the policy background.

Thus the president's role in civil rights policy is viewed as limited and reactive (Shull, 1989; Morgan, 1970). In their major theoretical work, Carmines and Stimson (1989) hardly see a role for the president in the evolution of civil rights issues. Page and Petracca (1983: 330) write this about presidents and civil rights: "[F]or presidents, public opinion must mostly be taken as a given, and as an impetus for action. . . . [P]residents articulated and acted upon demands that came from elsewhere." Leadership in civil rights policy making has been credited to the Supreme Court, Congress, and interest groups, not the president.

Such a view is predicated on a narrow reading of presidential action in civil rights, focusing on the latter stages of the public policymaking process, such as policy formulation, legitimation, and implementation (Jones, 1984; Bullock and Lamb, 1984). In this chapter, I demonstrate that presidents are important actors in the civil rights policy area through their ability to alter the public's agenda. By influencing the public agenda, presidents become important, if subtle, actors in the development of civil rights policy.

Ironically, I will also demonstrate that presidents are not responsive to public opinion on civil rights. This lack of responsiveness belies the reactive theory of presidential involvement in civil rights. At the agenda-setting stage, presidents lead, but do not follow the public in civil rights. The distinction between discretionary and required policy types (Walker, 1977) helps explain this asymmetry in presidential-public impact on each other. In the next section I present a general theory of presidential–public opinion interactions in the agenda-setting process.

PRESIDENTS, PUBLIC OPINION, AND PROBLEM AGENDAS

There are four major components to the model presented here: (1) characteristics of public thinking about public problems, (2) public expectations of the president, (3) presidential incentives, resources and behaviors, and (4) problem type.

Public Attention and Problem Type

Several characteristics describe public opinion with regard to public problems. First, the public can only attend to a few policy problems at one time (Baungarnter and Jones, 1992). The public's attentiveness to problems is thus constrained, selective, and serial. Second, public attention is easily diverted from one problem to another as objective conditions, scandals, accidents, and other high-publicity "events" appear. Attention may also be diverted as the public tires of a problem and as "issue attention cycle" dynamics set in (Downs, 1972). An underlying instability characterizes public attention to policy problems, and the many problems that exist must compete for the public's attention.

Some types of problems have, however, an easier time gaining and maintaining public attention than others. Walker (1977) and others (e.g., Kessel, 1974) term these "required" problems. Required problems are relatively persistent on the public's agenda, move onto that agenda relatively easily, and can restrict the access of other issues onto the agenda. Moreover, government usually has an institutionalized response to required problems, such as the annual budget and government agencies. Two policy areas, economic policy and foreign policy problems that raise questions of war and peace, are usually considered to be the key required problems on the public's agenda.

Civil rights is not a required problem. Rather, it has been characterized as discretionary (Shull, 1993). Discretionary problems, over the long haul, take a back seat to required ones. They have to fight harder to gain and maintain public attention and are easily pushed off of the public's problem agenda. The distinguishing characteristic of required versus discretionary problems is the easy access that required problems have to the public's agenda and the relative ease with which required problems can stay on the public's agenda in contrast to discretionary ones. Required and discretionary problems also evoke different public expectations of the president and place different incentives on the chief executive's behavior.

Public Expectations of the President and Problem Type

Public expectations are varied, often contradictory, and sometimes hard to fulfill (Cronin, 1980; Edwards, 1983; Wayne, 1982; Brace and Hinckley, 1992). The public expects the president to both lead and respond to the public's problem agenda. When the public feels strongly about a problem, it expects a presidential response. A response demonstrates that the president is behaving in a democratic manner, that he is listening to the people, and that there is a measure of democratic control over government.

The public also expects presidential leadership on policy problems. When the president talks about a problem, he signals that it has national significance. The public uses the president to sort important from unimportant problems. In Iyengar and Kinder's (1987) social psychology language, the president acts as a problem "primer." But presidential leadership also comforts the public, indicating that someone is in charge or ready to take charge of important national problems. The psychological distress that sets in when a policy problem is raised may be eased when presidents assume this leadership role (Edelman, 1964).

Public expectations may vary by problem type. While the public expects presidential action on all national problems, greater weight is given to required problems. Thus, (re)election and popularity implications are greater for required problems than discretionary ones. Administrations are more likely to be turned out of office (and their popularity ratings likely to plummet) if the economy is souring and/or a war is going on too long, than for any other problem. Other problems may fester and deteriorate without having such profound impact on the presidency.

Presidential Incentives and Behaviors

These facts of public opinion and public expectations form the public environment in which the president must act. They also structure the incentives for certain types of presidential activities. The president recognizes that the public expects him to act on problems that they deem important. His failure to do so may have negative popularity and/or electoral implications. Decreased popularity may harm his legislative program in Congress (Brace and Hinckley, 1992). At the same time, the president brings his own legislative or policy agenda to government. Much of that agenda may differ from the public's agenda. Mere responsiveness to public opinion not only undermines the public expectation for leadership, but limits the president's ability to move his agenda through Congress.

The president also recognizes that he possesses key leadership resources, such as access to the mass media, lack of competition from Congress and other elites to lead public opinion, and public readiness for his leadership. By taking advantage of these leadership resources, the president may be able to move public opinion such that its problem agenda comes to more closely resemble his.

Type of policy problem affects presidential responsiveness to and leadership of public opinion. Required policy areas and problems are relatively stable on the public's agenda. In setting the public's agenda on required problems, the president has strong competitors, such as the impact of these required problems on the lives of ordinary citizens, the news media, and attitudes rooted in experience.

Presidents do not face such competition when it comes to discretionary problems. The public needs "priming" (Iyengar and Kinder, 1987) to attend to a discretionary problem. The president may act as this primer due to his leadership resources (media access, etc.) and the fact that few other factors can play this role. Thus, presidential leadership prospects appear quite strong for discretionary problems.

In contrast, presidents do not possess much reason to follow the public on discretionary problems, unlike required ones. Discretionary problems, by their nature, are easily pushed out of the public's view. Being so unstable, they lack the popularity and electoral implications that required problems possess. Second, they occupy space on the public agenda that the president might prefer for his other agenda items. Thus, the president has an incentive to try to push these discretionary problems off of the public's agenda.

This theoretical outline suggests the following hypotheses concerning the relationship between the president's and the public's civil rights agendas:

HO1)   Presidents will be able to lead public opinion on civil rights. As presidential attention to civil rights increases, so will the public's.

HO2)   Presidents will not be responsive to public opinion on civil rights. Increased public attention to civil rights will not affect presidential attention to civil rights.

These hypotheses suggests a relationship between the president and the public on civil rights that differs strongly from the traditional view of presidents as reactive and minor actors in the civil rights policy arena. The next section presents data on presidential attention to civil rights policy, followed by tests of these hypotheses.

MEASURING PRESIDENTIAL ATTENTION TO CIVIL RIGHTS

I construct a measure of presidential policy problem emphasis by counting the number of sentences in presidents' State of the Union Addresses that refer to civil rights. Dividing by the total number of sentences that make any policy reference in a single speech gives us the percentage of policy sentences that focus on civil rights, a measure of the relative importance of civil rights to the president compared to all policy areas. This content analysis is performed on all State of the Union Addresses from 1953 through 1989.

The State of the Union Address is a good choice for determining presidential problem emphasis. Light (1982) argues persuasively that the Address not only presents the first look at the president's program, but that it also suggests the outline of presidential priorities (see also Kessel, 1974). It is eagerly awaited for information on what direction the administration will take in the upcoming year, and it has become institutionalized and routinized, making it comparable over the years.

The coding scheme employed here weights sentences equally. This assumes that each policy area has the probability of being mentioned in direct proportion to its importance to the president. Thus, as civil rights policy assumes greater importance, its probability of being mentioned will increase. Aggregating across sentences gives us a fair representation of the president's relative attention to civil rights policy.

Figure 1.1 presents a plot for the presidential series (minimum = 0%, maximum = 18%, mean = 6%, standard deviation = 5%). Presidents differ in their levels of symbolic attention to civil rights policy. On average, 5.9% of Eisenhower's sentences referred to civil rights, compared to 2.0% for Kennedy, 9.0% for Johnson, 6.2% for Nixon, 9.4% for Ford, 1.6% for Carter, 5.4% for Reagan, and 18.25% for Bush (1989 only).

Civil rights accounts for a significant proportion of the president's agenda three times (1968, 1976, 1989), though it never receives more than 20 percent of any one Address. On several occasions it fails even to attain presidential agenda status (1959, 1977, 1980, 1981), underscoring its discretionary nature.

We can contrast this pattern to that for the required areas of economic policy and international affairs. Foreign affairs and the economy always reach the agenda. The only exception relates to Nixon's addresses of 1969 and 1971.[1] Excluding the two Nixon Addresses that underplayed foreign affairs, we find that foreign policy always occupies at least 10 percent of the president's attention, and on the average accounts for 40 percent of

Figure 1.1
Presidential Attention to Civil Rights, 1953–1989

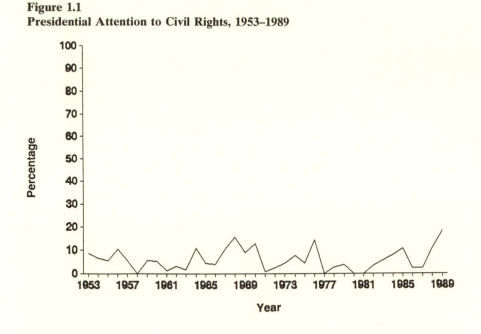

the problem agenda, nearly seven times the space given to civil rights. Economic policy is not quite so dominant, but still never fails to occupy at least 5 percent of the space in the Address, and on average occupies one-fourth of it, which is four times the space given to civil rights.

Sometimes economics or foreign policy are so important that they dominate the agenda, as illustrated in Table 1.1. For instance, six times foreign policy held 60 percent or more of the space on the president's Address (1958, 1961, 1962, 1963, 1966, 1980), while the economy held over one-half of the agenda twice (1973, 1981). Never does civil rights top 20 percent of the president's agenda. Together, foreign policy and the economy account for nearly two-thirds of the president's State of the Union Address on the average, demonstrating their power to attract and hold presidential attention. All other policy areas, including civil rights, must fight for the remainder.

PRESIDENTIAL LEADERSHIP OF PUBLIC OPINION ON CIVIL RIGHTS

Unlike past research, which generally downplays the role of the president in civil rights policymaking, this chapter, utilizing an agenda-setting focus on discretionary policy areas, suggests that presidents should affect the public's civil rights agenda. That is, presidents may lead opinion on civil rights.

Table 1.1
Descriptive Statistics for Presidential Economic, Foreign, and Civil Rights Policy Emphasis (in percentages)

Policy	Minimum	Maximum	Mean	SD
Economic	4.73	62.56	26.30	12.52
Foreign	10.90	85.98	40.74	18.37
Civil Rights	.00	18.18	6.00	4.66

Presidential capability to influence public opinion derives from his paramount position in the public's eye, his monopolization of the public space (Miroff, 1988), media attention, and public reliance on his leadership, especially in discretionary policy areas.

By their very nature, discretionary issues have a difficult time attaining agenda status. Therefore, the power of the president to focus attention should stimulate a stronger public reaction for discretionary than for required policy areas. On required issues, the public is already primed (Iyengar and Kinder, 1987). The president may be both primer and director on discretionary issues.

Our basic guiding hypothesis is that the more emphasis the president gives to civil rights, the more important that policy area becomes to the public. To test this hypothesis, we use the first public opinion reading from the Gallup "Most Important Problem" series, after the president has given his Address, and use the presidential attention series to predict the public opinion series.

However, the public is not dependent solely on the president in deciding to pay attention to civil rights. Other factors may also influence public concern. In particular, deterioration in the objective conditions of the economy and the international scene should push civil rights off of the public's agenda (Behr and Iyengar, 1985; Iyengar and Kinder, 1987; MacKuen, 1981).

Missing from this analysis are mass-media effects. A substantial literature has documented the impact of the mass-media on the public agenda using the Gallup "Most Important Problem" series (Funkhouser, 1973; MacKuen, 1981; Behr and Iyengar, 1985; Iyengar and Kinder, 1987). I do not include mass-media effects for the following reasons. First is the sheer magnitude of collecting mass-media data for this time series. Other studies employ shorter series (*e.g.*, Behr and Iyengar, 1985; MacKuen, 1981). Second, as the Behr-Iyengar results show, both media and presidential variables affect public opinion, and they appear to affect public opinion independently. Not including media effects, while underspecifying the model, should not affect the impact of the presidential variables on public opinion.

Table 1.2 presents regression results of the impact of presidential attention and objective conditions on the public's attention to civil rights. An AR1 estimation is used to correct for first-order correlation, which diagnostics indicated. Both significantly affect public concern. The estimation proved to be very powerful, with over 50% of the variance explained.

Specifically, each 1% increase in presidential attention to civil rights leads to a nearly .7% increase in public attention. Objective factor trade-offs are also apparent. Neither war nor inflation seems to divert attention from civil rights, but unemployment does so strongly. Each 1% increase in the unemployment rate reduces attention to civil rights by 1.5%, a massive impact.

These results are subject to one major threat, that the presidential effects are merely mediating prior public opinion. To control for this possibility, I added the public's civil rights ratings from the latest poll prior to the presidential Address. While introducing this control mutes the effects of presidential variables, presidential leadership of public opinion remains strong and significant (Table 1.2). Each 1% increase in presidential attention now moves public opinion a still-hefty .5%. Unemployment's impact decreases from 1.5% to .9% for each 1% change in the unemployment rate. Prior public attentiveness also strongly affects later public attentiveness: each 1% increase in public civil rights attention leads to a .57% increase in later public civil rights attention. The overall power of the equation also improves with the addition of the prior public opinion variable: the R^2 moves from .51 to .81.

Still, the important point is that presidential leadership of public opinion on civil rights is detected, is statistically significant, and persists in the face of statistical controls. Contrary to the pure reactive theory of presidential involvement in civil rights, presidents may play a leadership role—they help set the public's civil rights agenda. The reactive theory also suggests that presidents will react to public concern over civil rights. The agenda-setting theory offered here suggests the opposite. The next section tests that hypothesis.

PRESIDENTIAL RESPONSIVENESS TO PUBLIC OPINION

How responsive is the president to public concern with civil rights? The reactive theory suggests that the president will be strongly responsive to public opinion on civil rights matters. In contrast, the agenda-setting theory developed here suggests otherwise. I use the percentage citing civil

Table 1.2
Determinants of Public Attention to Civil Rights, 1953–1989

Variable	b	SE	t	b	SE	t
Constant	12.73	6.26	2.04	5.18	3.24	1.60
Inflation	-.35	.38	-.92	-.03	.17	-.18
Unemployment	-1.52	.90	-1.69	-.88	.46	-1.92
War	1.43	3.01	.47	.26	1.50	.17
President's Civil Rights Attention	.67	.27	2.48	.50	.16	3.04
Pub. Opinion $_{t-1}$	----			.57	.07	7.67
R^2/Adj.R^2	.51	/ .44	AR1	.81	/ .78	AR1

rights from last reading prior to the president's State of the Union Address from the Gallup "Most Important Problem" series to predict presidential attention to civil rights. The impact of the public opinion reading on the president's level of attention is used to test the presidential responsiveness hypothesis. I also control for other influences on presidential attention to civil rights.

First, objective conditions may affect presidential attention to civil rights. The most important objective conditions relate to the economy and foreign affairs, the areas not only of greatest concern to the mass public, but also the policy areas for which the public holds the president most responsible. Thus, when the economy or the international scene are deteriorating, presidents may be unable to avoid attending to them. Consequently, presidential attention to civil rights should decline in the presence of a deteriorating economy and/or international situation, as problems in those "required" policy areas deflect public attention away from discretionary policy areas. The level of inflation, unemployment, and the presence of war are used as indicators of the economy and the international scene.

Moreover, when presidents are more interested in the required areas, no matter their objective states, attention to discretionary areas should ebb. Thus, the greater the percentage of sentences in the president's Address referring to either the economy or international affairs, the less the president will attend to civil rights.

Third, the election cycle may also affect presidential attention to civil rights (Kessel, 1974, 1977). During election periods presidents focus on building their electoral coalitions. This should affect presidential attention to civil rights, as presidents offer civil rights policies to interested coalition elements. Thus, attention to civil rights should increase in the fourth year of the presidential cycle. Moreover, attention may stay high in the initial post-election year as presidents reaffirm the commitment made during the election campaign. However, the rotation in office of presidents and presidential parties may mute this effect, as new presidents may not feel bound by the promises that their predecessors made.

Table 1.3 presents results of the regression analysis of public opinion, objective conditions, presidential policy attention to economics and foreign policy, and election cycles on presidential attention to civil rights policy. Diagnostics indicated the presence of first-order autocorrelation, which was corrected with an AR1 estimation procedure.

First, the contention that presidents will pay little attention to public concerns for discretionary policy areas is supported. We observe no significant presidential responsiveness to public opinion for civil rights. The regression coefficient is a tiny .02, and its t-value is a paltry .30. Each 1% change in public opinion moves presidential attention a mere and imperceptible .02%.

But objective conditions, presidential attention to required policy, and election cycles all affect presidential attention to civil rights. Specifically, each 1% increase in presidential attention to foreign policy reduces presidential attention to civil rights by about .8%. However, attention to economic policy exhibits no impact. Also as expected, unemployment reduces presidential attention to civil rights. Each 1% increase in unemployment reduces presidential attentiveness to civil rights by nearly .9%, but inflation and war demonstrate no impact. Thus both required policy areas affect presidential attention to civil rights, though through different routes.

Lastly, civil rights displays classic election year dynamics. Presidents pay more attention to civil rights during the (re)election, fourth year in office, a 3% increase. Presidents may be playing campaign politics with civil rights, using civil rights rhetoric to attract voters. But the first year of each term shows no impact on civil rights attention, perhaps because of the lack of commitment effect noted above.

CONCLUSIONS

This chapter began with the observation that most studies of presidential involvement in civil rights view the president as a minor actor, often only reacting rather slowly and reluctantly to forceful events. Such a theory is used to explain Eisenhower's slowness to take action in the Little Rock incident and Kennedy's reluctance to intercede in civil rights matters until violence had erupted. In both cases, events forced the presidents' hands.

This study challenges that view, at least when looking at the agenda-setting stage of the policy process. The fact that civil rights policy is a

Table 1.3
Determinants of the President's Emphasis on Civil Rights in His State of the Union Address, 1953–1989

Constant	13.54	4.57	2.96
Inflation	-.16	.20	-.77
Unemployment	-.91	.55	-1.64
War	.29	1.81	.16
Year 1	-1.62	1.73	-.94
Year 4	3.42	1.56	2.19
Public Opinion-Civil Rights	.02	.08	.30
President's Economic Policy Attention	.02	.08	.31
President's Foreign Policy Attention	-.08	.04	-1.96
R^2/Adj.R^2	.44	.27	AR1

discretionary policy area means that presidents may have considerable influence over whether or not the public is concerned about that policy area. However, because civil rights is discretionary, the president is less responsive to the public than they are to him. Rather, the state of the economy, presidential concern with the foreign policy, and reelection year politics determine presidential attention to civil rights. The economic and foreign policy impacts suggest the ability of required policy areas to push discretionary areas off of the agenda. The reelection year effect demonstrates the attempt by presidents to use civil rights for reelection and political purposes, perhaps in an attempt to convert an unusual, nagging, divisive, and problematic policy area into normal distributional, coalitional, and interest group politics. The greater point, though, of this study is the revision of the view of the president as a minimal actor in civil rights policymaking and of the considerable power that the president has to influence the public agenda.

NOTE

1. In 1969, outgoing President Johnson gave the State of the Union Address, not Nixon, the customary practice. However, it is also traditional for an incoming president to give a State of the Union-like speech early in his administration. Nixon did so on April 14, 1969, but that speech focused only on domestic affairs; foreign policy matters were not mentioned except in passing. In 1971, Nixon attempted to create a two-Address system, one for the foreign policy area and the other for all other areas, but only the domestic speech was televised with the fanfare of the typical State of the Union Address.

2

Presidential Rhetoric in Civil Rights Policymaking, 1953–1992

STEVEN A. SHULL
AND ALBERT C. RINGELSTEIN

INTRODUCTION

Although often submerged throughout American history, civil rights issues have never been far from the surface. Perhaps because of its highly emotional content, civil rights has varied in salience over time. Certainly in the modern era, civil rights emerged as a prominent public policy concern (Walker, 1977; Carmines and Stimson, 1989). Occasionally, it has been the most salient domestic policy area. Civil rights was particularly visible in the last two generations, evolving rapidly during the postwar period. Yet, salience increased in the 1960s and 1980s and decreased in the 1950s and 1970s (see *Gallup Opinion Index*). The 1990s and Bush's temperament initially seemed likely to diminish its importance on the government's agenda. However, civil rights controversies involving both those inside and outside government remained highly salient during the Bush administration.

The rhetoric in public communications by presidents is an important way to influence public policy. Research suggests that presidents can use such messages to set their own, if not always the broader government agenda (Shull, 1989: ch. 3; Light, 1982). Much of what appears on the subsequent government agenda probably can be traced to presidential rhetoric. Public messages give presidents the opportunity to set the stage for policy innovations, which usually come from the White House (Light, 1982; Redford, 1969; Kingdon, 1984; Shull, 1989). Communications provide an important opportunity for presidents to "go public" in a highly discretionary issue area like civil rights.

Presidents play a crucial role in shaping civil rights policy through their messages because only with presidential support are major and lasting policy changes likely. Such communications are particularly important early in the policymaking process. Some presidential rhetoric, especially in an emotionally charged policy area such as civil rights, may be more symbolic than substantive (Denton, 1982; Ragsdale, 1984: 971). Yet, even symbolism can have important policy consequences by focusing public attention on the problem. Symbolic or not, communications may help presidents obtain support for their policy preferences. Such preferences as expressed in public rhetoric are often helpful in resolving societal conflicts (Eyestone, 1978: 3; Lindblom, 1980: 4). Because civil rights is highly conflictual, presidential remarks may be more symbolic than those in other policy areas (Shull, 1989: ch. 3).

"Presidents are symbolic and political as well as programmatic leaders" (Fishel, 1985: 8). Symbols are an important leadership tool to reassure or persuade the public (Elder and Cobb, 1983: 13–15). Perhaps because of its emotional content, civil rights seems to be a policy area ripe for symbolic leadership by presidents (Kessel, 1984: 113; Elder and Cobb, 1983: 2–4). Presidential communications should reveal varying degrees of symbolism. Symbolism through public rhetoric, then, is a potential source of presidential leadership in civil rights.

Apart from individual president differences, political party differences in presidential communications should also occur. Because cooperation among actors on civil rights policy often occurs, some might think that such policies usually are bipartisan. Although not as partisan as economic policy, partisanship over civil rights is growing. A possible explanation for this phenomenon is that civil rights is now the most distinguishable feature of the parties (Carmines and Stimson, 1989). Such increasing partisanship and diffused support generally for civil rights could lead to increased conflict in the future.

This chapter compares the public rhetoric of presidents Eisenhower through Bush as found in *Public Papers of the Presidents*.[1] To place such remarks in perspective, we assess the degree of attention, support, and symbolic nature of modern presidential communications. Does presidential attention to civil rights represent policy support, or is it merely symbolic rhetoric? Such statements are arrayed according to individual presidents and parties and also by groups targeted and issue areas within civil rights. This latter concern should reveal divergent attention within groups and among subissues and tell us about the changing nature of civil rights policy content.

MODERN PRESIDENTS' PUBLIC RHETORIC

Presidential communications on civil rights suggest several avenues for empirical inquiry. Considerable variation in attention, support, and symbolism is anticipated in presidential rhetoric. Presidents giving greater attention to civil rights should also voice greater support (or opposition) in their communications than will presidents for whom civil rights is less salient. We expect high attention and consistent support or opposition (less symbolism) from Presidents Kennedy, Johnson, Carter, and Reagan especially. Relatively low attention and mixed support (high symbolism) should emerge from Eisenhower, Nixon, Ford, and Bush. Our hypothesis is that Reagan should be the most ideologically extreme president, making many statements, but usually not being highly supportive of government action. He also may have called for more legislative and judicial action than most presidents, but to constrain rather than advance governmental intervention.

At the polar extreme of our hypothesis is Johnson, who also gave considerable attention to civil rights; but he should be the opposite of Reagan, ranking low on symbolism by being more consistent in attention, support, and calls for action by others in government. Both Nixon's and Bush's statements should be highly symbolic, with only moderate levels of support, but the latter should exhibit less attention to civil rights. These expectations for individual presidents and for party policy orientations are expressed graphically in Table 2.1.

Nathaniel Beck (1982) and Samuel Kernell (1986: 223) believe that policy agendas vary more by administration than by party. Yet, we expect dramatic differences by presidential party (see Table 2.1). Democratic presidents should reveal greater levels of attention and support (liberalism) for civil rights overall, consistent with the literature on party differences on broad social policy (Wayne, 1978; Orfield, 1975; Bullock and Lamb, 1984: 200). Democrats should more vocally favor interventionist civil rights policies and be more supportive than Republican presidents (Shull, 1989). This greater Democratic support may be due to ideological reasons or perceptions that presidents are serving their coalitions. Democrats are seen frequently as the party of "inclusive compromise" and Republicans of "exclusive compromise" (Mayhew, 1966). Therefore, Democrats probably request more affirmative civil rights legislation and adjudication than do Republicans.

Presidential attention should also vary by target group and issue area. Although civil rights was initially seen only as a racial issue, it has expanded to other groups in society (*e.g.*, the aged, women, the disabled, Hispanics/Native Americans, etc.). Thus, "racial" issues (education and voting) should be emphasized less after the 1970s than in the 1950s and 1960s. The history of the subissues suggests more presidential interest in employment than in housing, perhaps because employment affects many groups (Rodgers and Bullock, 1972: 164–65; Lamb, 1984: 148, 188; *Congress and the Nation*, vol. 2: 350).

Ideologically committed presidents, especially Lyndon Johnson, proba-

Table 2.1
Expected Nature of Presidential Statements

	Characteristic		
	Attention	Support	Symbolism
President			
Eisenhower	Lo	Mod	Mod
Kennedy	Mod	Hi	Mod
Johnson	Hi	Hi	Lo
Nixon	Mod	Lo	Hi
Ford	Lo	Lo	Mod
Carter	Hi	Hi	Lo
Reagan	Hi	Lo	Hi
Bush	Mod	Mod	HI
Presidential Party			
Democrats	Hi	Hi	Lo
Republicans	Lo	Lo	Hi

bly spread their attention broadly across categorical groups and issue areas, while less ideological presidents, such as Richard Nixon, probably emphasize African Americans and education. Similarly, Democrats as a whole should be attentive to more target groups and issue areas than Republicans, who probably are more narrowly focused. Obviously, the changing nature of civil rights influences these presidential and party preferences, however.

MEASUREMENT

The content of all presidential speeches, press conferences, letters, and other public communications as recorded in *Public Papers of the Presidents of the United States* was analyzed for presidential attention, support, and symbolism. Presidential statements were located by using "key words" on civil rights selected from the extensive index included in the annual editions of the *Public Papers*.[2] Number of "items" refers to the number of separate documents mentioning civil rights issues.[3] Policy "statements," as opposed to merely vague remarks, were also identified from presidential communications (items).

The number of policy statements per year, like the number of items, indicates the changing level of presidential attention. Such statements can be of any length but must specifically advocate policy rather than simply being vague generalizations. The explicit statement is usually a sentence but supporting wording varies considerably and number of "lines" (a measure of relative attention) is also reported.[4]

In addition to attention, the research includes a measure of presidential support toward civil rights. Each policy statement was coded as supportive, nonsupportive, or neutral. Favoring policies sought by civil rights activists and minorities is an example of a supportive position. More specifically, support could include advocating legislation or litigation directed against segregation or racial discrimination, as well as seeking such remedial tools as busing or stronger enforcement of civil rights statutes. Supportive positions, then, favor increased government involvement to ensure equality and are equated with the "liberalness" of positions.[5]

These measures help tap the amount of attention and support in civil rights communications. Many scholars view civil rights as highly symbolic (see, for example, Shull, 1989; Elder and Cobb, 1983: 2–4). Civil rights may be a policy area containing ambiguous referents and emotional content, referred to by Edelman as "condensation symbols" (1964: 6–9). To be attentive, presidents must make frequent and lengthy statements. Support will be ideological if it is highly consistent (strongly liberal or conservative). Admittedly, symbolism is the most difficult concept to operationalize but relates to attention and support. Statements are symbolic if they contain many mentions without specific policy statements and, thus, are largely devoid of policy content. Statements are also symbolic if they are very brief and rarely call for tangible actions by Congress or the courts.

FINDINGS

Table 2.2 presents several indicators of presidential attention and support. The overall (mean) measure provides a baseline for the various comparisons. On the average, presidents mention civil rights (number of items) 48 times per year in office and support civil rights 80 percent of the time. However, many mentions of civil rights (items) do not contain policy statements (45%), and thus, communications appear highly symbolic. These findings suggest relatively greater support for than attention to civil rights, but with variation explained by different indicators and aggregations of the data. Attention, support, and symbolism vary considerably across presidents and parties.

Civil rights clearly is more salient for some presidents than others; it was salient to Reagan, as expected, and especially to Bush, contrary to expectation. Johnson and Carter also show high attention, but among these four highly attentive presidents Reagan had far fewer policy statements on a yearly basis and, especially, few items containing policy statements. Some support appears for our expectations, since percent of statements to items is low, but length of statements relative to their number is high (see Table 2.2). Johnson and Carter have the highest support for civil rights (l00% and 96% respectively). Thus, they score high on

Table 2.2
Presidential Attention and Support on Civil Rights

	# Items /Pres.	Policy Statements		Length Policy Statement		Supportive Statements
		#/Pres.	% in Items	# Lines /Pres.	Mean Lines /Statements	% Liberal
Mean						
	48	22	45	756	33	80
	By Party					
Dems	54	27	50	855	32	99
Reps	46	19	41	713	34	69
By President[a]						
Eisenhower	16	5	31	112	22	97
Kennedy	38	18	47	453	25	100
Johnson	60	31	52	775	25	100
Nixon	23	15	65	580	39	62
Ford	28	14	50	348	25	43
Carter	58	29	50	1257	43	96
Reagan	79	17	16	717	42	72
Bush	83	43	39	1807	43	71

a. The number of years for which data are available and upon which calculations are based are DDE = 8, JFK = 3, LBJ = 5, RMN = 5.5, GRF = 2.5, JEC = 4, RWR = 8, GHWB = 4.

attention and low on symbolism. Surprisingly, George Bush is the president *most* attentive to civil rights. Bush had by far the highest number of items and substantive policy statements per year. He also issued the most lines per year and, along with Carter, had the longest average statements among these eight modern presidents. George Bush was fairly conservative, ranking well below average in percent support overall and about average among Republican presidents.

The assertion of high symbolism for Reagan deserves further scrutiny, given his higher than expected support. His seeming high attention (number of items per year) suggests considerable symbolism, especially since he had by far the lowest percent of policy statements to items, and, as previously noted, had relatively short statements. Reagan shows greater rhetorical support for civil rights than anticipated. In fact, he was more supportive than Nixon, Ford, or Bush. Perhaps it follows that a degree of at least rhetorical support is a requisite even for conservative presidents who now must deal with many more highly politicized groups. Thus, on several (but not all) measures Reagan ranks highest on symbolism and Johnson ranks lowest, as expected.

George Bush was quite willing to make policy statements and lengthy ones at that; they were by far the longest statements on a yearly basis of *any* modern president. Thus, contrary to what many might think, Bush was not a moderate on civil rights; he was actually more activist and slightly more conservative than was Ronald Reagan, the president to whom some attribute the modern conservative revolution on civil rights. Certainly, the "kinder, gentler" Bush on civil rights does not appear during his term in office.

Table 2.2 also reveals dramatic differences by presidential party. Democrats show greater attention on all measures as anticipated. Because Republicans had fewer statements per item and briefer statements (number of lines per year), their remarks appear more symbolic than those of Democrats. A particularly dramatic difference is the 30 percentage points greater support in Democratic versus Republican statements. Thus, by being much more consistent in their ideological preferences, Democratic presidents also seem less symbolic (and more substantive) than their Republican counterparts in their public communications on civil rights.

Notice in Table 2.3 that very few calls for legislative or judicial action are made by presidents. The few legislative calls and even fewer judicial calls per year suggest a high degree of symbolism in civil rights statements. Twenty-eight percent of policy statements contain legislative calls, while very few contain calls for judicial action. Surprisingly, presidents ask for little from other branches in the civil rights realm.

There is a somewhat gradual increase in the tendency to call for legislation, while the pattern for judicial calls appears to be in the opposite direction after Ford (see Table 2.3). The "trend" in legislative calls probably reflects the expansion of the civil rights subissues as well as recognition by presidents that they must deal with an increasingly resurgent Congress (Sundquist, 1981; LeLoup and Shull, 1993). The reasons why presidents now ask less of the courts in civil rights is less clear, but the broadening of groups and issues may require comprehensive legislation rather than the case-by-case judicial approach.

Democrats equivocate less in calls for action than do Republicans. These results, and those in Table 2.2, confirm the much greater symbolism of Republicans' statements relative to those of Democrats. Republicans make less than half the number of legislative and less than one-tenth the judicial calls that Democrats make. Variation is also considerable by individual presidents. Carter made by far the most calls for legislation— three times the average yearly rate, while Eisenhower made the fewest legislative calls. Calls for judicial action also varied, with Ford making the most and Bush making the fewest (in fact, none).[6]

Most policy statements were categorizable into target groups and issue areas, but recall that multiple counts are allowed. Some policy statements were too general to categorize (see notes to Tables 2.4 and 2.5). These tables show the changing nature of civil rights. The data reveal considerable attention to African Americans as a target group (60 percent, but

Table 2.3
Calls for Legislative and Judicial Action[a]

	Legislative		Judicial	
	No.	No/Year	No.	No/Year
Mean				
	31	6.2	3.5	.7
By Party				
Democrats	39	9.8	4.7	1.2
Republicans	26	4.6	2.8	.1
By President				
Eisenhower	6	.8	2	.3
Kennedy	6	2.0	4	1.3
Johnson	38	7.6	9	1.8
Nixon	22	4.0	1	.2
Ford	9	4.1	6	2.7
Carter	73	18.3	1	.3
Reagan	62	7.8	5	.6
Bush	30	7.5	0	0

a. We were quite generous in coding calls for both legislative and judicial actions. All the president must do is say that he has proposed such action or take a position on existing actions. Reference to a particular legislative bill or court case counts (including constitutional amendments and measures already passed into law). Even general references to the Supreme Court are tabulated as calls for judicial action.

diminishing since Ford) and, thus, relatively less attention to other groups. This finding is consistent with expectations. Limited data on age and Hispanics/Native Americans (but increasing emphasis since Ford) complicate the analysis but still reveal differences by president.

Eisenhower provided relatively much greater attention to age discrimination than any other president, while Kennedy gave more relative attention to Hispanics (based upon only two policy statements in 1961) than any other president. Attention to African Americans increased in the 1960s under Johnson. His two Republican successors, Nixon and, particularly, Ford, continued this trend. Carter and Reagan distributed their attention much more widely, but they were also more interested in the plight of women than was Johnson. This pattern partly reflects the changing agenda of civil rights away from race toward gender in the 1970s and 1980s. However, Bush and Johnson gave least attention to gender.

Perhaps more than any other president and, certainly more than his Republican predecessors, Reagan spread his attention more evenly across all groups, giving attention even to newly-emerging groups such as the

Table 2.4
Target Groups[a] (number mentions as percent of total)

	Blacks[b]	Hispanics/ Native Americans[c]	Women[d]	Agree	Other[f]	Total	
	%	%	%	%	%	N	%
Mean							
	60	5	19	8	9	635	100
By Party							
Democrats	47	6	33	5	11	226	100
Republicans	64	4	14	10	8	409	100
By President							
Eisenhower	60	5	15	20	5	20	100
Kennedy	56	13	25	0	6	16	100
Johnson	69	2	3	9	17	89	100
Nixon	78	2	10	7	3	59	100
Ford	81	0	19	0	0	26	100
Carter	31	4	55	3	6	121	99
Reagan	53	7	19	12	9	142	100
Bush	48	6	8	10	27	162	99

a. Vague references to "Equality for all citizens" or "equal protection under law" were left uncoded.

b. Color, segregation, busing, and any minority not specified.

c. Mexican-Americans, Indians.

d. Sex, gender, and any reference to the ERA.

e. Young and old.

f. Specific group like religion (or creed), disabled, institutionalized, and homeless.

disabled. Bush gave far more attention to "other" groups (especially the disabled and the homeless) than any other president. These recent presidents faced a different environment, perhaps explained by a "political period theory" based upon the expansion and maturation of the civil rights policy area.

Table 2.5 moves the emphasis from the target group to the issue areas of civil rights. Most of the policy statements were categorized into one or more subissues, but recall that multiple counts inflate these percentages.[7] Generally, we observe a somewhat more even distribution of policy statements by issue areas than was seen for target groups. Employment receives greatest emphasis (mentioned in 36% of policy statements), followed by

Table 2.5
Issue Areas[a] (number mentions as percent of total)

	Education[b]	Employment[c]	Housing[d]	Other[e]	Total	
	%	%	%	%	N	%
Mean						
	32	36	13	13	601	100
By Party						
Democrats	19	39	20	11	217	100
Republicans	40	32	9	13	384	100
By President						
Eisenhower	26	16	0	29	31	100
Kennedy	19	47	16	19	32	101
Johnson	22	30	17	16	114	100
Nixon	60	24	10	6	68	100
Ford	61	13	6	10	31	100
Carter	15	49	28	4	71	100
Reagan	34	54	12	10	111	101
Bush	19	55	15	11	143	100

a. Vague references to discrimination, equality of opportunity, intolerance were left uncoded.

b. General except for specific references to higher education, busing, school desegregation automatically refers to blacks.

c. Jobs, labor, pensions, affirmative action, federal employment, but not "enterprise."

d. Federal and private; subsidies, "fair" housing; includes renters.

e. Other specific issues like armed forces (DDE), health and pubic accommodations (LBJ), higher education (TWR and GHWB); voting (all presidents but Bush).

education (32%), housing (13%), and other (13%, including higher education, voting, health, public accommodations, and jury discrimination).

It is much harder to spot any trends in subissue emphases than for target groups; attention to education has decreased while attention to employment has increased. Most of these issue areas have had staying power in presidential policy statements. Only voting declined dramatically under Reagan and Bush after the extension of the Voting Rights Act; *no* voting policy statements were made after 1983. Voting dominated Eisenhower's policy statements but Bush made none at all. Kennedy focused more on employment but much less on the controversial education subissue than did most presidents. Johnson spread his attention quite evenly and, more than most presidents, delved into other subissues, such as health, public accommodations, and jury discrimination (other category). Nixon and Ford focused the preponderance of their policy statements, by far more than any other presidents, on education (particularly opposing the increasingly unpopular tool of "forced" busing). Carter gave the greatest attention of any president to housing, being least attentive to education and other, perhaps because he felt his preferred goals had already been attained in those subissues.

Reagan renewed the controversy of education by taking many nonsupportive positions and increasing its salience relative to what Carter had done.[8] Reagan also greatly *de*emphasized the controversial issue area of housing. He was the first president to oppose the Equal Rights Amendment. Bush expounded on housing and employment but significantly reduced attention to education, somewhat surprising since he said he wanted to be the "education president." Thus, as expected, the most ideologically committed president, Lyndon Johnson, spread considerable attention across several subissues and target groups.

Party differences also emerge by target group and issue area. Democrats (except Johnson) give much greater attention to women and other groups than do Republicans, except Reagan (see Table 2.4). However, Democrats give much less attention to African Americans and the aged than do Republicans. Democrats also emphasize housing and employment subissues (see Table 2.5). Republicans, on the other hand, continue to give major attention to education (a subissue that was predominantly African-American oriented during the time of those particular presidents). They gave somewhat less attention to employment than did Democrats. Party differences posited by issue areas are substantial on education and housing.

DISCUSSION

This chapter offers a comparative perspective on presidents' public rhetoric on civil rights on the dimensions of attention, support, and symbolism. Dramatic differences among presidents and between parties in tone and focus were revealed through our analysis, suggesting the importance of a time dimension in the salience of civil rights. Other research suggests that presidential communications may be cyclical (Shull, 1989), but that possibility is beyond our present concern. Differences among presidents and by parties also appeared in seeking action by others and in emphasis on target group and issue area.

All modern presidents made general statements about the desirability of equal opportunity, but civil rights seemed to vary greatly in salience.

Civil rights was just emerging as a salient area of public policy for Eisenhower, while it may have been impossible for Kennedy and Johnson to ignore it in the 1960s. Civil rights was less pressing in the 1970s and 1980s than in the late 1950s and 1960s. By 1970 there was general retrenchment in presidential civil rights advocacy. The Nixon and Ford approach was to encourage rather than force compliance. After a brief respite under Carter, that approach resumed in the 1980s and early 1990s as civil rights continued to be a salient policy area to presidents. Presumably they choose to make it so.

Presidents since the late 1960s had greater flexibility in whether and how much to communicate on civil rights. Ronald Reagan and George Bush were perhaps the presidents most adept at using public messages to assert leadership in the realm of civil rights. They not only renewed interest in civil rights, they also recast it. Probably more than any president, Reagan used public rhetoric to change the policy agenda in civil rights. Bush surprised many at being even more attentive to civil rights than was Reagan on just about every measure. He continued and pushed even further the Reagan legacy of going public and taking strong stands on civil rights matters. On most indicators, Bush's statements were less symbolic and less equivocal than were Reagan's. Johnson and Reagan gave civil rights considerable attention but differed dramatically on the symbolism of their communications. Reagan's and, particularly, Bush's frequent, lengthy, and conservative statements returned civil rights to a prominent place on the president's agenda,[9] and show that individual presidents matter. Although attention generally to civil rights decreased over Reagan's time in office, it was spread more evenly (some would say diffused) to other target groups and issue areas nearer the end of both his and Bush's terms. Bush greatly renewed attention to civil rights in presidential rhetoric. The party variable was particularly important in differentiating presidents' civil rights communications. Perhaps reflecting David Mayhew's (1966) notion of the "inclusiveness" of the Democratic party, Democrats are more consistent in their civil rights statements than are Republicans.

This chapter attempted to identify symbolism in presidential rhetoric. Attention, support, and statement length, as measures of symbolism, constitute useful components of presidential communications. Democratic presidents were shown to be less symbolic than Republicans. Calls for action by others in government and target group and issue area emphases are less clearly linked to symbolism. While some of the components fit together well, others are more elusive. Presumably purely symbolic statements are less likely to translate into tangible actions, and the linkages between statements, actions, and results may be seen elsewhere (Shull, 1993).

"Symbols play a vital role in the policy process" (Elder and Cobb, 1983: 142). They focus attention, legitimize power, and justify authority. Certainly it is true that the substance of presidential rhetoric may count for less than symbols. At the same time, presidents do make substantive policy recommendations, though make relatively few calls for legislative or judicial action. Presidents communicate to assert their policy preferences and to establish their leadership position for posterity. Such symbols may encourage political support for their preferences, and they appear to be a viable leadership strategy for the ideologically committed president. Symbolism perhaps is more important in civil rights than in other policy areas.

NOTES

1. We use *Public Papers of the Presidents* as the source for their communications. *Public Papers*, usually in two annual volumes, are available from presidents Hoover to the present (except for Franklin Roosevelt). When they are not yet available, we use *The Weekly Compilation of Presidential Documents*, which began in 1965 as a "companion publication to the Public Papers to provide a record of Presidential materials on a more timely basis. Beginning with the administration of Jimmy Carter, the Public Papers series has expanded its coverage to include all material printed in the Weekly Compilation. This expanded coverage now provides the full text of proclamations and Executive orders, announcements of appointments and nominations, as well as selected statements or remarks of senior administration officials," (*Public Papers of the Presidents*, 1977: viii). Since Carter, the two documents are essentially equivalent.

2. Key index words used to obtain remarks on race include Afro Americans, blacks, civil rights, colored, lynching, minorities, Negroes, slavery, and African slave trade. More specific words are used for target groups and issue areas (see Tables 2.4 and 2.5).

3. The *type* of message may also be an important research consideration. Light (1982) and Kessel (1974) used State of the Union messages exclusively in their studies of presidential agenda setting. My own research reveals that civil rights is not even mentioned in any of Kennedy's State of the Union messages. Thus, a wider array of documents is desirable. While civil rights is more important in other public messages, even these documents do not tell it all, particularly in an earlier era when civil rights had not reached the public policy agenda. Private communications and other sources from presidential libraries are also useful to scholars seeking to examine presidential policy preferences but they are, of course, frequently less subject to systematic examination.

4. The variety of print and column size in the *Public Papers* varies. To achieve parity on the number of lines measure, the data for Eisenhower and Ford were multiplied by a factor of 1.8.

5. By categorizing even neutral remarks as nonsupportive (conservative), there is greater assurance that the supportive (liberal) category is relatively pure.

6. Some might say that Ford made a large number of judicial calls because he was a lawyer. However, the only other lawyer in the group, Nixon, made the next fewest judicial calls. We surmise that Ford was frustrated by Congress in his conservative civil rights views and turned to the courts.

7. Originally included in this grouping was public accommodations, but perhaps

because of its local nature, it appeared in only four presidential statements (all Johnson). Because it has been a more or less closed subissue since the late 1960s, it was subsequently placed in the other category. The remaining 24 percent were too general to categorize.

8. In contrast to earlier presidents, Reagan and Bush emphasized higher education. Whereas Carter had sought to integrate predominately black colleges, Reagan and Bush took the more popular (less controversial) position of attempting to preserve their autonomy.

9. Reagan's need to defend his civil rights record may account for his higher-than-anticipated level of support, especially since he had the highest percentage of symbolic communications.

3

Moving with the Grain of History: An Examination of Presidential Action in the Civil Rights Domain from 1892 to 1968

RONALD E. BROWN

Richard Neustadt (1976: 251–54) contends that presidents want to implement public policies that allow them to move with the grain of history. None wish to be victims of history; instead, they wish to leave a legacy that helps define how future presidents ought to act in a given policy domain. In order to move with the grain of history, presidents must have a clear understanding of how past and present political dynamics shape and constrain policy choices (Skowronek, 1990: 118; Tulis, 1990: 50). An examination of presidential leadership in the civil rights domain from the period following Reconstruction until 1968 indicates that presidents mostly interpreted the racial climate as one in which the majority of white voters viewed blacks as second-class citizens. Yet, in 1948 the Truman administration went against the grain of history and sought to move blacks into the mainstream of American life. Following the Truman presidency, Eisenhower, Kennedy, and Johnson would cautiously lead the nation toward accepting black civil rights.

Three interrelated factors help describe how presidents came to interpret civil rights history. First, from 1865 until 1946, leading intellectuals, journalists, university professors, playwrights, and other political writers were instrumental in providing the framework that presidents used to interpret the racial milieu. While I do not propose a direct correlation between what was being written or performed on stage and presidential action, I do suggest that the nature of this discourse structured the policy choices available to presidents.

A second factor is that while most presidents did not adhere to social equality between African Americans and White Americans, none wished historical observers to write that their administrations were marred with racial strife—thus all sought to maintain some minimal form of racial harmony. As a result, some presidents would argue long before 1948 that blacks should have the same political rights enjoyed by whites.

The third factor is that by 1936 the Democratic Party realized that black voters in urban communities were in a strategic position to assist their party win close congressional and presidential elections. This motivated presidents to reestimate the cost and benefits of trying to hold on to white votes, particularly in the South, as they sought to secure the black vote.

INTERPRETING THE RACIAL ENVIRONMENT

In the mid 1830s the American Anti-Slavery Society sought radically to change the social contract between the African-American and White-American worlds by demanding equal civil privileges for blacks (Wiecek, 1989: 75). The term civil rights came to be used to describe the legal rights and immunities which were enjoyed by white persons under municipal law of the various states, but which were often denied in whole or part to free blacks. In addition, the Civil Rights Act of 1866 stated these very principles—that blacks at both the state and national level would have the same rights as whites. Thus civil liberties or civil rights in 1866 suggested the lessening of a racially stratified social order. This was not to be, for the *Plessy v. Ferguson* case in 1896 reinforced the dominant view among White Americans, namely that the federal government could not guarantee social equality if the people in the states did not desire it. The prevailing White-American sentiment was that race and culture defined American citizenship; people of African descent were not deemed worthy of first-class citizenship (Smith, 1993).

John Hope Franklin (1989: 10–11) maintains that historians—laymen and professionals alike—sought historical explanations for the social and political experiment that was Reconstruction. The predominant view of southern white intellectuals and their northern allies was that federal Reconstruction policy was an affront to southern white culture. Edwin L. Godkin, editor of the *Nation*, wrote his friend, Charles Elliot Norton, four days after Appomattox, and stated that "he did not oppose enfranchising those blacks who could prove their fitness by a moral as well as an educational test" (Armstrong, 1974: 74). Something very similar is true of Godkin's sometime collaborator, Charles Francis Adams, Jr., though Adams did not limit his displeasure to blacks in government. "Universal suffrage," Adams said, "can only mean in plain English the government of ignorance and vice—it means a European, and especially Celtic, proletariat on the Atlantic Coast, an African proletariat on the shores of the Gulf, and a Chinese proletariat on the Pacific" (Armstrong, 1974: 74).

James Shepherd Pike, a journalist for the *New York Tribune*, wrote a series of articles on South Carolina politics in 1872 (Durden, 1954: 106–7). These articles were organized into a manuscript-length book entitled *The Prostate State*. Pike's articles were written before he had visited South Carolina, and his interviews were mostly with whites. Nonetheless, Pike concluded that the state of South Carolina should not remain in the control of its black rulers. To do so "would be a testimony against the claims of Anglo-Saxon blood" (Durden, 1954: 106–7).

Pike was said to be dismayed at the corruption in the Grant Administration and that the articles and book on South Carolina politics were used to illustrate the extent of the corruption (Durden, 1954: 106). Pike's articles were given wide editorial support in northern and southern newspapers. The *New York Tribune*, the *Pittsburgh Dispatch*, and the *Savannah Republican* all endorsed his position (Durden, 1954: 93). *The Prostate State* was positively reviewed in leading national magazines such as the *Literary World*, and in Godson's *Nation* in 1874 (Durden, 1954: 95). Pike's work also reached the halls of Congress. In 1876 a bloody race riot broke out in Hamburg, South Carolina. In attempting to explain the causes of the riot, a Democratic House member from Maine cited Pike's book as an authority on South Carolina politics and maintained that the corruption of native Africans was responsible for the racial unrest. Finally, leading historians such as James Ford Rhodes and William Dunning would cite Pike extensively in their scholarship on Reconstruction politics.

Thomas Dixon Jr., a lay historian from the South, greatly contributed to shaping white public and elite opinion about the Reconstruction era (see Franklin, 1989: 10–23). From 1903 to 1907 he wrote a Reconstruction trilogy which linked the social, moral, political, and economic woes of the South to the problems created by trying to make black men equal to white men. Publication of these materials made Dixon a sought-after lecturer all over the nation. One of his novels, *The Clansman*, in 1905 was produced as a dramatic play that was shown all over the nation. With the assistance of David W. Griffin, this play became the movie "Birth of a Nation." While opposition to "Birth of a Nation" was formidable, President Wilson, a classmate of Dixon at Johns Hopkins, agreed to a private showing of the movie on February 18, 1915, shortly after members of the Supreme Court and many members of the United States Congress also viewed the movie in a private setting (Franklin, 1989: 16–17).

From these men and their intellectual allies came the scholarly and psychological framework that later embodied the core policy of racial stratification which would dominate the United States in the early part of this century. Their view, which increasingly permeated social thinking, was that Reconstruction was a mistake because blacks and whites could never be incorporated into the same polity on a basis of legal equality and majority rule. Blacks were inherently, biogenetically, incapable of exercising the citizenship function. Kenneth Stampp (1965) characterizes Reconstruction as being thought the "ultimate shame of the American people." It was the epoch that most Americans wanted to forget. Intellectuals accepted the white supremacist view that black equality was a chimera, that seeking it was a mistaken policy, and that Reconstruction was a brutal infliction upon the white South and a source of corruption in politics.

The anxiety about African rule, whether proletarian, as Adams feared, or otherwise, was soon to express itself most powerfully in the writings of historians trained under Herbert Baxter Adams at Johns Hopkins and William A. Dunning at Columbia University (Ayers, 1992: 423). These university professors trained a generation of scholars who used the latest techniques of Germanic scholarship to "discover that southern slavery had been benign and that Reconstruction had been unjust" (Ayers, 1992: 423). A minority of white Southern history professors, such as Andrew Sledd of Emory College in Atlanta and John Basset of Trinity College in North Carolina, used the same scientific methods to demonstrate the positive benefits of Reconstruction (see Ayers, 1992: 422–24; Link, 1992: 46). Sledd's article in the *Atlantic Monthly* (1902) and Basset's article in the *South Atlantic Quarterly* (1903) called for an end to racial violence directed toward the black community. They maintained that African Americans should be given the same rights as White Americans. According to the authors, white attitudes toward blacks needed to change so that blacks could be treated as equal citizens. These scholars were forced to resign from their respective positions and go north.

African-American historian W.E.B. Du Bois also published works challenging the view that the Reconstruction was a failure. In 1910 he published an essay in the *American Historical Review* entitled "Reconstruction and its Benefits," which posited that out of Reconstruction came educational opportunities, constitutional protection for all citizens, and the beginning of political activity for those who were formerly enslaved (Franklin, 1989: 389). Furthermore, in the same year, John Lynch, an African-American member of the Mississippi House of Representatives and former member of Congress, published a work on the Reconstruction suggesting that African Americans were competent political leaders (Franklin, 1989: 389).

In 1935, Du Bois published a more in-depth piece that discussed the positive aspects of the Reconstruction. It took to task historical observers such as Adams and Dunning, who used scientific methods to prove their point that African Americans did not deserve equal rights (Du Bois, 1986: 1026–29). He also stated that leading research universities such as Johns Hopkins and Columbia were not admitting African-American students into their programs. As a consequence, Du Bois argued that the southern racists' perspective on Reconstruction was dominating the social science curriculum.

Du Bois had every reason to be alarmed, for between 1867 and 1919 institutions such as Columbia, Johns Hopkins, the University of Michigan, the University of Wisconsin, and others reorganized their graduate programs and began offering Ph.D.s in history and political science (Ricci, 1984: 42). Ayers (1992: 422) notes that in 1901, 236 out of the 456 advanced students at Johns Hopkins had come from the South. These were future social science professors who would shape White-American attitudes toward African Americans. Du Bois' examination of textbook materials on African Americans in the 1930s indicated that the dominant view was that African Americans were inferior to White Americans, unfit to rule, and that Reconstruction was a failure (Du Bois, 1986: 1026–28).

The southern intellectual view that the Reconstruction was a failure had its effect on public policy. What became known as the "Magnolia Strategy" (Cross, 1984: 138–39) effectively took the vote away from black citizens. The Mississippi Constitution in 1891 required all voters to pay a $2.00 poll tax; additionally, voters had to pass a literacy test in order to vote (Cross, 1984: 138). By 1940 the black registration rate was only 3.1 percent (Jaynes and James, 1989: 233).

In conclusion, the overwhelming intellectual sentiment that blacks were inferior to whites greatly influenced the political life of the South so that blacks would enter the twentieth century with very little political power. Unfortunately, the political powerlessness of southern blacks did not stop southern whites from using political violence as an instrument of political control. Outcries from those opposed to this form of majority tyranny and the need to have some form of social peace moved some presidents to address the question of black civil rights.

THE NEED FOR SOCIAL PEACE AND RACIAL SEMI-HARMONY

A dominant theme in Dixon's *Clansman* and Griffin's "Birth of a Nation" was that as long as southern black men could vote, white women would be at the mercy of immoral black men. Political terrorism, in the form of lynching, was often used by southern white males to terrorize blacks. Between 1892 and 1922 more than 50 blacks a year were lynched in the United States (McAdam, 1982: 89). This form of political terrorism presented a policy dilemma for presidents, for the rule of law had to be obeyed and mob rule could not be allowed to determine the social boundaries between the black and white worlds. Yet, the white southern vote was needed to win elections and southern House and Senate members held powerful positions in Congress. What could be done to address this moral as well as explosive political issue?

Political rhetoric would be used most often by presidents in reaction to public outcries against lynching. A number of presidents moved cautiously against southern white sentiment by stating that blacks had the same God-given natural rights as whites. President Harrison, in his Fourth Annual Message to Congress on December 6, 1892, stated that every citizen qualified by law had a right to cast a ballot and that the public sentiment should be mobilized against the frequent lynching of "colored people" (Bureau of National Literature, 1897: 5767). In an address before Congress on December 3, 1906, President Theodore Roosevelt echoed similar sentiments. He stated that regardless of race, class, or social position, all men were entitled to fair treatment under the law. Like Harrison, Roosevelt called upon American citizens to voice their opposition to the lynching of black citizens (Bureau of National Literature, 1897: 7029, 7030–31). Roosevelt's disdain for those who did not play by the rules is evident by his statement that "Every Christian patriot in America needs to lift up his voice in loud and eternal protest against the mob spirit that threatens the integrity of the Republic" (Bureau of National Literature, 1897: 7030).

In 1921 President Harding gave a speech in Birmingham, Alabama, in which he stated that blacks deserved the right to vote (see Du Bois, 1986: 1188–94). The president also urged Congress to take action to curb political terrorism in the South. Finally, President Coolidge, in his first Annual Message to Congress in 1923, posited that it was both a private and public duty to protect the rights of blacks and that Congress ought to exercise all its powers and pass legislation that would make lynching a federal crime (Schlesinger and Israel, 1966: 2648, 2664, 2688, 2702).

Using the God-given natural rights argument may have had something to do with the fact that African-American voters were still playing a minor but somewhat significant role in southern Republican party politics. For example, John Lynch of Mississippi was a delegate to the Republican national conventions in 1884, 1888, 1892, and 1900 (Franklin, 1989: 261). Also, during this era (from 1892 to 1930), black delegates to the Republican conventions used what little power they had to ensure that Republican presidential candidates were aware of their demands. With the exception of the Republican conventions in 1904 and 1916, Republican delegates from 1892 to 1952 adopted party planks that called for blacks to have the right to vote and to be free from political terrorism (Johnson, 1978).

Republican presidents may have spoken out against lynching because they wanted to convey the message to progressive white voters in the South that the Democratic Party did not know how to play by the rules of the game. Their goal may have been to convince white voters that the social constitution between the black and white worlds could be maintained even if southern blacks were given the right to vote. While Republican presidents spoke for black voting rights and against the use of violence as a tool for maintaining social order, none would issue an executive order to send federal troops to the South to protect black rights. Thus, although these chief executives were outraged by mob violence and the systematic exclusion of blacks from the ballot box, all would retreat from a strong defense of black rights.

Neustadt (1976: ch. 3) maintains that political capital must be guarded because it is not renewable; therefore a president can ill afford to alienate future allies by only thinking about a present crisis or situation. The behavior of these presidents, as well as President Hoover in 1930, illustrates this point. During the Hoover presidency, William Trotter, an African-American activist and founder of the National Equal Rights League, and William White, Executive Director of the NAACP, lobbied the president to make public statements against lynching (Lisio, 1985: 256–57). Hoover, realizing that African-American voters were growing more distrustful of his administration, took an initially bold step, issuing a memorandum to the attorney general asking about the political feasibility of deploying federal troops in the South, where lynching was most prevalent. Hoover's aides strongly discouraged such a policy; he was told that such a policy would alienate southern white congressional leaders and possibly lead to his losing the presidential nomination. Hoover remained silent on the lynching question. Franklin D. Roosevelt's refusal in 1937 to offer public support for an anti-lynching bill that was being supported by sixty Congressional Democrats and Republicans also illuminates the principle that political capital is not renewable. Some theorize that President Roosevelt did not want his economic program held hostage by white southern Democrats in the Senate (Weiss, 1983: 119; Holden, forthcoming). Thus a political calculus took precedence over moral outrage regarding the hideous crime of lynching (Weiss, 1983: 119). Three other interrelated factors may also have influenced Roosevelt's behavior. First, he must have been aware that in 1922 an anti-lynching bill which passed the House fell victim to a filibuster by white southern Democrats; this was still a possibility in 1937. Second, civil rights was not a major concern of the Democratic Party. There was no mention of civil rights in the Democratic Party platform in 1932 or in 1936 (Johnson, 1978: 331–33, 360–63). Third, the electoral fallout from supporting an anti-lynching bill was real. According to a Gallup Poll survey conducted between October 30–November 4, 1937, only 57% of southerners felt that Congress should pass a law that would make lynching against federal law, as compared to over 75% of the respondents who lived in the New England and midwestern states. While this survey did not break down the respondents by race, a Gallup survey conducted between January 1–12, 1940 does provide data on how blacks felt in comparison to white southerners. In that survey, 45% of white southerners and 89% of blacks were in support of a federal anti-lynching law.

President Truman would be the first president to move beyond public speeches to secure black civil liberties. On December 4, 1946, Truman was at a meeting with the National Emergency Committee against Mob Violence. At this meeting he was told of the blinding of a black sergeant, and

Truman stated, "My God. I had no idea it was as terrible as that. We've got to do something!" (Leuchtenburg, 1991: 58). The very next day, on December 5, 1946, Truman signed an executive order creating the President's Committee on Civil Rights. This commission was directed to look at the entire universe of civil rights (Leuchtenburg, 1991: 58) The committee, led by Charles E. Wilson, the president of General Electric, consisted of fifteen citizens. Only two were from the South, and both were conspicuous liberals (Leuchtenburg, 1991: 58). Truman's Civil Rights Commission is said to have relied heavily on Gunner Mydral's *An American Dilemma*, a seminal piece on American race relations published in 1944, which called for the implementation of public policies that would provide blacks with full social and political rights (Southern, 1987: 113). The recommendations of this commission marked a departure from the "failed Reconstruction ethos" that had so dominated presidential leadership in the civil rights arena. At the 1948 Democratic Convention, Truman supported the adoption of a civil rights plank which called for not only full and equal political participation, but also equal opportunity in employment, the right to be secure from the threat of lynching, and equal protection in the services and defense of our nation (Johnson, 1978: 430–35).

Supreme Court rulings in 1954 and 1955 declaring public school segregation as illegal also eventually redefined the social contract between blacks and whites. The refusal of white southern political leaders and citizens to accept these Supreme Court rulings as legitimate forced presidents to ensure the civil rights of blacks. President Eisenhower was the first to come to grips with the phenomenon, although he did not favor federal intervention into state or local issues dealing with race (see Stern, 1989b: 722; Shull, 1989: 49). Nonetheless, the Republican and Democratic Party platforms in 1956 respectively pledged their support to the 1954 *Brown* ruling by the Supreme Court that outlawed racial segregation (Johnson, 1978: 453).

The Republican Party agreed that racial discrimination in public schools must be progressively eliminated, and it supported involvement of local federal district courts to accomplish the task with all deliberate speed (Johnson, 1978: 453). Additionally, the Republican Party Platform Committee adopted language which stated its belief that true progress could be attained through "intellectual study and education," and that the use of violence by any group or agency would only tend to worsen the many problems inherent in trying to integrate southern public schools (Johnson, 1978: 453).

If we focus on the decision in 1956 by the Republican Party to uphold the Supreme Court's ruling, such support was a risky endeavor. A Gallup Poll survey conducted from November 17–22, 1956, revealed that southern whites did not endorse the *Brown* decision. Eighty percent of southern whites disapproved of the Supreme Court's ruling. In addition, Gallup surveys in 1953 and 1954 revealed that civil rights and segregation were mentioned by southerners as the most important problems facing the nation (*Gallup Poll*, 1972).

Again, although President Eisenhower did not favor federal intervention into state affairs, once the Supreme Court decision was handed down, the president in a press conference stated that "the Supreme Court has spoken, and I am sworn to uphold the Constitutional process in this country" (Stern, 1989b: 787). Thus, the decision to send federal troops to keep order in the desegregation of Central High School in Little Rock, Arkansas (Schuman, Steeh, and Bobo, 1985: 40–41) reflected the president's strong commitment to uphold the authority of the federal government. For Eisenhower, this meant upholding the Supreme Court ruling.

President John F. Kennedy found himself in similar situations in 1962 and 1963. In both cases southern state officials sought to defy federal court rulings that would allow black students to attend white universities (Schuman, Steeh, and Bobo, 1985: 23). Much like his predecessor, Kennedy was forced to use power bestowed on him as chief executive if he were to keep the peace.

Nationwide civil disobedience by blacks in the 1950s and 1960s threatened to undo the delicate biracial electoral coalitions of both Republican and Democratic Party candidates. Eventually this had a major impact on how presidents dealt with civil rights issues. In six of eleven national public opinion polls conducted between 1961 and 1965, civil rights was identified as the most important problem confronting the country (McAdam, 1982: 159–60). Asher's (1992: ch. 5) exploration of important policy issues among self-identified Democrats and Republicans in presidential elections from 1960 to 1988 shows a similar pattern. From 1960 to 1968, civil rights emerged among both self-identified Democrats and Republicans as one of the top five problems facing the nation.

Essentially, until the Truman presidency political speeches were used to convey the message that blacks should be treated as political equals. The Civil Rights Commission Report, the Democratic Party platform, and the Brown decisions would extend the boundaries of the social contract between the black and white worlds.

The migration of African Americans from the rural South to urban centers in the North and the South would also affect the political decision-making of both major parties, and in particular the Democratic Party. This phenomenon is discussed to show how it influenced presidential leadership in black civil rights.

THE NEED FOR BLACK VOTERS, PRESIDENTIAL ACTION, AND REACTION FROM THE WHITE WORLD

Weiss (1983: ch. 9) maintains that the 1936 election was the first election in the twentieth century in which the Democratic Party aggressively pursued the black vote. The Democratic party seated ten black delegates and twenty-two alternates from twelve states at its national convention. Another first was that an African-American clergyman, Marshall L. Shepherd, pastor of Mt. Olivet Tabernacle Baptist Church in Philadelphia and a member of the Pennsylvania legislature, delivered the invocation at a convention session (Weiss, 1983: 185). Moreover, the Democratic Party and the Republican Party advertised extensively in the black press by taking out full-page advertisements in newspapers and magazines to extol the virtues of their candidates (Weiss, 1983: 187).

Although the majority of blacks at this time lived in the South and were disenfranchised, between 1910 and 1960 a total of 4.1 million blacks migrated from the South to eight northern states, where they would have the right to vote (McAdam, 1982: 78–79). What made the black vote attractive was its concentraioñ in major urban areas. Weiss (1983: 205) states that in 1936, the Democratic tactic of targeting black voters in northern cities paid off. Roosevelt won anywhere from 60 to 250 percent more votes in black congressional districts in 1936 than in 1932 in the following cities: Chicago, Cincinnati, Cleveland, Detroit, Knoxville, New York, Philadelphia, and Pittsburgh. The pivotal positioning of blacks in these urban districts no doubt convinced Democrats that black voters could play a central role in determining the outcome of electoral college votes in a close presidential race (Huckfeldt and Kohfeld, 1989: 4–5). Furthermore, black votes could be used to elect liberal northern congressional leaders who would be sympathetic to Roosevelt's New Deal legislation (Weiss, 1983: ch. 9).

The competition for the black vote in 1940 led the Democratic Party, for the first time in the twentieth century, to include in its party platform a category entitled "Negroes" (Johnson, 1978: 381–86). Included in this section was a call for legislation to safeguard against discrimination in government services and benefits and for blacks to have an equal chance to get jobs in the defense industry. Also mentioned was a pledge to uphold due process and equal protection under the law, and the need for aid for the employment of black youth. The Republican Party went one step further, calling for full suffrage for black voters (Johnson, 1978: 381–86). By 1944, both parties' platforms pledged support for voting rights for African Americans.

When the Republicans still entertained the concept of competition for black votes, the Eisenhower administration, following Truman, eventually deemed it necessary to support legislation that became the Civil Rights Act of 1957. The Kennedy and Johnson administrations would also sponsor and support legislation that would become the 1964 Civil Rights Act and the 1965 Voting Rights Act. All in all these laws destroyed the institutional and legal barriers that had restricted the social, economic, and political mobility of African Americans.

Aggressively pursuing black voters did have a negative effect on both parties, with Truman's support of the civil rights plank resulting in the convention walkout of Strom Thurmond and the Dixiecrats (Huckfelt and Kohfeld, 1989: 6). In the ensuing three elections (1952, 1956, and 1960), Adlai Stevenson and Kennedy attempted to solidify the bond between the northern black vote and the Democratic Party, but they also attempted to avoid offending white southern Democrats (Huckfelt and Kohfeld, 1989: 6).

The same behavior existed during the Eisenhower administration. Whereas the president recognized the importance of the northern black vote, he also recognized the need for making political inroads into the South. President Eisenhower did not publicly meet with black civil rights leaders in his first term. His first meeting with black civil rights leaders was June 23, 1958 (Stern, 1989a: 780). Kennedy, much like Eisenhower, was concerned about the political fallout which would occur if he was perceived as being too closely linked with civil rights leaders. During the transition from the Eisenhower to the Kennedy administration, Martin Luther King was not invited to the inauguration. King's name was too sensitive at the time, too closely associated with ongoing demonstrations that were vexing politicians in the South (Branch, 1988: 381). Nor was Roy Wilkins, the executive director of the NAACP, granted a private audience with the president-elect to present his civil rights agenda (Branch, 1988: 381). The administration sought to stay clear of civil rights; Kennedy only devoted one sentence to civil rights in his first State of the Union Address to Congress (Stern, 1988: 815).

Kennedy had no intention of making civil rights a high priority in the first term of his presidency. According to staff members who worked under President Kennedy, civil rights was not among the most important domestic programs pushed by the president. Aid to education, Medicare, unemployment, and area redevelopment were all deemed more important (King and Ragsdale, 1988: 67). What moved Kennedy to act were the protest-demand actions of black activists, the violent reaction of southern whites to Supreme Court decisions, and a growing concern that the United States would have a difficult time moving developing nations into the western pro-democracy camp if the civil rights of African Americans were not protected. President Kennedy did not wish to be a victim of history. Maintaining some degree of racial harmony between the black and white worlds and holding on to future black votes meant getting involved in the civil rights struggle.

President Johnson, much like Truman, would use his influence to push black civil rights. The National Party Platform in 1964 affirmed its 1960 civil rights pledge to create an affirmative new atmosphere in which to deal with racial divisions and inequalities. These divisions threatened both the integrity of American democracy and the proposition that all men are created equal (Johnson, 1978: 645, 671). The 1964 Democratic Party platform also stated that because the party was concerned with the opportunity for people to be equal, it would carry the War on Poverty forward in opposition to human want (Johnson, 1978: 645).

Goodwin's (1991: 214–15) biography of President Johnson suggests that it was not only the strategic need for black votes that drove President Johnson to support civil rights; it was also a moral sense. Johnson strongly believed in social equality for African Americans. Goodwin maintains that Johnson's idea was that America was a nation in which every person shared in the progress and the responsibilities of the country. President Johnson wished to change radically the social status of blacks. His commitment to civil rights is also shown in Shull's (1989: 78) findings that Johnson took positions on civil rights legislation nearly three times more frequently than Nixon, the next closest, and twenty times more frequently than Kennedy.

The Johnson presidency would not only change the political landscape in terms of the commitment of blacks to the Democratic Party; it would also mark a strategic shift by the Republican Party. Presidential candidates Barry Goldwater in 1964 and Richard Nixon in 1968 both targeted white southern voters and ignored the black vote. In 1964, the Republican Party platform charged that the Johnson administration had "exploited interracial tensions by extravagant campaign promises, that were not fulfilled." In 1968, Republican presidential delegates recognized that racial inequality existed, but maintained that civil disorder in American cities would not be tolerated (Johnson, 1978: 682, 749–50).

In contrast, the Democratic platform in 1968 stated that it would play a leadership role in making sure that those who had patiently lived with hope long-deferred would not have to wait any longer (Johnson, 1978: 718). This platform language sounds much like the poems, "As I Grow Old" and "Deferred," written by African-American poet Langston Hughes. By 1968, the African-American intellectual voice crying for social and political equality had found its way into the Democratic platform.

Unfortunately for the black civil rights movement, Republican candidate Richard Nixon won the election partially because he pledged to restore "law and order" by putting an end to the violence that was rocking the nation. Moreover, when President Nixon took office in 1968, White Americans were clearly against busing as a tool to integrate schools. Schuman, Steeh, and Bobo (1985: 148–49) show that in 1964 close to 40 percent of whites favored federal intervention to achieve school integration, but by 1968 it had dropped to about 35 percent.

President Nixon was very much aware of the white public outcry against busing. In a closed meeting with southern delegates to the Republican convention in 1968, he stated that he wanted men on the Supreme Court who were "strict constitutionalists," men who interpret law and don't try to make the law (Edsall and Edsall, 1991: 74). Nixon went on to say that he didn't think that there was any court in this country, or any judge in this country, either local or on the Supreme Court, as qualified as a local school board to grapple with the school integration issue (Edsall and Edsall, 1991: 76). President Nixon demonstrated his commitment to slowing down the pace of integration in the nation's schools by having the Department of Justice and the Department of Health, Education and Welfare drop their strict compliance with timetables for school integration (Edsall and Edsall, 1991: 81).

CONCLUSION

As we near the close of the twentieth century, racial polarization continues to plague the nation. Bobo and Kluegel's (1991) analysis of data from the 1990 General Social Survey indicates that many white respondents hold very negative views of blacks. Whites tend to rate blacks as being lazier than whites, more prone to violence, and less intelligent. These findings may help explain why the vast majority of White Americans are opposed to equality of outcome programs that would redistribute governmental resources based upon race (McClosky and Zaller, 1984: ch. 3).

The debate over the wisdom of federal government involvement in the civil rights domain also continues. Edsall and Edsall (1991: 72) maintain that 1964 was a pivotal year because it marked the beginning of the end of the traditional Democratic Party coalition. Their point is that conservative and moderate white voters equated the riots, the Black Power movement, and antiwar demonstrations as part of a social revolution with which they did not want to associate. In addition, Edsall and Edsall (1991: 283) state that competing in a global economic market where there are scarce resources increases racial tensions. Thus a Democratic Party presidential candidate can ill afford to run a campaign that pledges to assist poverty-stricken blacks but does little to assist the struggling white working and middle classes.

Is President Clinton seeking to establish himself as a Democratic president who can manage the race question? The attack on Sister Souljah during the presidential campaign, the ill-fated Lani Guinier nomination, and the push for welfare reform can be viewed as attempts by Clinton to demonstrate his independence from the liberal wing of the Democratic Party. At the same time, President Clinton has appointed four African Americans to high-level positions and has been able to maintain high ratings from African-American civil rights organizations. Only time will tell whether the Clinton presidency redefines the social and political boundaries between black and white worlds. Nonetheless, an examination of presidential behavior between 1892 and 1968 suggests that the ability of any president to maintain a coalition of White-American and African-American voters means treading cautiously in the civil rights policy domain.

PART II

Institutions, the President, and Civil Rights

4

Presidential Leadership Style and Civil Rights Legislation: The Civil Rights Act of 1957 and the Voting Rights Act of 1965

——————————————————— JAMES D. KING AND
JAMES W. RIDDLESPERGER, JR.

The American system of government offers the president a choice of avenues for bringing about policy change. The president can act alone within the executive branch, directing his subordinates to modify policies and practices through executive orders. This approach allowed presidents from Franklin Roosevelt to Lyndon Johnson to combat racial discrimination in employment and housing (Morgan, 1970). The president may also opt for a judicial strategy, seeking to influence policy through appointments to the federal courts and through Justice Department involvement in civil rights litigation as a party to the case or a friend of the court (Scigliano, 1971).

Much can be said in favor of executive and judicial strategies for policy change, but both have drawbacks which limit their effectiveness. First, the scope of the executive orders is restricted to activities within the executive branch. While federal government contracts can be used to extend the reach of executive order-based policy into the private sector, the length of that reach will typically fall short of touching all segments of society. The appropriations needed for full implementation may also be lacking (Morgan, 1970: 31–32). In the judicial arena, a president may find himself with few opportunities to appoint Supreme Court justices and Appeals Court judges, and find his control over appointments to lower federal courts curtailed significantly by congressional involvement in the process (Mackenzie, 1981). Additionally, the Justice Department may lack the statutory authority to initiate lawsuits in a particular field or may not find cases filed by other parties which enable it to achieve the administration's objectives with amicus curiae briefs. Even if favorable rulings do result from administration efforts, compliance with Court directives is by no means assured (Wasby, 1970).

While an imperfect tool for policy adoption, the legislative approach offers the president greater opportunities to effect change. If majorities can be mustered to enact administration proposals, the resulting legislation can extend the reach of the policy throughout American society and provide the funds and statutory base necessary for full implementation. This, of course, is a big "If." Presidents' success in convincing Congress to enact their proposals has generally been limited. From 1953 to 1975 only 46 percent of the proposals submitted by presidents were passed into law. Of the presidents of this era, only Johnson—noted for his legislative skill and working with substantial partisan majorities in both houses of Congress—managed to win approval for more than one-half of his initiatives (Edwards, 1980: 14). Furthermore, Shull's (1983: 115–34) analysis of initiatives between 1953 and 1982 in a number of domestic policy areas showed presidents being less successful in securing adoption of proposals in the area of civil rights than any area except antitrust.

The president's success in securing approval for his legislative proposals hinges on his ability to attract votes from individual members of Congress. This may seem like a statement of the obvious, but it is nonetheless true. Legislative majorities are composed of individual legislators. Thus the extent to which a president can attract support for his proposals from members of Congress serves as one indication of his ability to lead the nation in establishing public policy. As Fleisher and Bond (1983: 746) note, "Programmatic success is certainly an important aspect of presidential-congressional relations, but individual support is, nonetheless, a necessary first ingredient."

This chapter examines the support Dwight Eisenhower and Lyndon Johnson generated for their proposals, which ultimately resulted in the Civil Rights Act of 1957 and the Voting Rights Act of 1965. These two presidents were selected because of their very different styles of leadership and because they operated under very different conditions (Eisenhower facing a Congress controlled by the opposition party, Johnson having substantial majorities in both houses). After a review of Eisenhower's and Johnson's leadership styles, we examine levels of and determinants of support for their proposals in the House of Representatives.

STYLES OF POLITICAL LEADERSHIP

As president, Eisenhower and Johnson presented dramatically contrasting styles of political leadership. Eisenhower had a passion for organization and a desire to avoid (at least publicly) the "grit" of politics, while Johnson was, by all accounts, a political animal who reveled in the limelight and individual-level politicking. This difference in the level of activity is reflected in Barber's (1992) classification of Eisenhower as a *passive*-negative president and Johnson as an *active*-negative one. Yet each was president at a time of passage of momentous civil rights legislation and each played a significant role in its enactment. For Eisenhower, the most dramatic legislation came in the Civil Rights Act of 1957, which was the first comprehensive civil rights legislation passed by Congress since the end of Reconstruction. As majority leader of the Senate, Johnson played a role in the passage of this act. As president, he pushed for adoption of the Civil Rights Act of 1964, the most broad-sweeping piece of civil rights legislation ever passed, and the Voting Rights Act of 1965.

The literature on Eisenhower's leadership has had two distinct phases. In the period immediately following his terms, Eisenhower was often characterized as a president of great popularity who had little real political skill. The politicians' perspective of Eisenhower's skill was summed up by his predecessor, Harry Truman, who once commented, "He'll sit here [in the Oval Office] and he'll say, 'Do this! Do that!' And nothing will happen. Poor Ike—it won't be a bit like the army. He'll find it very frustrating" (Neustadt, 1960: 9). Academics tended to view Eisenhower as, in the words of McAuliffe (1981: 625), "the dull leader of a complacent and uninteresting era. He was unintelligent, inarticulate, bland, passive, and captive to the influence of corporate executives, who used him for their own ends." Wolk (1971: 221) concluded that in the field of civil rights Eisenhower "could not envisage himself using the power of the Presidency to forcefully bring about something that he thought could best be effectuated through persuasion and education."

This traditional view of Eisenhower as a political leader has been challenged in recent years. Most notable among the revisionist perspectives of the Eisenhower presidency is Greenstein's (1982) description of Eisenhower's "hidden hand" style of leadership.[1] As a hidden-hand leader, Eisenhower often resorted to quiet, off-the-record negotiation or made his feelings known only in the private world of cabinet politics. Greenstein cites an example of this leadership style in a note from the president to Maxwell Rabb, his minority group relations advisor, concerning the enforcement of the desegregation of federal facilities in South Carolina, in which Eisenhower wrote that "Our job is to convince not to publicize" (Greenstein, 1988: 93). According to this perspective, while Eisenhower preferred to operate through a formal staffing procedure, he nonetheless was the clear policy leader of his administration. In the area of civil rights policy, Stern (1989b: 789), in his analysis of the first years of the Eisenhower presidency, concludes that within his views of the limits of the federal role, Eisenhower "moved to aid the black civil rights cause," and that his leadership "appeared to be a very successful and a well-crafted balancing act of party building and policy leadership."

Eisenhower's image as a legislative leader has undergone a transformation similar to those of his overall leadership and leadership on civil rights. The traditional view of Eisenhower's ability to work effectively is represented by Edwards' assessment that Eisenhower was the antithesis of Johnson. According to Edwards (1980: 135), Eisenhower was "notable for his seeming lack of concern for or involvement in getting many of his programs passed. He failed to give priority to programs, thus losing the opportunity to communicate his special interests in and desires for programs and his willingness to aid their enactment into law." More recent assessments of Eisenhower portray him as a more careful legislative strategist, one who "achieved much by limiting the targets of his interest and efforts" (Peterson, 1990: 235). Although limited in its time frame, Cavalli's (1992) examination of presidents' activities indicates that Eisenhower devoted almost as much time to legislative activities as did Johnson. Jackson and Riddlesperger's (1993) study of the passage of the 1957 Civil Rights Act exemplifies the revisionist image of Eisenhower as a legislative leader. They found Eisenhower to have been intimately involved in developing the content of the legislation and well aware of the nuances of the legislative process. However, the public and personalized leadership of the administration's initiative was left to others, most notably Attorney General Herbert Brownell, with the president remaining in the background.

In contrast to Eisenhower's reluctance to engage in personalized leadership, Johnson defined leadership in a personal way. As president, Johnson involved himself in every major decision of the administration. He could not—or would not—rely on a chief of staff or delegate authority as Eisenhower had. Additionally, because of his experience on Capitol Hill, Johnson saw himself as the best legislative liaison he could have. As a result, he was intimately involved in the proposing of legislation, the compromising that he viewed necessary to secure passage, and ultimately in the personal contacting of members of Congress to persuade them to vote for the legislation he supported. After leaving the White House, Johnson described his personal approach to working with Congress: "The challenge was to learn what it was that mattered to each of these men, understand which issues were critical to whom and why. Without that understanding nothing is possible. Knowing the leaders and understanding their organizational needs let me shape my legislative to fit both their needs and mine" (Kearns, 1976: 186). Without question, Johnson was widely seen as the most brilliant legislative strategist ever to occupy the White House. Berman (1988: 136) noted that in 1965, at the height of his effectiveness, Johnson "embodied creative leadership in the modern presidency, combining formidable personal political skills with the extraordinary powers of his office."

Moreover, after a mixed record on racial matters as a congressman and senator, Johnson became committed to the cause of civil rights, pursuing an active and comprehensive legislative agenda (Stern, 1992). As a result,

Amaker (1988: 19) argued that "the presidency of Lyndon Johnson exhibited the greatest amount of sustained executive leadership in this field in the nation's history." The combination of this personal commitment, his extraordinary popularity during 1964 and 1965, and his willingness to use personal leadership to its fullest contributed to the perception of Johnson as an almost invincible legislative leader.

CIVIL RIGHTS LEGISLATION IN 1957 AND 1965

Our analysis of presidential influence on congressional civil rights policy focuses on the Civil Rights Act of 1957 and the Voting Rights Act of 1965. Although some congressmen introduced civil rights legislation at roughly the same time, the bills which ultimately became law were presidential initiatives. The two acts concerned voting rights, although each took a different approach. The 1957 act (the first civil rights legislation passed by Congress since Reconstruction) created the Commission on Civil Rights, upgraded the Civil Rights section of the Justice Department to divisional status, and empowered the Justice Department to initiate civil law suits to protect voting rights of blacks. As majority leader, Johnson played a key role in forging the compromise which enabled the bill to pass the Senate, although the Eisenhower administration was displeased by an amendment which provided for jury trials in certain cases involving voting rights (Lawson, 1991: 57–58; Sundquist, 1968: 235–38). As finally enacted, the Civil Rights Act of 1957 reflected "a combination of presidential moderation and Democratic party factionalism" (Lawson, 1991: 56). The reactions of leaders in the civil rights movement were mixed. For example, Roy Wilkins of the NAACP viewed the act as an important first step in the legislative struggle for equal rights, while SCLC President Martin Luther King, Jr. saw it as a lesson that blacks could not depend on white political institutions to provide meaningful civil rights legislation (Branch, 1988: 221–22). The Civil Rights Act of 1960 attempted to close certain loopholes of the 1957 act by expanding judicial supervision of the suffrage process.

In contrast to the judicial remedies of the 1957 and 1960 acts, the Voting Rights Act of 1965 gave the Justice Department far-reaching powers to assure voting rights. It suspended state literacy tests, allowed the attorney general to dispatch registrars to recalcitrant counties in the South, required states to have changes in their electoral laws approved by the U.S. District Court in Washington, D.C., to assure that reforms did not place undue burdens on blacks, and eliminated the use of poll taxes in nonfederal elections in the states which still used them (Lawson, 1991: 115). The 1965 act was passed into law quite rapidly in the weeks following the violent events of Selma, Alabama. Powledge (1991: 628) concludes that the ease with which it was enacted was a "clear product of Selma."

SUPPORT FOR CIVIL RIGHTS INITIATIVES: 1957 AND 1965

To what extent did these presidents with such different styles receive support for their proposals for civil rights legislation? To address this question, we develop a measure of support by members of the House of Representatives on civil rights legislation in 1957 and 1965 relative to expected levels of support for presidential initiatives. No president's proposals are considered and voted upon in a vacuum. Rather, they are taken up by Congress under varying conditions. The political context under which proposals are considered will determine to some extent the level of support the president receives (Bond and Fleisher, 1980; Peterson, 1990; Shull, 1983, 1989). Thus, the first step in evaluating Eisenhower's and Johnson's support on civil rights legislation is developing a measure of presidential support in the context of the existing political environment.

Measuring of Civil Rights Support

We operationally define presidential support on civil rights (PSCR)—the dependent variable for this analysis—as the difference between the percentage of votes cast in accordance with the president's public position on roll calls relating to civil rights (CRS) and the expected level of overall presidential support (EPS):

$$PSCR_i = CRS_i - EPS_i$$

with separate measures calculated for each representative (**i**) serving in 1957 and in 1965. This measure provides an indication of a representative's support for the president's civil rights legislation relative to what we would anticipate given the existing political environment. A positive PSCR score results when the representative is more supportive of the president on civil rights legislation than overall conditions would predict, and is indicative of success on the part of the president in drawing the member to his coalition. A negative PSCR score denotes a representative who is less supportive of the president than expected, and a failure to bring the member into the administration's coalition.

Members' support for civil rights (CRS) are based on a series of roll calls taken on the bills which resulted in the 1957 Civil Rights Act and the 1965 Voting Rights Act. The House debates on the proposals offered by Eisenhower in 1957 and Johnson in 1965 each resulted in four roll calls.[2] An individual member's (CRS) score is the percentage of votes cast in accordance with the president's public position. Members failing to vote or pair on all four roll calls were excluded from the analysis. As a result, 377 and 370 members were included in the analyses for 1957 and 1965, respectively. The limited number of votes on which this component of the presidential support measure is based causes some concern. The more general and commonly-used presidential support scores computed by *Congressional Quarterly* are typically based on a hundred roll calls or more. But to insist on a larger base would prohibit any consideration of votes on civil rights legislation, since few roll calls on the issue are taken during any given Congress.

The expected level of presidential support (EPS) is produced from the model developed and tested by Bond and Fleisher (1980).[3] Their model to explain presidential support in the House of Representatives is grounded on the notions that (1) popular presidents receive greater support than do unpopular ones, (2) congressmen are more likely to support the initiatives of presidents with whom they share an ideological perspective, and (3) members of the president's party are more likely to cast supporting votes than are members of the opposition party. While not originally developed to predict levels of presidential support, the model is nonetheless appropriate for this purpose (Fleisher and Bond, 1992: 528-29).[4] Replications of Bond and Fleisher's model give us our measures of expected presidential support for members serving in 1957 and 1965.

Levels of Support for Presidential Initiatives

Table 4.1 presents the mean PSCR scores for 1957 and 1965. The most obvious conclusion to be drawn from these data is that, given their popularity and general ideological perspectives, Dwight Eisenhower and Lyndon Johnson fared similarly well in attracting support for their civil rights legislative proposals. The average representative's civil rights support in 1957 and 1965 was, respectively, 11.90 and 16.43 percentage points above expected levels of presidential support. While Eisenhower's mean score was slightly lower than Johnson's, the difference is of little significance.

The similarities between the two chief executives continues to be evident when the support they garnered from various partisan subgroups is considered. First, both Eisenhower and Johnson were most successful in attracting support from the dominant faction of the opposition party. In 1957, the average northern Democrat's support for the president's proposal was more than 35 points above the baseline; similarly, the average eastern Republican's support score was more than 40 points above the standard in 1965. Secondly, the lowest positive PSCR scores are found for the groups closest to the president's own ideological position: non-eastern Republicans for Eisenhower and northern Democrats for Johnson. This, of course, is of no surprise as we would expect these groups to support the president on civil rights as they would other legislation. Finally, both Eisenhower and Johnson failed to attract the support of southern Democrats. As with the prominent regional groups in the parties, this was to

Table 4.1
Support for Presidential Civil Rights Proposals

	Eisenhower		Johnson	
	Mean	N	Mean	N
Total	11.90	377	16.43	371
Democrat	-.05	210	9.00	251
Republican	26.93	167	31.99	120
	eta=.34*		eta=.36*	
Northern Democrat	36.48	114	24.71	173
Southern Democrat	-43.44	96	-25.85	78
Eastern Republican	31.91	69	40.51	35
Noneastern Republican	23.40	98	28.48	85
	eta=.83*		eta=.75	
Nonsouth	32.55	274	29.95	277
South	-43.04	103	-23.38	94
	eta=.85*		eta=.79*	
< 10% black	32.09	246	30.18	246
10-20% black	-7.36	64	11.54	68
> 20% black	-43.82	67	-37.07	57
	eta=.75*		eta=.81*	

*p<.0001

Entries are mean Presidential Support on Civil Rights (PSCR) scores (see text).

be expected; the 1957 and 1965 acts targeted racial segregation and discrimination in the South.

The extremely low levels for support for civil rights by southern Democrats is reflected in two additional subgroupings. Representatives from the South (mostly but not entirely Democrats) gave significantly less support to presidential initiatives than did their colleagues from other regions. Similarly, representatives from states in which more than 20 percent of the population was black (also mostly southern Democrats) were the least supportive of the presidents' civil rights legislation. For both the regional and racial classifications the differences among subgroups were greater in 1957 than in 1965.[5]

The more broad-sweeping nature of the 1965 act would suggest that southern resistance would be greater in that year. The higher level of southern resistance in 1957 may have been a product of the newness of civil rights legislation. The 1957 law was the first major civil rights act passed since Reconstruction. On the other hand, the 1965 act was the fourth piece of major civil rights legislation to go before Congress in less than a decade and the second extensive bill in two years. Also, the enfranchisement of blacks through the 1957 and 1960 Civil Rights Acts and voter registration activities of various civil rights groups may have had the effect of alerting southern congressmen to the need to support civil rights legislation. Alternatively, the differences between support for the 1957 and 1965 acts by southerners and representatives of states with substantial black populations may be traceable to differing presidential styles. Johnson's more direct involvement in constructing the winning coalition may have been an important factor in attracting southern votes.

Determinants of Support for Presidential Initiatives

To identify more specific determinants of support for presidents' civil rights proposals, we test a multivariate model using ordinary least squares (OLS) regression which incorporate the three key elements of Bond and Fleisher's (1980) model—presidential popularity, ideology, and party—plus one variable unique to this policy area—race.

The empirical link between presidential popularity and support for presidents on roll calls has been demonstrated repeatedly. Following the lead of other studies in which individual congressmen serve as the units of analysis, presidential popularity is operationalized as the vote in the representative's district in the 1956 or 1964 election, as appropriate (e.g., Edwards, 1980: 100–8; Schwarz and Fenmore, 1977). Secondly, ideology plays a role in congressmen's decisions on roll calls (Kingdon, 1973: 247–54). The Conservative Coalition Support score computed by *Congressional Quarterly* serves as our operationalization of ideology. The score measures the level of agreement with the coalition of a majority of Republicans and a majority of southern Democrats. It is unidimensional (Poole, 1981) with a high score indicating a conservative voting record, a low score a liberal one. Thirdly, members of the president's party tend to be more supportive of presidential initiatives, either because they are open to his influence or are from shared policy preferences (Cooper and Bombardier, 1968; Clausen, 1973: 206–8; Kingdon, 1973: 169–78). Party is measured as a dummy variable, with one signifying a member of the opposition party. This will highlight the response of opposition party members and provide an indication of the president's success in attracting votes from the other side of the aisle to his coalition. Finally, because of the issue at hand and the relationship between race and support evident in Table 4.1, the percentage of blacks in the state's population is included in the model.

The model is specified as follows:

$$PSCR_i = a + b_1 VOTE^s_i + b_2 VOTE^o_i + b_3 IDEOL^s_i$$
$$+ b_4 IDEOL^o_i + b_5 PARTY_i + b_6 RACE_i$$

where

$PSCR_i$	=	Presidential Support on Civil Rights for member i;
$VOTE^s_i$ =		Presidential Vote in the state if member i's party is the same as the president and 0 otherwise;
$VOTE^o_i$	=	Presidential Vote in the state if member i is from the opposition party and 0 otherwise;
$IDEOL^s_i$	=	Conservative Coalition Support score if member i's party is the same as the president and 0 otherwise;
$IDEOL^o_i$	=	Conservative Coalition Support score if member i is from the opposition party and 0 otherwise;
$PARTY_i$	=	1 if member i is of the opposition party and 0 otherwise;
$RACE_i$	=	Percent Black in the population of member i's state.

Two variables for presidential vote and representative's ideology are included, as the relationships between these concepts and support for civil rights legislation are expected to be conditioned by partisanship (Wright, 1976). Because the two presidents were of opposing political parties, it is expected that the regression coefficients for the vote and ideology variables will differ (a variable with a positive coefficient for the Eisenhower model should have a negative coefficient for the Johnson model and vice versa). Only for the race variable should the regression coefficients be in the same direction, in this case negative in both the 1957 and 1965 models.

The estimates from the least squares model are presented in Table 4.2. As with the first table, the most striking feature is the similarity between models estimated for 1957 and 1965. For both Eisenhower and Johnson there is a significant relationship between ideology and presidential support for members of the Democratic party (reflected by the significant coefficients for $IDEOL^o$ in 1957 and $IDEOL^s$ in 1965). Very clearly, liberals were more supportive of civil rights legislation than conservatives.

In both 1957 and 1965, representatives from states with large black populations—generally southern states—provided less support for civil rights legislation than Bond and Fleisher's general model of presidential support would predict. Of course, this product of the multivariate analysis confirms what was revealed by the bivariate analysis reported in Table 4.1. However, by controlling for other factors, the OLS analysis demonstrates that the resistance to civil rights legislation exhibited by representatives resulted from more than an ideological difference between themselves and the president.

Table 4.2
Effects of Presidential Vote, Ideology, Part, and Race on Support for Presidential Proposals on Civil Rights

	Eisenhower	Johnson
VOTE^S	.28	-.12
VOTE^O	(.33)	(.10)
	-.14	.66**
	(.17)	(.16)
IDEOLOGY^S	.05	-.43**
	(.07)	(.04)
IDEOLOGY^O	-.50**	.01
	(.06)	(.07)
PARTY	36.57	-39.99*
	(21.57)	(13.67)
RACE	-2.03**	-1.41**
	(.22)	(.14)
Constant	19.07	46.21
R =	.755	.856
R^2 =	.571	.733
Adjusted R^2 =	.564	.728

*p<.05

**p<.001

Entries are unstandardized regression coefficients.
Standard errors of the estimates are in parentheses.

Somewhat surprisingly, presidential popularity as measured by the 1956 vote had no bearing on support for Eisenhower's civil rights initiative. As expected, Republicans from districts which voted heavily for Johnson in 1964 were significantly more supportive of his 1965 proposal. The negative (albeit not statistically significant) relationship between the 1965 vote and support for civil rights among the president's partisans undoubtedly results from the overall agreement between Johnson and northern Democrats. As noted above, there is little a liberal president must do to attract the liberals of his party to his policy position. Furthermore, a landslide election such as 1965 will yield districts which give substantial majorities to the president but elect more conservative representatives.

CONCLUSION

It is difficult to imagine two presidents with such diverse leadership styles as Dwight Eisenhower and Lyndon Johnson. One preferred to operate in the background, avoiding the political spotlight, at times deliberately making himself appear less than competent. The other reveled in the rough and tumble of legislative politics, both publicly and privately. And yet both succeeded in enlisting sufficient support to enact major civil rights legislation.

What role did leadership style play in building and maintaining the coalitions in the House of Representatives which resulted in passage of the Civil Rights Act of 1957 and the Voting Rights Act of 1965? A definitive answer to this question cannot be given. Too many factors affect the legislative process and too much time has passed to isolate the role of a single element. However, the analysis reported here suggests that each president's leadership style served him well in the political environment of the times.

Eisenhower's 1957 legislative proposal was clearly less ambitious than that offered by Johnson in 1965. But Johnson had the advantage of promoting the fourth—not the first—major civil rights bill of the decade. He also had the opportunity to work with substantial partisan majorities in each chamber rather than facing a Congress dominated by the opposition party. Operating under less favorable conditions, Eisenhower proposed less far-reaching legislation, but legislation for which he could garner support. Both Eisenhower and Johnson demonstrated the ability to draw legislative support for their civil rights proposals above the levels to be expected for presidents of their standing with the public (and both Eisenhower and Johnson were very popular at the time) and their ideological perspectives (relative to members of the House), despite the different leadership styles reflected in Barber's (1992) typology. Additionally, each attracted votes from the dominant wing of the opposition party while retaining support (or in Eisenhower's case increasing support) from within his own party. The latter facet of coalition building should not be underestimated, for a president who fails to maintain support from his own legislative party is likely to find himself in a partisan crossfire which produces little but stalemate. The Bush administration, whose first-year efforts to find common ground with the opposition party cost it support from its own partisan base, illustrates the problems produced by a misjudgment in selecting a legislative strategy (Fleisher and Bond, 1992).

Perhaps the lesson of Eisenhower's and Johnson's leadership in enacting civil rights legislation in 1957 and 1965 is that success is more likely to be forthcoming when leadership style and the political context mesh. An aggressive, arm-twisting strategy in support of a far-reaching proposal is unlikely to succeed in the face of an opposition party in the majority; that majority would surely oblige the president by engaging in open warfare. A limited proposal guided through the legislative process by a hidden-hand approach is also likely to fail when the president possesses a strong partisan majority; that majority is certain to flex its muscles and press for more comprehensive legislation than the president prefers. Thus, it is not the leadership style or the context alone which produces the desired results. Rather, it is the proper mixture of the two which yields success.

APPENDIX: DATA SOURCES

Civil Rights Support (CRS) 1957—Roll call votes #11, #13, #15, #19. In each instance, a "yea" was a vote in support of the president's position. Representatives pairing for or against the motion were coded as voting "yea" or "nay." Those announcing a position for or against and those not voting were coded as missing. Source: *Congressional Quarterly Almanac 1957* (pp. 428–31, 434–35).

Civil Rights Support (CRS) 1965—Roll call votes #82, #86, #87, #107. A "yea" was a vote in support of the president's position on all motions except #86, where a "nay" vote supported the president's position. Representatives pairing for or against the motion were coded as voting "yea" or "nay." Those announcing a position for or against and those not voting were coded as missing. Source: *Congressional Quarterly Almanac 1965* (pp. 976–77, 984–85).

Conservative Coalition Support Score (IDEOL) 1957—The Conservative Coalition Support score measures the percentage of roll calls on which a representative voted in agreement with the conservative coalition, defined as a majority of Republicans and a majority of southern Democrats. Source: Authors' calculations based on sixteen roll call votes held in 1957 and reported in *Congressional Quarterly Almanac 1965* which meet the above criteria.

Conservative Coalition Support Score (IDEOL) 1965—The Conservative Coalition Support score measures the percentage of roll calls on which a representative voted in agreement with the conservative coalition, defined as a majority of Republicans and a majority of southern Democrats. Source: *Congressional Quarterly Almanac 1965* (pp. 1092–93).

Presidential Vote (VOTE)—Percent of the two-party vote received by Eisenhower in 1956 and Johnson in 1964 in the representative's district. Sources: *Congressional Quarterly Almanac 1957* (pp. 144–78); *Congressional Quarterly Almanac 1964* (pp. 1024–68).

Presidential Popularity—Mean percentage of the population responding approvingly to the question "Overall, do you approve or disapprove of the way (Eisenhower, Johnson) is handling his job as president" in 1957 and 1965. Source: *The Gallup Opinion Index* (Report No. 1982, October–November 1980).

Racial Composition of the Population (RACE)—Percent black in population of the representative's state. Source: U.S. Bureau of the Census (1963).

NOTES

1. A similar perspective of Eisenhower's political skills, discussed in the context of subsequent presidents, is found in Henderson (1988).

2. Data sources are listed in the Appendix.

3. Using data from a random sample of 500 representatives serving from 1959 to 1974 and ordinary least squares regression techniques, Bond and Fleisher produced a model for assessing presidential support. The model's regression coefficients can, in turn, be used to compute predicted presidential support scores by inserting values appropriate for individual members for each independent variable. For a complete description of the model and the coefficients used to predict expected presidential support, see Bond and Fleisher (1980: 71–75).

4. Fleisher and Bond (1983 and 1992) used a similar approach to assess the overall legislative leadership of Presidents Carter, Reagan, and Bush in the first years of their respective terms.

5. "South" is defined here as the eleven states of the old Confederacy. An analysis of differences in support for presidents' civil rights proposals was conducted using four regional categories: Northeast, Midwest, West, and South. The results indicated no differences among representatives from the first three regions. Therefore, the more parsimonious, dichotomous regional breakdown is used. Additionally, the relationship between PSCR and race was tested using both percent black in the representative's state and percent black in the representative's district. In both 1957 and 1965, the stronger correlation is found between the dependent variable and the former. Apparently representatives opposing civil rights legislation were sensitive to the impact of such laws on their states rather than their individual districts.

5

Affirmative Action and Business Deregulation: On the Reagan Administration's Failure to Revise Executive Order No. 11246

ROBERT R. DETLEFSEN

INTRODUCTION

Occasionally, in the course of studying or discussing policy one finds Executive Order No. 11246 referred to as "the affirmative action order." But this reflexive tendency to identify this order with affirmative action stems more from the Department of Labor's guidelines for implementing the order than from the text of the order itself. During the Reagan years, those Labor Department guidelines became the source of a major policy dispute within the executive administration. This chapter explores the nature of the order, its implementation guidelines as developed over the years by the Department of Labor, the controversy surrounding a Reagan administration proposal to reformulate those guidelines, and the reasons why the proposal was ultimately abandoned by Reagan administration officials.

CIVIL RIGHTS EXECUTIVE ORDERS IN HISTORICAL PERSPECTIVE

Franklin Roosevelt was the first President to use the executive order to advance the cause of civil rights. Issued in 1941 as Executive Order No. 8802, the Roosevelt order banned employment discrimination by firms having defense contracts with the federal government (Morgan, 1970: 87–88). In the years that followed, more civil rights-related orders would be issued from the Oval Office, not only by Roosevelt, but by Presidents Truman, Eisenhower, Kennedy, and Johnson as well. These executive orders tended to be similar in two respects: first, they were aimed at the problem of racial discrimination in those sectors of American society over which the president could plausibly claim some constitutional authority. Thus, the "commander in chief" and "take care" clauses of Article II were invoked in support of orders that asserted a policy of nondiscrimination in the civil service agencies of the federal government, in the armed services, in federally-assisted housing, and, as in the case of the Roosevelt order, in private firms under contract to the federal government. Several of the orders that followed Roosevelt's were concerned with implementation and enforcement, and so created new administrative agencies for that purpose, often transferring such authority from preexisting agencies (Morgan, 1970).

The second common feature of the executive orders from Roosevelt through Johnson is that, with the exception of Johnson, each order substituted for a presidentially-sponsored legislative program. Among this group of presidents, only Lyndon Johnson made the passage of fair-employment legislation a high priority of his administration; the others preferred to address the sensitive issue of civil rights by means of the direct and relatively discreet instrument of the executive order.

Some modern critics might be tempted to criticize the recourse to executive orders in such an important policy area. For one thing, an executive order may seem to represent a circumvention of congressional authority, and it might be argued that in an area as morally freighted as civil rights, policymaking ought properly to occur with the full knowledge and cooperation of the legislative branch. A more practical objection is that, compared to statutory law, executive orders are difficult to enforce; among the notable disadvantages of the executive order as a policymaking tool is that criminal sanctions are not available for coercing compliance and punishing violators. Yet at least one scholar has concluded that executive orders offer unique advantages over legislation in civil rights policymaking. Reflecting in 1970 on the use of executive orders in the area of civil rights, Ruth Morgan (1970: 84) noted approvingly that the executive order "provides a more flexible, adaptive framework than the relatively permanent molds of statutory law," and suggested further that they satisfied "a need . . . for experimental programs at the national level. . . . "

The virtues of flexibility and adaptability stemmed in part, it seemed, from the ease with which future presidents could modify, revise, or cancel the "experimental programs" that were inherited from previous administrations and conceived under the authority of preexisting executive orders. That, at least, is what intuition would suggest. After all, if one administration were able to initiate an executive order unilaterally, that is, without the consent of Congress or the courts, then it should have been just as easy for a subsequent administration, acting in accordance with its prerogative, to revise or eliminate a preexisting order. As we shall see, however, the Reagan administration's failure to revise Executive Order No.

11246 suggests that, intuition notwithstanding, preexisting executive orders are not always so easy to change. Ronald Reagan was a popular president whose view of civil rights was most definitely in conflict with an executive-order program inherited from previous administrations. Yet despite having the legal and constitutional wherewithal to bring the order into line with his own administration's views on civil rights issues, Reagan apparently felt obliged to maintain the status quo.

THE REAGAN ADMINISTRATION'S POSITION ON CIVIL RIGHTS

The cornerstone of the Reagan administration's approach to civil rights policy was opposition to affirmative action. In the eyes of key officials within the administration, affirmative action had degenerated into a racial spoils system in which individuals were accorded preferential treatment by virtue of their membership in a racial or ethnic group that was deemed (usually by a court or administrative agency) to be oppressed or disadvantaged. The other side of the affirmative action coin (as these officials understood it) was the phenomenon of "reverse discrimination," whereby individuals not belonging to one of the "preferred" groups (most often, but not always, white males) were subject to adverse treatment in law and public policy.

In place of affirmative action, the Reagan administration sought to reintroduce the notion that law and public policy should mandate "color-blindness," and should itself be color-blind. Thus key administration officials repeatedly voiced opposition to race- and gender-conscious, group-oriented civil rights policies. Of these, probably none was more outspoken than William Bradford Reynolds. As assistant attorney general for civil rights in the Department of Justice, Reynolds was better situated than any member of the administration other than Reagan himself to affect change in the scope and direction of civil rights policy. In a candid interview given in the summer of 1984, he outlined his agenda:

I think we should bring the behavior of the government on all levels into line with the idea of according equal opportunity for all individuals without regard to race, color, or ethnic background. In my view this means that we should remove whatever kinds of race- or gender-conscious remedies and techniques that exist in the regulatory framework, to ensure that the remedies that are put in place are sensitive to the non-discrimination mandate that is in the laws. We've got a ways to go before we get there (Chavez and Green, 1984: 34).

Shortly before beginning his second term as president, Reagan appointed his domestic policy advisor and longtime friend, Edwin Meese, to head the Department of Justice. As attorney general, Meese further am-

plified the administration's opposition to race-conscious civil rights policies, and made clear its determination to serve as a catalyst for reform.
Soon after assuming the attorney general's post, Meese began presiding
over the development of new rules for enforcing the 1965 Voting Rights
Act. Among other changes, the new rules would have shifted the burden
of proof in voting rights disputes from state and local government officials
to those alleging illegal voting discrimination; they would also have per-
mitted certain changes in local election procedures and in legislative re-
districting even if such changes resulted in a "dilution" of minority-group
voting strength (Pear, 1985b). Moreover, Meese had taken to speaking out
publicly against the use of racial preferences in employment and school
admissions, telling one audience that

the idea that you can use discrimination in the form of racially preferential quotas,
goals, and set-asides to remedy the lingering social effects of past discrimination
makes no sense in principle; in practice, it is nothing short of a legal, moral, and
constitutional tragedy (Shenon, 1985).

During the Reagan administration, the Justice Department would for
the first time file legal briefs in support of white firefighters (*Firefighters
Local No. 1784 v. Stotts*, 1984), school teachers (*Wygant v. Jackson Board
of Education*, 1986), and others who had lost their jobs or been denied
promotion because of government-mandated affirmative action programs.
As for Executive Order No. 11246, by the time Reagan was elected in
1980 it had evolved into precisely the sort of race-conscious, group-
oriented civil rights policy that Reynolds and Meese had criticized. There
was thus every reason to anticipate that the Reagan administration would
substantially revise or eliminate the order.

AFFIRMATIVE ACTION AND EXECUTIVE ORDER
NO. 11246

Executive orders are rarely cast as specific policy directives, and President John F. Kennedy's use of the term "affirmative action" in Executive
Order No. 10925—a precursor of Executive Order No. 11246—was typically imprecise. The Kennedy order declared simply that "it is the policy
of the Executive branch to encourage by positive measures equal opportunity for all persons . . . " and that federal contractors should take "affirmative steps" to ensure that objective (Goldstein, 1984: 20). President
Johnson expanded the scope of the coverage of the contractual provision
of the earlier executive order when he signed Executive Order No. 11246
in 1965. The Johnson version also assigned responsibility for the implementation of the order's equal opportunity mandate to the Department

of Labor, which in turn created the Office of Federal Contract Compliance Programs (OFCCP) to carry out that function.

Although proponents of affirmative action often trace the policy's origin to Executive Order No. 11246, and accordingly regard affirmative action as one of the great civil rights victories of the Johnson administration, the Johnson order itself did nothing to alter the common understanding that affirmative action meant merely that employers, in addition to hiring without regard to the race or ethnicity of job-seekers (both the Kennedy and Johnson executive orders are unequivocal on this point), should also publicize job vacancies and seek to encourage job applications from members of those groups (principally blacks) that might otherwise be discouraged from applying because of widespread discrimination against them in the past. In other words, "affirmative action" was understood to mean that employers should aggressively spread the news that the bad old days of racial discrimination were over, and that now all applications for employment would be treated in the same manner.

In 1968 President Johnson added "sex" to the list of prohibited forms of discrimination mentioned in Executive Order No. 11246, and OFCCP issued implementing regulations that for the first time required all government contractors with contracts worth at least $50,000 (thus including, by 1986, some 15,000 companies employing 23 million workers at 73,000 installations) to develop written affirmative action plans (Pear, 1986a: 9). The regulations also expanded further upon the meaning of affirmative action:

A necessary prerequisite to the development of a satisfactory affirmative action program is the identification and analysis of problem areas inherent in minority employment and an evaluation of opportunities for utilization of minority group personnel. The contractor's program shall provide in detail for specific steps to guarantee equal opportunity keyed to the problems and needs of minority groups, including, when there are deficiencies, the development of specific goals and timetables for the prompt achievement of full and equal employment opportunity. Each contractor shall include in his affirmative action compliance program a table of job classifications. . . . The evaluation of utilization of minority group personnel shall include . . . an analysis of minority group representation in all categories (Glazer, 1975: 46–47).

The regulations' use of the word "deficiencies" adumbrated one of the guiding presuppositions of affirmative action doctrine—that absent discrimination, statistical parity among racial and ethnic groups would be the norm. Although not explicit, a "deficiency," as the word is used here, would seem to denote any state of affairs in which this norm is not realized. It remained for yet another set of guidelines, issued under the Nixon administration in 1971 as "Revised Order No. 4," to confirm this interpretation. While retaining much of the wording of the previous guidelines, the new version required employers to undertake:

an analysis of all major classifications at the facility, with explanations if minorities and women are currently being underutilized in any one or more job classifications. . . . "Underutilization" is defined as having fewer minorities and women in a particular job classification than would reasonably be expected by their availability (Glazer, 1975: 49).

In March 1986, the *New York Times* published an article which strongly suggested that OFCCP regulators tended to equate "underutilization" of minorities and women with the absence of statistical group parity in particular job categories within a given firm. The story concerned a small Kansas construction company that employed fifteen hourly workers, including two truck drivers who were white males, and three workers of minority background. Following a Labor Department investigation, the company received a letter from the department accusing it of having "failed to exert adequate good faith efforts to achieve the minimum minority utilization goal of 12.7 percent for truck drivers and minimum female utilization goal of 6.9 percent for carpenters, heavy equipment operators, iron workers, truck drivers, and laborers." The letter noted that the "remedy" was to "recruit and hire qualified minorities and females until such time as the required utilization goals have been met" (Noble, 1986b: 1). OFCCP regulations provide for the debarment of contractors who fail to affect the prescribed remedies for documented instances of minority and female underutilization.

THE REAGAN YEARS

The Reagan administration's philosophic opposition to affirmative action has already been noted. I have suggested that the administration might have revised or eliminated Executive Order No. 11246 on the basis of its philosophical position alone. There may, however, have been additional reasons for a president who had sworn to "faithfully execute the laws" to feel uneasy about the OFCCP guidelines his administration had inherited from the administrations of Nixon, Ford, and Carter, for it is at least arguable that the guidelines were illegal. Section 703(j) of the Civil Rights Act of 1964 expressly prohibits giving

preferential treatment to any individual or group . . . on account of an imbalance which may exist with respect to the total or percentage of persons of any race, color, religion, sex, or national origin employed . . . in any comparison with the total number or percentage in any community, state, section or other area or in the available workforce or community.

What is most striking about this language is the remarkable prescience with which it anticipates and rejects the policy agenda embodied in Revised Order No. 4. It was as if the Nixon administration had, in effect, unilaterally repealed an Act of Congress and replaced it with its own contrary policy. The argument for revising the order appears even stronger when one considers that in 1956, the Supreme Court ruled that an executive order may be held invalid if it conflicts with provisions either of the Constitution or of a statute (*Cole v. Young*, 1956). To the extent that presidents generally prefer to avoid the prospect of legal challenges to executive branch policy, Reagan (or any other president) may have wished to revise the order for no other reason than to avert a potential conflict with the judicial branch.

Despite Ronald Reagan's reputation as a "great communicator" with regard to matters such as national defense and economic policy, he was largely silent on the question of affirmative action, leaving the struggle over civil rights policy to be waged by surrogates such as Attorney General Edwin Meese and Assistant Attorney General for Civil Rights William Bradford Reynolds. It was thus Meese and Reynolds who spearheaded the effort within the administration to eliminate the reference to numerical goals and timetables from the guidelines for implementing Executive Order No. 11246. That effort, however, would be forcefully opposed by the administration's Secretary of Labor, William Brock.

From mid-1985 until mid-1986, Brock led a faction within the administration that opposed the Meese-Reynolds proposal to reformulate the OFCCP regulations (Pear, 1986b: 1). Although this was one of the few areas of civil rights policy in which the administration could have acted unilaterally, the president could not or would not resolve the dispute within his cabinet. Hence the status quo was maintained through inertia, and the Brock forces, in effect, won. However, it was not merely disagreement among executive branch officials that produced this stalemate; interest-group lobbying was responsible as well.

INTEREST-GROUP POLITICS: BIG BUSINESS VERSUS SMALL BUSINESS

At first glance, one might expect that virtually the entire business community would be elated by the prospect of the sort of deregulation embodied in the Meese-Reynolds proposal. By no longer requiring firms under contract to the federal government to follow rigid numerical goals and timetables for the hiring and promotion of minorities and women, the administration would have relieved employers of what would seem to be an onerous burden. But the American business community is not a political monolith, and hence when the administration began to hint that it might revise or amend the executive order guidelines, business groups began lobbying both for and against the proposed changes.

In August 1985 the administration let it be known that it had drafted an executive order that, as reported by the *New York Times*, "would prevent the Labor Department from requiring any companies to set numerical goals. It would also forbid the use of statistical evidence to measure compliance with laws against discrimination" (Pear, 1985a: 10). Accordingly, the draft contained the following language:

Nothing in this executive order shall be interpreted to require or provide a legal basis for a government contractor or subcontractor to utilize any numerical quota, goal, or ratio, or otherwise to discriminate against, or grant any preference to, any individual or group on the basis of race, color, religion, sex, or national origin with respect to any aspect of employment . . . (quoted in Fisher, 1985: 27).

It is important to note that the proposed draft would not have prevented employers from using racial goals, quotas, or other forms of preference on a voluntary basis. Its only effect would be to prevent the Labor Department from requiring their use by federal contractors. But while the administration might nevertheless have anticipated that Richard T. Seymour of the Lawyer's Committee for Civil Rights would call the draft "an astonishingly extreme document," or that Ralph Neas of the Leadership Conference on Civil Rights would simply label it "unconscionable" ("Plan to end minority hiring," 1985: 18), the administration was no doubt surprised by the negative response that the draft received from a substantial segment of the business community.

In a survey taken among chief executive officers of large corporations (most of them in the Fortune 500), more than 90 percent—116 out of 127 respondents—said that the "numerical objectives" in their company's affirmative action program were established partly to satisfy "corporate objectives unrelated to government regulations." In response to a related question—"Do you plan to continue to use numerical objectives to track the progress of women and minorities in your corporation, regardless of government requirements?"—slightly more than 95 percent said yes (Fisher, 1985: 28). Like many survey questions, this one is worded ambiguously enough to warrant caution in interpreting the results; to at least some of the respondents, using statistics to "track the progress" of female and minority employees may not have meant the same thing as hiring and promoting members of these groups according to predetermined numerical quotas and timetables.

Yet many businesses did make clear their intentions in no uncertain terms. John L. Hulck, chairman of Merck and Company, a large pharmaceutical company located in Rahway, New Jersey, declared that "we will continue goals and timetables no matter what the government does.

They are part of our culture and corporate procedures." John M. Stafford, president and CEO of Pillsbury, voiced a similar sentiment: "It has become clear to us that an aggressive affirmative action program makes a lot of sense. So if the executive order is issued, it wouldn't affect us" (Fisher, 1985: 28).

If these and other companies intended to proceed with their affirmative action efforts even if not required by government to do so, one might have expected them to be indifferent to the possible removal of a such a requirement, much as one would be indifferent to the repeal of a law requiring citizens to breathe. And yet many of the nation's largest companies, led by the National Association of Manufacturers, the traditional lobbying arm of "big business," mounted a major campaign to dissuade the administration from adopting the draft proposal (Noble, 1986a: 13). Why should they have bothered? There appear to be two reasons. The first can be deduced from the section of the draft that disclaims a legal basis in the executive order for the use of racial preferences. In an increasingly litigious society, employers have an interest in maintaining legal certainty and predictability, in discrimination law no less than in other areas of business-related law. As long as the Labor Department requires federal contractors to use goals and timetables that have the effect of favoring minorities and women in hiring and promotion, the firms using these methods will be virtually invulnerable to "reverse discrimination" suits brought by white males who believe they have been unfairly denied a job or promotion. Remove the governmental requirement, however, and the legal climate may change. At the very least, more white males may be encouraged to bring such suits, and defending against them would be more difficult—and expensive.

The simple solution for such firms would have been to drop their race- and gender-based employment procedures altogether, as the draft proposal apparently intended them to do. But that too would have created serious problems. As a perceptive article in *Fortune* magazine pointed out at the time, "most large companies have an entrenched affirmative action bureaucracy in the personnel department," and many of the people who staff these bureaucracies are themselves minority group members and feminists with close ties to the organized civil rights community (Fisher, 1985: 28). In addition to overseeing their companies' minority and female recruitment, retention, and promotion efforts, these in-house affirmative action professionals are often given free reign to organize "workshops" and "seminars" to generate support for affirmative action principles. Thus, according to the *New York Times*:

since 1981 all Merck employees have been required to attend a day-long session to discuss such issues as racial stereotypes, sexual harassment and problems of the handicapped. The company offers "assertiveness training programs" for women and courses in English as a second language. Merck also recruits extensively at historically black colleges and has a special executive program for women, blacks and Hispanic people (Noble, 1986a: 13).

If an IBM, an AT&T, or a Merck were suddenly to announce the cessation of its race- and gender-conscious employment techniques—which would, of course, entail the shutting down of the company's in-house affirmative action bureaucracy—it is unlikely that these affirmative action professionals would leave quietly. To the contrary, one can imagine the outcry, the recriminations, the demonstrations, and threats of consumer boycotts.

The outrage of the displaced affirmative action professionals would likely be shared by their clients in the company, the minorities and women who have been encouraged in the belief that their fate is directly linked to the fate of affirmative action. As one corporate affirmative action professional put it, "now that minorities have come in the door, the job of affirmative action is to oversee the upward mobility of these people. That is the focus in the 1980s" (Fisher, 1985: 30). Thus, according to *Fortune*, "once a company has an affirmative action program in operation, it cannot stop or even retreat noticeably without stirring grievances and impairing morale among women and minorities on the payroll" (Fisher, 1985: 28).

If the executive order draft were enacted, large companies with entrenched affirmative action bureaucracies would be faced with a Hobson's choice: they could either retain their affirmative action programs and risk exposure to lawsuits brought by disgruntled white males, or they could eliminate that risk by dropping their affirmative action programs, thereby incurring the wrath of the displaced affirmative action professionals, their clients within the company, and possibly the organized civil rights community in the form of demonstrations and boycotts. That alone would be enough for many large companies to view the executive order draft with alarm.

There is still another reason why large businesses of the sort represented by the National Association of Manufacturers would have an incentive to keep the existing Labor Department rules intact. That reason becomes easy to discern when one considers that the businesses that lobbied in favor of the administration's draft tended to be small firms with low profit margins and hence a heightened interest in maintaining low overhead costs. These firms, whose lobbying arm in the debate over the draft was the United States Chamber of Commerce (Noble, 1986a: 13), tended not to have entrenched affirmative action bureaucracies in their personnel departments; indeed, they might not even have had personnel departments per se. For them, staying abreast of changes in particular goals and time-tables prescribed by the OFCCP, conducting extensive minority and female recruitment efforts, and filing the reams of government forms that are part and parcel of the compliance effort often constituted an intolerable burden. The comparatively adverse impact of these compliance costs could put a small firm at a competitive disadvantage against a larger rival in the bidding for government contracts. Hence larger firms had a very sound business reason to lobby against any changes that would have the effect of decreasing the disadvantage under which their smaller rivals were forced to operate. Eugene Bardach and Robert Kagan have observed this phenomenon across the spectrum of regulated industries, and it sometimes makes for strange political bedfellows. According to Bardach and Kagan:

[a]ntibusiness social groups are often joined in pushing for more protective regulation by distinctly "probusiness" groups and, in fact, by businesses. Regulation usually affects competitors unevenly, imposing relatively higher costs on some than on others and creating advantages for low-compliance-cost firms. It also creates markets for suppliers of whatever is needed to comply with the regulations (1982: 18).

Moreover,

[t]he available stock of proregulation political sentiments can also be exploited by business interests seeking competitive advantages. While firms may not always be able to predict how they would fare under the specific terms that might emerge in a new regulatory program, once the regulations are in place the distribution of relative advantages and disadvantages becomes apparent. Proposals to ease regulatory restrictions, at that point, stimulate opposition from the specific interests that foresee losing some advantage. This opposition can conveniently ally itself with more diffusely ideological proprotection interests (1982: 200).

Bardach and Kagan developed these rules of thumb in the course of studying the impact of consumer, environmental, and worker health and safety regulations on businesses, but they apply with equal validity to the present case. Here an alliance of large business groups and the already formidable civil rights lobby—combined with internal division within the White House—were enough to kill the executive order draft.

CONCLUSION

Business firms are often assumed to be uniformly opposed to regulation that has the effect of reducing profits and interfering with the prerogatives of business managers. However, when viewed as an attempt by a conservative, pro-business administration to deregulate the business community, the Reagan administration's ill-fated attempt to revise Executive Order No. 11246 illustrates the tendency of regulated firms to resist deregulation under some circumstances. In the present case, one such circumstance was the establishment of a regulatory regime that mandated hiring and promotion policies which, over time, became entrenched to the point where rescinding those policies would have been highly disruptive. Continuation of the regulatory regime was therefore desirable, inasmuch as the regulations served to legitimate the firms' entrenched affirmative action policies. A second circumstance was the likelihood that deregulation would cancel the asymmetrical distribution of compliance costs among competing firms. In the future, affirmative action employment policies are likely to persist, in part because influential actors have powerful incentives to resist their abolition.

6

A Transformed Triangle: Court, Congress, and Presidency in Civil Rights

——————————————————— STEPHEN L. WASBY

INTRODUCTION

The subject to be examined is the triangle formed by the Supreme Court, Congress, and the president, with which interest groups must learn to deal in order to achieve their goals—the old notion of checks and balances from a different perspective. This triangle is more fluid than the "iron triangles"—consisting of government agency, legislative subcommittee, and interest groups—said to have dominated policymaking in particular policy domains. One can also envisage the relationship as a diamond, with interest groups as the fourth point. Indeed, one can imagine two diamonds touching, with interest groups as the common point—one diamond representing national-level activity (Supreme Court, Congress, president), the other representing activity at the state level (Salokar, 1992). As relations among the elements change, the diamonds change shape; instead of being impermeable, they are malleable. In this chapter, our attention is restricted to the "federal diamond" [federal triangle?].

Over time, the relative permeability of the triangle's three elements to demands by particular interests has varied. With respect to civil rights, for almost two decades after World War II the Supreme Court became the "arena of choice" as Congress remained resistant to any initiatives, either presidential or from within itself, and even presidents who might have desired to do so could accomplish little. Then, while the Court continued to remain accessible, for a brief time (1963–1966) the two politically elected branches also became accessible to and supportive of civil rights groups' claims. But starting in the late 1960s, with the exception of Carter's presidency, executive branch support declined and congressional support moderated. When the Supreme Court also adopted presidents' conservative stance and limited rights, Congress acted to overturn the Court, even over presidential vetoes.

Certainly in the 1950s and into the early 1960s, one could not have imagined Congress, with or without the president's assistance, providing strong support for civil rights while the Supreme Court refused to provide such support. Yet there has now been a reversal of position with respect to the relations between the Court, Congress, and the president on civil rights, with a shift from a situation of limited presidential action and resistance by Congress (which prompted Supreme Court action in aid of rights) to one in which the Court limits rights and Congress restores them. In this chapter, brief overviews of civil rights groups' use of litigation and of the Supreme Court's support of civil rights are followed by an analysis of changes in litigation position from one administration to the next ("flip-flops") and of the changed relation between Court and Congress in the protection of civil rights.

CIVIL RIGHTS GROUPS AND LITIGATION

Civil rights groups have often turned to litigation to achieve their goals, with favorable precedents from the United States Supreme Court often a particular goal. The campaign by the National Association for the Advancement of Colored People (NAACP) and the NAACP Legal Defense and Educational Fund leading up to the landmark 1954 school desegregation ruling, *Brown v. Board of Education* (see Kluger, 1976), along with the parallel campaign to eliminate racial restrictive covenants in housing, leading to *Shelley v. Kraemer* (1948) (see Vose, 1959), remains the model of activity by racial minorities to achieve their goals through the courts. So dominant is the "*Brown* model" of litigation that it became the basis for litigation in which other groups—women, Hispanics, Native Americans, the handicapped, and gays and lesbians—have sought to fight discrimination and achieve equal treatment.

The symbolic importance of *Brown v. Board of Education* focused attention on civil rights groups' use of litigation, although they had also sought goals through legislative lobbying, as could be seen in the NAACP's campaign for an anti-lynching law (Zangrando, 1980). Indeed, the name of Clarence Mitchell, long the NAACP's chief Washington lobbyist, was as important as that of Thurgood Marshall, the group's chief lawyer. Yet until well beyond *Brown*, the successes civil rights groups could achieve came primarily through the courts because the groups were politically disadvantaged. The long-standing Democratic dominance of Congress and its racially conservative white southern committee chairmen led civil rights groups to focus their efforts on the courts. In a sense, southern legislators almost forced the NAACP into court; that is, with the legislative avenue closed, litigation was the only path available.[1] Later, the presence of liberal Democratic committee chairmen, who blocked a conservative "social agenda," would similarly force President Reagan to devote substantial attention to the courts.

THE TRIANGLE AND ITS SHIFT

The Court and Support for Civil Rights

Before the 1950s and *Brown v. Board of Education*, the Supreme Court was not known for its civil rights stance. But because the Court sometimes did act when the racial situation was especially unconscionable, it did provide some victories for proponents of civil rights. Included were elimination of the whites-only primary election (*Smith v. Allwright*, 1944); invalidation of court enforcement of racial restrictive covenants (*Shelley*, 1948); and invalidation of segregation in graduate education, as in the *Sweatt* and *McLaurin* cases (1950). Thus, even before *Brown*, the Court was the place where civil rights groups sought refuge, both because Congress was hostile and because help from the president was limited—either because the president could do little in the face of a recalcitrant Congress or because the president himself was hesitant. The Supreme Court therefore became "the place to go" for whatever civil rights gains could be achieved, despite its own less-than-vigorous activity in that area.

The Supreme Court's support for civil rights after the 1954 *Brown* ruling has been seriously overstated. The second *Brown* ruling, providing the standard of "all deliberate speed" for school desegregation and indicating a laundry list of factors that school boards could use as excuses, was retrogressive rather than supportive of the first *Brown* ruling. Moreover, except for rulings in the Little Rock (*Cooper v. Aaron*, 1958) and Prince Edward County (*Griffin v. Board of Education*, 1964) cases, both involving extreme situations, the Court generally failed to provide either guidance or leadership in the school desegregation effort. Although finding many ways to reverse convictions of African Americans for their sit-in challenges to proprietors who discriminated on the basis of race, the Court never was willing to rule unconstitutional a proprietor's invoking the help of police to enforce trespass laws (see Grossman, 1969; Wasby et al., 1977). In avoiding confronting that "state action" question in the sit-in cases, the justices were aware that Congress was considering a public accommodations statute, and knew that a ruling from a Congress that was finally prepared to act would be more acceptable to the nation than a ruling from the unelected Supreme Court.

The Court's hesitation to support civil rights fully prompted justified criticism of its actions as "two steps forward, two steps back, and sidestep, sidestep" (Steel, 1968). Indeed, one wonders what would have happened to advance school desegregation had it not been for the strong pro-desegregation stance of moderate Republican judges in the Fifth Circuit, appointed by President Eisenhower—although not appointed *to* bring about desegregation. Without judges like John Minor Wisdom, Elbert Tuttle, Richard Rives, and Frank Johnson, there would have been little basis for later action by Court and Congress; the Fifth Circuit took a far more assertive position on school desegregation than did its judicial superiors.

When Congress finally did adopt a public accommodations law in the Civil Rights Act of 1964, the Court readily upheld it—in *Heart of Atlanta Motel v. United States* (1964)—and then read the law to apply to pending appeals of sit-in convictions, in *Hamm v. City of Rock Hill* (1964), thus further avoiding the sticky and not-resolved legal issue posed earlier. Only after Congress had enacted major civil rights statutes and President Johnson had taken supportive administrative action did the Supreme Court reenter the civil rights fray with strong statements supporting desegregation (see *Green v. County School Board*, 1968). There is irony that, at the point when many in the black community were tiring of trying to achieve civil rights through litigation because of inaction by the Court and others, the Court finally had a liberal majority that took strong action in other areas of rights. But with Congress finally acting, the Court was shifted to a secondary role, of interpreting statutes rather than making ground-breaking law. Attention thus shifted to Congress and the executive branch.

The Transformed Triangle

The pre- and immediately post-*Brown* hesitation of presidents to support civil rights can be seen in Eisenhower's unwillingness to support the solicitor general's call for an end to "separate but equal" at the reargument of *Brown* and his failure to make any statements in support of *Brown*. Despite more liberal civil rights campaign rhetoric, John F. Kennedy was also at best reluctant to act on that rhetoric and, at worst, acted in a counterproductive fashion through some of his appointments to the federal bench in the South.[2] Yet there was some limited executive-legislative cooperation concerning civil rights even before the peak of support for civil rights initiatives in 1963–1966. An example is the efforts of Republican President Eisenhower and Democratic Senate Majority Leader Lyndon Johnson, which together provided the groundwork for the Voting Rights Act of 1957 (Jackson and Riddlesperger, 1990) and the Voting Rights Act of 1960.

The mid-1960s were heady times for those seeking support for civil rights. President Johnson's support for civil rights was matched by a congressional majority that produced the first major civil rights laws since Reconstruction.[3] Coupled with the administrative regulations developed for their implementation, these statutes meant that civil rights groups had to expand their focus from the courts, where they had been seeking victories on constitutional grounds, to include Congress and the executive branch.

Presidential and congressional support for civil rights lasted only a short time before eroding in a backlash. Because of the difficulty of getting all three corners of the triangle to act for a common purpose, tribranch support of civil rights like that which characterized the mid-1960s is rare. It is therefore not surprising that it was not to last. As efforts to enforce *Brown* moved north, liberal Democratic members of Congress "abandoned ship" and joined conservative Republicans (and conservative Democrats) in seeking to limit "forced busing." Increased involvement in Vietnam and the negative reaction to the war increasingly absorbed President Johnson's attention. Thus, despite passage of the 1968 open housing law, the shift away from strong presidential and congressional support for civil rights had begun even before Richard Nixon became president, as can be seen in the antiriot provision of the 1968 act.

Transitions Between Administrations

Changes in administration are key factors in the transformation of the triangle as it affects civil rights policy, because administrative and litigative enforcement actions have varied from one presidency to the next.[4] One apparent disjuncture between administrations was in the Johnson/Nixon transition, seen in the Nixon administration's efforts to defer school desegregation in Mississippi. For the first time since *Brown*, this put a presidential administration and the NAACP Legal Defense Fund on opposite sides of a school desegregation case before the Supreme Court (*Alexander v. Holmes County*, 1969). Yet civil rights groups' rhetoric suggested far more damage than occurred in that transition.

President Gerald Ford, a moderate on civil rights, generally continued the Nixon administration's position, including continued opposition to busing, which was reflected in threats to intervene in the Boston school case, and the low priority given to enforcing housing discrimination rules (see Lamb, 1991). Although the Carter administration was definitely more supportive of civil rights than the Ford administration and was liberal by comparison with the country's increasingly conservative tone, the Carter administration's shift from its Republican predecessors was not of large magnitude because, like its predecessor, it was moderate in tone and action. The Carter administration was, however, particularly supportive of the work of civil rights organizations. In some measure this resulted from drawing on those organizations to staff important executive branch positions—for example, appointing former NAACP Legal Defense Fund attorney Drew Days III as Assistant Attorney General for Civil Rights.

Moreover, the Carter administration made the strongest commitment in our history to affirmative action in selecting federal judges.

The Carter-to-Reagan transition provided a clear and most severe disjuncture—a stark juxtaposition—in presidential support for civil rights. Where the Carter administration, itself supportive of civil rights and with a supportive constituency in the civil rights community, had been moderate and relatively nonideological, the Reagan administration was strongly conservative and committed to pursuing an ideological social agenda, which included explicit opposition to affirmative action programs ("quotas") and less visible efforts to make the federal courts less accessible to those wishing to pursue civil rights litigation. The Reagan administration's attention to conservative ideology (masked as "judicial self-restraint") in its judicial selection meant another abrupt change as we returned to a largely white-male judiciary. The distinctiveness of the Carter-to-Reagan transition, far more detrimental to the goals of the civil rights community than earlier transitions, shows the importance of taking a long-term view in any examination of the presidency and civil rights.

The Supreme Court's Shift

At least through the early 1970s, while civil rights organizations were encountering reduced congressional and presidential support, they received continued support from the Supreme Court. The Johnson-to-Nixon transition in civil rights was eased by the Supreme Court's continuation until the mid-1970s of its commitment to civil rights. It was the new Nixon-appointed Chief Justice, Warren Burger, who refused to accept the administration's desire for further delay in desegregation and announced the end of "all deliberate speed" for the Court in *Alexander v. Holmes County* (1969). It was Burger who also wrote for the Court in upholding lower courts judges' discretion to issue remedies, including busing, in school desegregation cases, and in giving Title VII of the 1964 Civil Rights Act a broad reading (the "disparate impact" test) in *Griggs v. Duke Power Co.* (1971). The Court's first northern school case, from Denver, was also a civil rights victory.

Only in 1974 did we see the Court draw back. It did so in the first Detroit case, *Milliken v. Bradley*, when it refused to allow interdistrict busing for school desegregation. The Court's withdrawal was visible not only in the result—a decision against claims by civil rights organizations—but in the majority's highly formalistic treatment of those claims—in particular, its rejection of the connection between housing discrimination and segregated schools and its strong adherence to existing school district boundaries. The Court's ruling that interdistrict remedies were permissible only if the other districts had also discriminated, along with the Court's earlier ruling making it extremely difficult to test suburbs' exclusionary zoning rules (*Warth v. Seldin*, 1975), gave white suburbs further incentives to exclude minorities and made the achievement of metropolitan area desegregation almost impossible. The new Supreme Court majority also drew back in the employment area. After at first indicating its willingness to allow retroactive job seniority in employment discrimination cases, in the 1977 *Teamsters* case the justices showed their unwillingness to allow full seniority to those who had been the objects of employment discrimination.

That the Court later upheld desegregation plans for central-city Detroit and made the state pay for remedial programs (*Milliken v. Bradley*, 1977) removed little of the sting of the first Detroit case because the suburbs remained closed to desegregation. However, further indicating the nonlinear progression of the Court's rulings, two years after the second Detroit decision the Court strongly supported lower court orders to desegregate Dayton and Columbus, Ohio, schools on the grounds they had engaged in official segregative acts since *Brown* (*Dayton Board of Education v. Brinkman*, 1979; *Columbus Board of Education v. Penick*, 1979).

In contemplating the Court's future course, we should keep in mind that there remains a high surprise level in its rulings and thus there often will be exceptions to the established pattern perceived by observers. Just as the Columbus and Dayton cases followed the retrogressive first Detroit decision, so in 1992 the Court, over only a single dissent, ruled that Mississippi's system of higher education remained segregated and that action must be taken to desegregate it effectively (*United States v. Fordice*, 1992). That this was a ruling sought not only by civil rights groups but also by the Bush administration illustrates that fluidity in the policymaking triangle can indeed be considerable.

LITIGATION: STABILITY AND SHIFT

Stability in Litigators' Environment

When organizations like the American Civil Liberties Union or the NAACP Legal Defense Fund begin litigation, and particularly when they initiate a set of cases in a specific area of the law, they appear to assume that their legal environment will remain relatively stable. That the Supreme Court did not immediately shift as expected with Nixon's appointments to the Court, except perhaps in the criminal procedure area, may have reinforced litigators' assumption of continuity in the Court's position at that time. Yet when litigation is extended, as it has been with school and employment cases, there is great likelihood that the Court will shift position, thus changing the legal environment during a campaign. This makes shifts in the Court's posture an important part of litigation dynamics.

In addition, civil rights groups' prior attention to the courts to achieve their goals and their victories there have produced a momentum (a type of inertia) that has led lawyers to attempt to achieve successes in court even after the atmosphere had become far less favorable. The momentum means that more attention has continued to be focused on the courts than is warranted by the decreasing payoff, as the Supreme Court has become less supportive of civil rights, and there was a considerable lag before that "excess" effort was shifted to the legislative branch. Yet the Court's conservatism and the administration's abandonment of civil rights meant civil rights groups had to fight defensive battles in the Court and with the administration, and had to seek all the help they could obtain from Congress.

That litigants proceed along well-worn paths reinforces the notion that the legal environment is stable. Continuity in the legal environment is further reinforced by the view that it is not wise for a litigant, whether a private civil rights organization or a government agency, to appear to have changed positions in mid-litigation. Judges are quick to point out such changes, doing so not to applaud but observing tartly, "The parties have changed their position at every stage of the litigation," or letting fly barbs like Justice Stevens' "The Equal Employment Opportunity Commission has staunchly argued both sides of this policy question at different stages of this litigation."[5] The Court may recognize the need for the government to change position when the presidency changes hands,[6] but does not always accept this as an excuse, because of the notion that "the law" is, or should be, stable. This serves as a constraint on change, and helps to explain why the professional image of the solicitor general's office suffers if an administration alters its position significantly from its predecessor's stance (see Caplan, 1988).

Flip-Flops: Shifts in Administration Litigation Posture

Administration changes in litigation position provide a basis for the courts, including the Supreme Court, to shift their stance. The Court will not necessarily go along, but it may move closer to the administration's new position, and it has done so, particularly in areas where the justices have tended to take their lead from the government's stance—for example, voting rights (see Wasby, 1982). Judicial movement toward executive policy is quite likely if the new administration has been able to place some nominees on the Court, as Presidents Reagan and Bush were able to do.

Significant changes in the administration's litigation position can produce major problems for litigating interest groups. When a new administration abandons enforcement efforts which have served to assist the litigating interest group, a substantial caseload increase for the group can result. The organization's workload will also be very much heavier if the new administration seeks to reopen litigation once thought to have been resolved on terms favorable to the group. A major example is the Reagan administration's reopening of consent decrees (reached in the Carter administration and earlier) to resolve complaints of discrimination in municipal employment.

"Flip-flops" in the executive branch's litigation position also can occur within a single administration. For example, the Bush administration, after first filing a brief challenging the spending of more money on historically black colleges and universities in the attempt to bring about desegregation, supported a new brief in which the positive role of such colleges and universities was explicitly recognized (Jaschik, 1991; Blumenstyk, 1991). In another instance, Reagan's Justice Department had agreed to settle a voting rights case on terms less desirable than what civil rights groups wished; intervenors seeking the strong position were able to get a federal court to turn down the settlement, and when the case was appealed, "Justice reversed its position, although with little evidence of enthusiasm, and supported the district court's stand" (*City of Port Arthur v. United States*, 1982) (Bullock and Butler, 1985: 40).

However, flip-flops are more likely between administrations. Changes in policy from one administration to another may take place with some frequency, but changes in position in individual cases which continue to be litigated are thought to be far less frequent. A new administration will be more likely not to pursue on appeal cases initiated by its predecessor and to abandon an area of litigation than to engage in flip-flops. Nonetheless, the latter are a significant part of the dynamics of litigation. They are more likely with an interparty change in administrations, and particularly when there is a distinct ideological shift such as that particularly evident when President Reagan took office.

A flip-flop can, of course, be favorable to civil rights organizations. As one can see in the Ford-to-Carter transition, changes in administration may lead to greater government willingness to settle cases in which the organization earlier opposed the government. More significant, however, have been shifts from executive branch support of civil rights organizations' position—with government and interest group perhaps even being on the same side of the case—to divergence of government and interest group or even strong opposition. The extent of the shift in litigation position from one administration to the next has varied from only a modest alteration in emphasis, as in the shift from Truman to Eisenhower or (with the benefit of hindsight) Johnson to Nixon, to a distinct reversal of position, as in the change from Carter to Reagan.

Several examples of an administration reversing its predecessor's position are found in the Carter-to-Reagan transition, when the Reagan administration abandoned Carter administration positions while cases were pending before the Supreme Court instead of waiting to press its position in new cases. As the Leadership Conference on Civil Rights (1982: 3, 14) asserted, the new Reagan Justice Department had "abruptly switched sides in cases pending before the Supreme Court and announced that it would seek the overturning of Supreme Court decisions of very recent vintage, in disregard of the importance of certainty and continuity in the law."

One major change involved the controversy over whether private schools that based their racial discrimination on religion should be deprived of their tax-exempt status because of that discrimination (see Caplan, 1988: 51–62). The government had won a lower court challenge to the revocation of Bob Jones University's tax exemption. Although the acting solicitor general felt the government had properly won the case, the initial reaction of the solicitor general's office to the university's appeal was to acquiesce in the Supreme Court's hearing the case. However, a group of high-level Justice Department officials then persuaded Attorney General William French Smith to adopt as the government's position the claim that the Internal Revenue Service lacked authority for revoking the exemption. When the administration then argued in its brief that the case was moot, the Court was left with no party to argue the position initially advocated by the government. The Court appointed an *amicus curiae* to do so—choosing William Coleman, former Cabinet member *and* chairman of the NAACP Legal Defense Fund. The Court then ruled against the Reagan administration.

Another flip-flop came in the Seattle school desegregation case. There the Carter Justice Department had supported a major busing plan, but the Reagan administration changed sides. The Supreme Court, in *Washington v. Seattle School District No. 1* (1982), noting that the government "has changed its position during the course of this litigation, and now supports the State" (which opposed the busing plan), upheld the initial, not subsequent, government position, just as it had in the *Bob Jones University* case (1983). In a voting rights example, the *City of Lockhart* case (1983), in the lower courts the Carter Justice Department had supported minority voters challenging certain election changes. Here the Reagan administration argued that voters were not worse off from the changes and that the pre-1982 version of Section 2 of the Voting Rights Act should be applied. However, in 1983 the Court accepted the new administration's position on nonretrogression.

CONGRESS AND THE RESCUE OF CIVIL RIGHTS

As the Court became the place where civil liberties and civil rights are limited, there was, finally, a shift from civil rights advocates turning to the Court (because Congress was resistant) to their turning to Congress to overturn a resistant Supreme Court which a conservative president aided through positions taken before the Court in key cases and appointments to the Court. When the Court has abandoned support of civil rights, going to Congress to protect the policies earlier legitimated or adopted by the Court becomes important. Congress is needed to undo the position of the Court *and* the president, at times when the justices have adopted an administration flip-flop. In this "transformed triangle," Congress has increasingly responded positively, restoring what the Court has refused to give or has taken away. Congress even overrode the president in order to restore protection of rights sought by those unsuccessful in the Supreme Court. In the last two decades, Congress *has* come to the aid of civil rights groups.

Congressional support for civil rights groups has not come solely from spontaneous combustion. The groups were aided by Democratic control of the House throughout the Reagan and Bush presidencies, with only six years of a Republican Senate majority. Under the umbrella of the Leadership Conference for Civil Rights, civil rights organizations worked hard to bring about positive results. Although always interested in a favorable legislative atmosphere, the groups' greater attention to lobbying came largely from an effort to undo the Supreme Court's actions that resulted from its decreasing receptivity to the groups' arguments. The linkage between negative Supreme Court rulings and civil rights organizations' increased attention to Congress can perhaps be best seen in the aftermath of the Court's ruling in *City of Mobile v. Bolden* (1980), requiring a showing of intent to prove a Section 2 Voting Rights Act violation. The ensuing effort to overturn the ruling included using major voting rights litigators like Frank Parker and Armand Derfner as lobbyists to bring the law back to its pre-*City of Mobile* position. As part of this activity, the Lawyers Committee for Civil Rights Under Law moved its Voting Rights Project from Mississippi to Washington, D.C. That instance provided a major reversal of the Court—the law was returned to an earlier test that was easier for plaintiffs to satisfy—that attracted considerable attention because the Reagan administration changed positions during the debate.

Congress's first modern "rescue" of civil rights groups from adverse Supreme Court rulings came in 1976. In *Alyeska Pipeline Service Co. v. Wilderness Society* (1975), the Court had severely limited federal courts' award of attorneys fees to those successful in litigation. In response, Congress passed the Civil Rights Attorneys Fees Act of 1976, providing attorney fees to the prevailing party in civil rights cases. That statute, despite the difficulty of persuading some judges to award fees, provides a major source of funding for civil rights litigation, thus facilitating civil rights litigation generally. Another instance was the overturning, in the aptly-titled Civil Rights Restoration Act, of the Court's ruling in the *Grove City College* case (1984) that the antidiscrimination provision of Title IX (sex discrimination in education) applied only to specific programs that received federal funds, not to the entire institution. Congress instead said that if an institution received any federal funds, the antidiscrimination laws applied to the entire institution.

The most striking instance of Congress's reversing the Supreme Court in the civil rights area came in response to June 1989 rulings in which the Court significantly limited employees' ability to prove discrimination in employment. It did so by changing the standard for proving a violation of Title VII, by ruling that racial harassment on the job and denial of promotions based on race were not actionable under the post–Civil War civil rights laws, and by facilitating the reopening of employment discrimination consent decrees by white males claiming "reverse discrimination." While conceding that some of the rulings should be reversed, the Bush administration put up considerable resistance to the proposed Civil Rights Act of 1990, arguing that the proposal to reinstate the prior standard for providing "disparate impact" discrimination would require "quotas" in employment. President Bush vetoed the first version of the law before ultimately agreeing to a new version, the Civil Rights Act of 1991. At the heart of the new statute was a provision that restored the Court's 1971 employment discrimination standard, which it had significantly limited in *Wards Cove Packing Co. v. Atonio* (1989). The lapse of two years between the Supreme Court rulings and their reversal allowed Congress, in the same law, to reverse two more Supreme Court rulings from 1991.[7]

Post-Reversal Interaction

A crucial part of the "triangle" of Court, Congress, and president is continuing interaction between Court and Congress over the latter's reversals of the Court's decisions. When the Court interprets a statute in a way that displeases a congressional majority to the point that the legislators rewrite the law, the Court's usual response is to accept the congressional reversal—in what one might say is good grace—and to go on about applying the new statute. One can see that in the Court's recognition of the reversal of its *City of Mobile* ruling and its attempt to apply the new (or old) "effects" standard to claims of vote dilution in *Thornburg v. Gingles* (1986).

At times, however, the Court appears to resist full acceptance of the letter and spirit of congressional action. For example, the Court has generally applied the spirit of the Civil Rights Attorneys Fees Act, but one of the cases leading to a reversal in the Civil Rights Act of 1991 illustrates a different stance by the Court. In *West Virginia University Hospitals v. Casey* (1991), Justice Scalia, for the Court, recognized that members of Congress saw the Act (§1988) as a response to the *Alyeska* ruling. However, he said, "It is a considerable step . . . from this proposition to the conclusion . . . that §1988 should be read as a reversal of *Alyeska* in all respects," and then declared "that, in many respects, §1988 was not meant to return us precisely to the pre-*Alyeska* regime" (at 1146). The Court then ruled that fees were not available for expert witnesses in connection with civil rights cases. This ruling was overturned by Congress in 1991.

It then became an open question how the increasingly conservative Supreme Court would treat the Civil Rights Act of 1991. Particularly at issue was whether the standard adopted to overturn *Wards Cove* was to be applied to employment discrimination cases brought between that 1989 ruling and the effective date of the 1991 reversal legislation. Most civil rights statutes have been granted retroactivity. However, the present Court, reluctant to facilitate the bringing of civil rights claims in the employment area, showed it was not hesitant to exhibit resistance by reading the new statute narrowly. The Bush administration, having only reluctantly agreed to the statute, then argued against its retroactive application, and, toward that end, gave up a victory in which a lower court applied a different civil rights statute which was also silent on the retroactivity question (see Greenhouse, 1992a). Following the administration's lead, the Court then did deny retroactivity.[8]

CONCLUSION

Policy is not static; in some sense it is like the weather: if you wait a bit, it will change. We have seen the administration engage in such changes in the course of litigation, including notable Reagan administration flip-flops during civil rights litigation. However, it is not only the substance of policy that varies over time. Relations between principal policymaking bodies also change. The relative access to interest groups provided by government institutions likewise varies. This provides support for the proposition that "if one door is closed, there are two others that might be opened" for interest groups seeking entry (Rebecca Salokar to author, June 23, 1992) and confirmation that multiple access points assist the achievement of civil rights policies (Perry, 1991).

Development of civil rights policy by Congress, president, and Supreme Court over the last fifty or so years provides clear evidence that we have moved from (1) a lack of presidential enthusiasm for civil rights initiatives and congressional resistance to civil rights legislation, coupled with the Court's increasing support for civil rights, through (2) a brief period of tripartite support for major elements of the civil rights community's agenda, into (3) a period of presidential and legislative withdrawal coupled with moderated judicial support, and then to (4) presidential opposition to civil rights claims and efforts to roll them back through the courts, with Congress ultimately giving shelter to civil rights organizations by legislatively reversing the Court over the president's objections. The situation is largely a function of divided government, in which one political party controls the presidency and appointments to the Supreme Court and the other has a congressional majority. Were the same ideological faction to become dominant in all three branches—if the Republicans were to win control of Congress—civil rights groups would face a uniformly bleak situation. Yet that change is unlikely, at least in the foreseeable future; with an entrenched Supreme Court conservative majority (but see Greenhouse, 1992b, on moderating tendencies), a Democratic presidency probably would change the situation only marginally from the present.

NOTES

I am indebted to several people for invaluable substantive and editorial comments on earlier versions of this chapter: Susan Daly, Donald Jackson, and Rebecca Salokar.

1. I am indebted to Michael Adams for part of this formulation.

2. See Navasky (1971). On the Kennedy administration's hesitancy to deal with Southern violence aimed at civil rights workers, a hesitancy tied in part to a prior ruling by the Supreme Court, see Belknap (1987).

3. Murphy and Tanenhaus (1990: 1018) observe that "one might ask whether the Civil Rights Act of 1964 and the Voting Rights Act of 1965 did not function as congressional and Presidential legitimations of the Supreme Court decisions on race—legitimations backed up by the use and threat of greater use of federal force."

4. This is illustrated well in studies of the effect of political control of the bureaucracy, which encompass the Equal Employment Opportunity Commission. See B. Dan Wood and Richard W. Waterman, "The dynamics of political control of the bureaucracy," *American Political Science Review* 85 (September 1991): 801–28, particularly pp. 806–7, and Wood, "Does politics make a difference at the EEOC?" *American Journal of Political Science* 34 (May 1990): 503–30.

5. *Northwest Airlines v. Transport Workers Union*, 451 U.S. 77, 89 (1981).

6. We can see this in an example from outside the civil rights area. In discussing why nonmutual collateral estoppel should not be applied to the government, Justice Rehnquist wrote for the Court: "The panoply of important public issues raised in government litigation may quite properly lead successive Administrations of the Executive Branch to take differing positions with respect to the resolution of a particular issue. . . . Such policy choices are made by one Administration, and often reevaluated by another Administration." *United States v. Mendoza*, 464 U.S. 154, 161 (1984).

7. In addition to *Wards Cove*, 490 U.S. 642 (1989), also reversed in the Civil Rights Act of 1991 were *Lorance v. AT&T Technologies*, 490 U.S. 900 (1989)(holding that the statute of limitations for complaints about new seniority systems ran from adoption of the system, not from when someone might recognize they were adversely affected); *Patterson v. McLean Credit Union*, 491 U.S. 164 (1989)(racial harassment); *Price Waterhouse v. Hopkins*, 490 U.S. 228 (1989)(standard to be

used in gender discrimination cases); *Martin v. Wilks*, 490 U.S. 755 (1989)(consent decrees); *West Virginia University Hospitals v. Casey*, 499 U.S. 83 (1991)(fees for expert witnesses); and *E.E.O.C. v. Arabian American Oil*, 499 U.S. 254 (1991)(limiting extraterritorial effect of Title VII).

8. *Landgraf v. USI Film Products*, 114 S.Ct. 1483 (1994); *Rivers v. Roadway Express*, 114 S.Ct. 1510 (1994).

PART III

Policy Arenas, the President, and Civil Rights

7

Presidential Decision-Making in Two Desegregation Crises: Little Rock Central High School and the University of Mississippi

Mark Stern

INTRODUCTION

This chapter examines how Presidents Dwight D. Eisenhower and John F. Kennedy dealt with similar policy crises: the use of federal troops to enforce federal school desegregation court orders which were openly defied by state governments. Both episodes, the desegregation of Little Rock Central High School in 1957 and the University of Mississippi (Ole Miss) in 1962, developed in remarkably parallel fashion as state governors defied the federal courts and then maneuvered to deceive the president of the United States. This chapter also examines the Kennedy administration approach to the desegregation crisis at the University of Mississippi, given the precedent set by the Little Rock crisis. Finally, this chapter examines the basis for both presidents' reluctance to use federal troops to resolve these crises and the consequence that their decisions had for the federal-state relationship.

Crises, that is, situations demanding a quick response by decision-makers, often lack routine. They are also often unpredictable with accompanying ad-hoc decision making. Time is of the essence during crises as decisions are often forced upon a limited array of participants who usually choose from among a brief set of options which yield what is often hoped to be, at best, a "satisficing" solution. The latter solution solves the problem at hand in a reasonable, if not most desired, fashion. Crises truncate the consultation as well as the systematic exploration of policy alternatives.[1] By contrast, major policy innovation, as Nelson Polsby points out, is often first brought forward in open debate during elections in the United States, and is the product of subsequent discussion and negotiation among many actors in the political system.[2] In addition, as Charles Lindblom and others have pointed out, most policy change is incremental and fairly routinized, a matter of bargaining and minor adjustments, again often with a host of major political players involved in the final resolution of the issue.[3] In national domestic crises the president, after consultation with a small, intimate group of advisers, is often the key, final decision-maker. As such, the president's values and the context of the crisis as he and a limited array of advisers view it usually become the major determinants of action in these crises. Crises bring attention to a problem, frequently, as John W. Kingdon notes, through a "focusing event."[4]

The Eisenhower and Kennedy administrations each had a "focusing event" which forced them to use federal troops to resolve school desegregation crises: open gubernatorial defiance of a federal court order. The Kennedy administration had the precedent of the Little Rock integration crisis from which it could and did draw lessons to be applied in its handling of the integration crisis at the University of Mississippi. The Kennedy White House viewed the crisis at the University of Mississippi as parallel to the crisis at Little Rock, but they saw it as a chance to handle the matter differently than their predecessors' handling of Little Rock.

EISENHOWER AND LITTLE ROCK

President Eisenhower's approach to the desegregation crisis at Little Rock Central High School mirrored his beliefs about race relations, the nature of law and people, and the federal government's role under the Constitution.[5] Eisenhower believed in the equality of the races, but he also believed that equal treatment for racial minorities was a matter that would be achieved between individuals, and law could not mandate such matters. While he believed that federal law was supreme, and must be enforced, he tied this to a respect for the traditional bounds of the federal-state relationship.

Eisenhower and his attorney general, Herbert Brownell, reviewed the federal government's brief that was submitted to the Supreme Court for its implementation of the 1954 desegregation decision, *Brown v. Board of Education, et al.*[6] The executive branch supported the plaintiffs.[7] Eisenhower sent a telegram to the 1954 Annual Meeting of the National Association for the Advancement of Colored People (NAACP), in which he stated that he regarded the *Brown* decision as a "milestone of social advance." But he warned, "we must have patience without compromise of principle. We must have understanding without disregard for differences which actually exist. We must have continued social progress, calmly but persistently made. . . . "[8] Eisenhower continually maintained the latter position, albeit with a more empathetic understanding of the southern white need for gradualism than the southern black need for speed.

As the Supreme Court worked on the *Brown* implementation decision, Eisenhower wrote to a close friend that the desegregation issue would "become acute or tend to die out according to the character of the procedure orders that the Court will... issue."[9] Southern political leaders overwhelmingly opposed *Brown*, and the implementation ruling did not lessen their opposition despite the Court's allowance for the local execution of the desegregation process with "all deliberate speed."

Despite the intensity of southern opposition to *Brown*, and his sympathy for the southern position, Eisenhower consistently maintained that the Court's mandate would be upheld. On March 14, 1956, three days after 101 southern members of the United States Senate and House of Representatives issued the "Southern Manifesto," they voiced opposition to any enforcement of the school desegregation order and called for state "nullification" of federal law. Eisenhower publicly stated, "the [southern white] people who have this deep emotional reaction... were not acting over the past three generations in defiance of law. They were acting in compliance with the law as interpreted by the Supreme Court [in *Plessy v. Ferguson*]." *Brown* "completely reversed" the earlier case, "and it is going to take time for them to adjust their thinking and their progress to that.... I don't know anything about the length of time it will take." The president warned, however, that "nullification" of federal law by a state was unacceptable. "There," he noted, "would be a place where we get to a very bad spot for the simple reason I am sworn to defend and uphold the Constitution of the United States and, of course, I can never abandon or refuse to carry out my duty."[10] Soon afterwards he told his cabinet, "in the long run the Constitution is going to be enforced. That's my duty, but the Supreme Court gave us some time. Our complaint is that time is not being used [wisely]. Instead states have merely sat down and said 'we defy.'"[11] How long "the long run" was going to take was an open matter.

Neither in public nor in private did Eisenhower personally endorse the substance of *Brown* during his presidential tenure. Privately, he occasionally indicated a lack of support. For example, when the Platform Committee at the 1956 Republican National Convention proposed to state that "the Eisenhower Administration" supported the *Brown* decision, the president called his attorney general, who was at the drafting sessions, and told him the statement had to be deleted or he would not attend the convention. It was removed from the platform document. The president indicated to Brownell that "because of the Supreme Court's ruling the whole issue has been set back, and badly."[12] Yet, he wrote to his friend, Swede Hazlett, "if the day comes when we can obey the orders of our Courts only when we personally approve of them, the end of the American system... will not be far off."[13] And that was the nub of the issue for Eisenhower. Whether or not he supported the substance of the *Brown* decision was irrelevant; preservation of the federal-state constitutional relationship was the relevant issue. While he would not voice an opinion on the substance of *Brown*, he maintained that it would be upheld as the law of the land.[14]

Of the southern states, only Arkansas and Texas took steps to begin the desegregation of public schools in 1956, the school year following the implementation decision, and in both cases the state and local authorities backed away from the desegregation process in the face of public agitation.[15] When asked at a September 6, 1956 news conference what his administration planned to do about the active opposition to school desegregation by state and local officials in Texas and Tennessee, the president answered that the district judges had "the primary responsibility for insuring that progress . . . was made." He continued, "it is difficult through laws and through force to change a man's heart." Everyone had a responsibility to "bring a change in spirit so . . . [there] is recognition of the equality of men." Asked if he endorsed the *Brown* decision, the president replied that it made "no difference whether I endorse it. The Constitution is as the Supreme Court interprets it; and I must conform to that and do my best to see that it is carried out in this country."[16] On September 11, 1956, again in response to a journalist's question about federal efforts to stop the public turmoil which blocked school desegregation in Texas, the president responded that the federal government could only intervene if "called upon by the Governor of a state."[17]

Over the next year, as southern opposition kept school desegregation efforts at a near standstill, the president was repeatedly asked about his administration's intent to use federal troops if necessary to enforce *Brown*. In July of 1957, Eisenhower responded, "I can't imagine any set of circumstances that would ever induce me to send Federal troops . . . into an area to enforce the orders of a Federal court. . . . " He followed this up by stating he "would never believe it would be a wise thing to do in this country."[18] That fall Eisenhower found the circumstances such that he had to send federal troops into Little Rock to enforce a federal court order for school desegregation.

When the 1957 school year commenced, Governor Orval E. Faubus of Arkansas used his state's National Guard to block the desegregation of Little Rock Central High School. On September 3, Eisenhower publicly stated that he doubted the Department of Justice would intervene.[19] Two days later the governor asked the president for his understanding as he defied the Court. The president replied, "the only assurance I can give you is that the Federal Constitution will be upheld by me by every legal means at my command."[20] On September 11, Arkansas congressman Brooks Hays, with Faubus's agreement, requested that presidential assistant Sherman Adams arrange for the president to meet with the governor. Eisenhower was assured that the governor intended "to comply with the order that has been issued by the District Court in this case . . . ," and he acceded to the request.[21] Brownell warned the president not to hold the meeting. He believed the governor would double-cross his chief.[22] Brownell believed that Faubus would use his meeting with Eisenhower to enhance his reelection chances in the upcoming Arkansas gubernatorial elections. A confrontation with the president would solidify the governor's leadership of the anti-integration forces, and the latter forces were riding high with the Arkansas electorate. The governor, Brownell told his boss, was not about to accede to integration.[23] Eisenhower still went forward with the meeting.

Governor Faubus visited with the president on September 14 at his vacation residence in Newport, Rhode Island. After the meeting was over, Eisenhower wrote in his diary that he believed Faubus was "going back to Arkansas to act within a matter of hours to revoke his orders to the guard to prevent re-entry of the Negro children into the school."[24] Eisenhower also told the governor, "I did not believe that it was beneficial to anybody to have a test of strength between the President and a Governor because in any area where the Federal government had assumed jurisdiction and this was upheld by the Supreme Court there could be only one outcome—that is, the state would lose, and I did not want to see any Governor humiliated."[25] Within days, the president learned that the governor "was not going to carry out the order of the court. . . . "[26] On September 23, the president issued a proclamation which warned, "I will use the full power of the United States including whatever force may be necessary to prevent any obstruction of the law and to carry out the orders of the Federal Court."[27] Faubus remained defiant.

The next day Eisenhower returned to the White House, informed his staff of his intention to use federal troops to enforce the court order, and went on national television to inform the nation of his decision. He stated that "under the leadership of demagogic extremists, disorderly mobs have prevented the carrying out of proper orders from a Federal Court. Local authorities have not eliminated that violent opposition. . . . Whenever normal agencies prove inadequate to the task and it becomes necessary for the Executive Branch of the Federal Government to use its powers and authority to uphold Federal Courts, the President's responsibility is inescapable." Eisenhower continued, "with that responsibility, I have today issued an Executive Order directing the use of troops under Federal authority to aid in the execution of Federal law at Little Rock, Arkansas," to enforce "the Court's order relating to the admission of Negro children to school."[28] He noted, "this became necessary when my proclamation of yesterday was not observed, and the obstruction of justice still continues."

Eisenhower explained his position further, "[My] personal opinions about the [Court's desegregation] decision have no bearing on the matter of enforcement; the responsibility and authority of the Supreme Court to interpret the Constitution are very clear." The Federal Courts had "issue[d] such orders and decrees as might be necessary to achieve admission to the public schools without regard to race—and with all deliberate speed. ... When large gatherings of obstructionists made it impossible for the decrees of the Court to be carried out, both the law and the national interest demanded that the President take action." He argued, "The very basis of our individual rights and freedoms rests upon the certainty that the President and the Executive branch of Government will support and insure the carrying out of decisions of the Federal Courts, even, when necessary with all the means at the President's command. Unless the President did so, anarchy would result." The president maintained, "from intimate personal knowledge, I know that the overwhelming majority of the people in the South—including those of Arkansas and of Little Rock—are of good will and respect the law even when they disagree with it. They do not sympathize with mob rule." He described how he understood the basis of southern concern with desegregation. He ended by asking "the citizens of the State of Arkansas to assist in bringing to an immediate end all interference with the law and its processes. If resistance to the Federal Court orders ceases at once, the further presence of Federal troops will be unnecessary." However, in fact the troops remained in Little Rock throughout the school year.

On October 3, 1957, Eisenhower told a press conference, "No one can deplore more than I do the sending of Federal troops anywhere. It is not good for the troops; it is not good for the locality. It is not really American except as it becomes absolutely necessary for the support of the institutions that are vital to our form of government."[29] The president understood the violence that the use of federal troops over state objection inevitably wrought upon the federal-state relationship. Yet, his belief in the supremacy of federal law, and the Supreme Court as the interpreter of law under the Constitution, brought him to resolve this crisis in a manner he had previously thought to be almost unimaginable. Brownell believed, "there never was any doubt after Little Rock that the Constitution, as defined by the Supreme Court in *Brown I* would be upheld by the full powers of the Federal government."[30] Yet, once again federal troops were to be deployed to enforce *Brown* as the governor of Mississippi confronted Eisenhower's successor in a more violent affair.

KENNEDY AND OLE MISS

President Kennedy's approach to the desegregation crisis which occurred at the University of Mississippi in 1962 reflected his beliefs about race relations, the nature of law and people, and the federal government's role under the Constitution, as well as the lessons of the Little Rock crisis as he understood them. JFK believed that differences over issues could be solved rationally, with individuals coming to agreement over logical, reasonable solutions. Civil rights and race relations were the most passionate, obstinate, and irrational issues in American history and politics, and Kennedy had little contact with them prior to his presidency, save as brief campaign matters.[31] Martin Luther King, Jr. recalled of his first meeting with Kennedy in June of 1960, "at the time I was impressed with his concern and I was impressed with his willingness to learn more about civil rights. He did not have the grasp and the comprehension of the depths and dimensions of the problem at that time. . . . "[32] After a brief discussion of racial matters with JFK in August 1960, Harris Wofford, a friend of King and a Kennedy adviser, concluded, "he considered it [race relations] irrational. He was not knowledgeable about it. It was alien to his experience."[33] In October 1961, Kennedy, at the urging of his brother-in-law, Sargent Shriver, made an impromptu telephone call to Coretta Scott King to express his concern and support for her and her husband when he was arrested and jailed for picketing a segregated department store, in violation of a condition of parole stemming from a previous traffic violation. This event, which helped JFK win black votes in the 1960 presidential election, was the only civil rights occurrence with which he had a direct experience. JFK was to have much more direct experience with the race issue as his administration grappled with the nation's reactions to the ever more forceful stirring of the civil rights movement.

President Kennedy publicly endorsed the substance of the *Brown* decision and made it clear that he believed segregation was morally and legally unjust.[34] The civil rights voice of the president was often that of his brother, Robert—the attorney general, and his most trusted political confidante. King recalled, "Whenever I talked with the Attorney General, I always felt he was talking for the President. . . . "[35] Harris Wofford notes, "most of [JFK's] key decisions . . . in civil rights, were made with Bob Kennedy, and you really didn't know what happened."[36] Roy Wilkins put it succinctly, "I think we were able to say 'the Kennedys' because I don't think there was any difference between Robert and Jack."[37]

Initially the Kennedy administration depended on the vigorous enforcement of civil rights law through the judicial process, but it also tried to negotiate desegregation plans with southern school systems. In the fall of 1960, when the New Orleans public school system, supported by the state legislature, refused to comply with a desegregation order, Robert Kennedy strongly backed Assistant Attorney General for Civil Rights Burke Marshall as the latter brought contempt proceedings against the responsible public officials. New Orleans soon began to desegregate its public school system.[38]

Both nationally and within the South Robert Kennedy articulated the administration's school desegregation position. On May 6, 1961, he courageously told a Law Day audience at the University of Georgia that he personally believed in school desegregation, "but my belief does not matter—it is now the law." He continued, "I say to you today that if the orders of the court are circumvented, the Department of Justice will act."[39] On the other hand, the administration leaders made it clear that they understood the South's position and they preferred negotiated settlements of desegregation disputes. In an interview published in the March 28, 1961 *Look* magazine, Robert Kennedy acknowledged that white southerners "have grown up with totally different backgrounds and mores, which we can't change overnight."[40] On January 2, 1962, he told a House appropriations subcommittee, "I feel very strongly that this problem [integration] is not going to be solved by just passing some laws. It will require some understanding." Quiet discussions and "good will," RFK argued, were the best tools for bringing about change in this area.[41]

While the Kennedy's understanding of the South's plight and the utility of passing legislation to deal with race relations sounded much like Eisenhower's understanding of these matters, they believed the Eisenhower administration's use of troops to enforce desegregation marked a substantial policy failure. In the *Look* interview noted above, Robert Kennedy stated that he could not imagine "ever sending troops to any part of this country." He could not "conceive of this administration's letting the situation deteriorate to that level." Kennedy's deputy attorney general, Nicholas deB Katzenbach, recalled, "they both [JFK and RFK], and particularly the President, had a real conviction that it was wrong to send troops in. . . . [JFK] felt that Little Rock was a great failure in the Eisenhower administration . . . because they sent in troops."[42] The Kennedys believed this would never occur while they held the White House.

On September 13, 1962, Federal District Court Judge Sidney C. Mize issued an order for the admission of James C. Meredith, an African-American young man, into the University of Mississippi. That night Mississippi's governor, Ross Barnett, in a statewide televised broadcast, spoke of a federal policy of "racial genocide," his code words for integration. He called for resistance to this policy and cited the 1832 South Carolina Act of Nullification, which declared federal laws that violated a given state's laws to be null and void within that state, as the basis for his refusal to allow Meredith to enter the University of Mississippi. The Justice Department moved to enter the case. The administration understood a crisis was imminent, given the vocal opposition of Mississippi's governor to the integrated schools.[43]

From September 15, when the attorney general first spoke directly with the governor and was assured there would be no violence, until after the president addressed the nation at 9:00 P.M. on September 30, with a plea for calm at Ole Miss as rioting broke out on the campus, the Kennedys and Barnett remained in contact. A vain, and at times burlesquelike effort ensued to avert the use of federal troops.

On September 20, the governor personally denied Meredith's attempt to register at the university. Mississippi highway patrolmen escorted Meredith, several U.S. marshals, and Justice Department attorneys from the campus while a crowd jeered and threw rocks at them.[44] On September 24, the university trustees, under court order from Judge Mize, agreed to register Meredith. Barnett let Robert Kennedy know that he still would not let Meredith register for classes at Ole Miss.

On September 25, Assistant Attorney General John Doar and Chief U.S. Marshal James McShane escorted Meredith to the Federal Building in downtown Jackson, Mississippi, where the university registrar had agreed to sign the papers of admission. The registrar was not there. Robert Kennedy spoke with the governor and he was assured "they're not going to bother him [Meredith]." The justice team then went with Meredith to the state legislative building. There, John Doar met the governor and a crowd of Mississippi state legislators, with radio microphones and television cameras set to carry the confrontation live across the state. Barnett proclaimed the right of "interposition" on behalf of the State of Mississippi and personally "finally" denied him admission to the University of Mississippi. Amid Mississippi's legislators' jeers and taunts directed at Meredith and the federal officials, and cheers directed at the governor, the registration mission was aborted. That evening, Robert Kennedy called Barnett and angrily told him that Meredith would be registered at Ole Miss. Later that night the Justice Department secured an order for the governor to appear before the Fifth Circuit Court for a contempt hearing.

The next day, September 26, while the *New York Times* headlines read: "U.S. IS PREPARED TO SEND TROOPS AS MISSISSIPPI GOVERNOR DEFIES COURTS AND BARS NEGRO STUDENT," Meredith, McShane, and Marshall went to Oxford.[45] Meredith's third attempt to register met with failure. This time Lieutenant Governor Paul Johnson, backed by state troopers and sheriffs, rebuffed the registration effort. Robert Kennedy and Ross Barnett now discussed a new scenario: a force of about twenty-five U.S. Marshals, guns drawn, would confront the governor and force him to yield.

Kennedy: I hate to have them all draw their guns as I think it would create hard feelings. Isn't it sufficient if I have one man draw his gun and the others keep their hands on their holsters?

Barnett: They must all draw their guns. Then they should point their guns at us and then we could step aside.

Kennedy: There will be no problem?

Barnett: Everyone pull your guns and point them and we will stand aside and you will go right through.

Kennedy: You will make sure not the marshals but the state police will preserve order?

Barnett: There won't be any violence.

That discussion took place at 2:50 P.M. At 6:35 P.M., after two additional conversations between the governor and the attorney general, the following exchange took place:

Barnett: General, I'm worried. . . . You don't realize what's going on. There are several thousand people here with cars, trucks. . . . We don't know these people.

Kennedy: I had better send them [the marshals] back.

Barnett: There is liable to be a hundred people killed here. It would ruin all of us. . . . We can't control people like that. A lot of people are going to get killed. It would be embarrassing to me.

Kennedy: I don't know if it would be embarrassing—that would not be the feeling.

Barnett: It would be bad all over the nation.

Kennedy: I'll send them back.[46]

On September 28, the administration raised the ante when it publicly announced that the Justice Department had consulted with Major General Creighton Abrams, assistant deputy army chief of staff for military operations, about the possible use of troops in Mississippi. In addition, the Fifth Circuit Court of Appeals, with Assistant Attorney General for Civil Rights Burke Marshall presenting the federal government's argument, found Barnett guilty of contempt of court. The governor had until October 2 to purge himself or face arrest and a fine of $10,000 for each day he remained in contempt of the court.[47]

On the same day, September 28, Theodore Sorensen, counsel to the president and a long-time aide, wrote to JFK: "You and the Attorney General have been handling the whole [Ole Miss desegregation] affair excellently. . . . I concur in your judgement to stay out of it personally for the time being." Sorensen advised, "I hope you will continue your policy of 'keep moving but move slowly.' There can be some action every day, preferably in Court, without requiring Meredith to make any more approaches which it is known will be rebuffed—and without sending troops to Mississippi until all litigation (including, if possible, a Supreme Court decision) and all other avenues of action are at dead end. In contrast to you predecessor," Sorensen reminded JFK, "you are demonstrating how many graduated steps there are between inaction and troops."[48] But Sorensen wrote to his chief from a hospital bed, and thus during this crisis he was out of the minute-to-minute White House decision-making loop.

The president believed his direct intervention was now directly required and that court options were no longer available to him. On September 29 he personally telephoned Barnett and spoke with him twice in a desperate attempt to work out a deal. Barnett, however, refused to guarantee Meredith's safety and these discussions came to naught. At 7:00 P.M. Barnett called the president and assured him that if Meredith were secretly registered in Jackson the state police would guarantee his safety. JFK agreed to the deal. Three hours later, after attending an Ole Miss football game held in Jackson, Mississippi, and telling a roaring crowd, "I love Mississippi. I love our people. I love our customs," Barnett told the president he could not go through with the latest deal.[49] At midnight, Norbert Schlei of the Office of Legal Counsel brought JFK a proclamation which ordered any and all individuals who were obstructing justice in Mississippi to cease and disperse. Another document federalized the Mississippi National Guard. Arthur Schlesinger, Jr., who was with JFK at the time, reports that the president asked Schlei, "Is this pretty much what Ike signed in 1957 with the Little Rock thing?" With minor changes it was. Schlesinger reports, "Kennedy signed, snapped off the light, and headed into the hall."[50]

The next morning, September 30, Barnett called the attorney general and proposed a staged surrender of Mississippi forces to armed Federal troops. RFK derisively called this "a foolish and dangerous show." He also told Barnett, "The president is going on TV tonight. . . . He will have to say why he called up the National Guard; that you had an agreement to permit Meredith to go to Jackson to register. . . . " Barnett responded, "That won't do at all." "You broke your word to him," the attorney general interjected. With great anxiety Barnett continued, "Don't say that. Please don't mention it. . . . We will go on and do it in any way. Let's agree to it now and forget it. I won't want the President saying I broke my word. . . . We will cooperate with you." The governor and the attorney general agreed to a Sunday registration. Few students would be on campus. "You won't mind if I raise cain about it?" asked Barnett. "I don't mind that," RFK answered, "just say law and order will be maintained."[51]

The administration leadership believed that the crisis was going to be resolved peacefully. Robert Kennedy agreed to keep the governor abreast of all developments in Meredith's registration. The governor agreed to let Kennedy clear the statement he planned to make to the people of Mississippi apprising them of his capitulation. At 7:30 P.M., Mississippi time, Barnett "urged" a statewide television audience "to preserve peace and to avoid violence in any form." He went on, "surrounded on all sides by the oppressive power of the armed forces of the United States of America, my courage and my convictions do not waver. My heart still says 'Never,' but my calm judgement abhors the bloodshed that would follow [armed resistance]."[52] At about the same time the governor was giving his talk to Mississippi's citizens, the Mississippi state troopers were withdrawing from the Ole Miss campus.

JFK ordered Theodore Sorensen to draft a speech for him to deliver to a national television audience that evening.[53] The president went on television that Sunday night of September 30, at 9:00 P.M.[54] He told the nation, "The orders of the court in the case of *Meredith versus Fair* are beginning to be carried out. Mr. James Meredith is now in residence at the campus of the University of Mississippi." JFK emphasized this was being done "without the use of the National Guard or other troops." Paralleling Eisenhower's national address during the Little Rock crisis, Kennedy stated, "our nation is founded on the principle that the observance of law is the eternal safeguard of liberty and defiance of law is the surest road to tyranny. The law which we obey includes the final rulings of the courts. . . . [F]ew laws are universally loved, but they are uniformly respected and not resisted. Americans are free, in short, to disagree with the law but not to disobey it." He continued, "If any man or group of men by force or threat of force could long defy the commands of our court and our Constitution, then no law would stand free from doubt . . . and no citizen would be safe from his neighbors."

Kennedy, again like Eisenhower, distanced his administration from the substantive matter at hand by arguing, "In this case in which the United States Government was not until recently involved, Mr. Meredith brought a suit in Federal Court against those who were excluding him from the University." The federal courts ordered his admission into Ole Miss, not the Kennedy administration.

When those orders were defied, and those who sought to implement them threatened with arrest and violence . . . the[ir] enforcement . . . had become an obligation of the United States Government. Even though this Government had not been a party to the case, my responsibility as President was therefore inescapable. I accept it. My responsibility under the Constitution . . . is to implement the orders of the court with whatever means are necessary. It is for this reason that I federalized the Mississippi National Guard . . . while the United States marshals carried out the orders of the court and prepared to back them up with whatever other civil or military enforcement might have been required.[55]

JFK noted that integration at public universities in nine other southern states had proceeded without recourse to armed federal intervention and "I recognize the present period of transition and adjustment in our Nation's Southland is a hard one for many people. Neither Mississippi nor any other southern State deserves to be charged with all the accumulated wrongs of the last hundred years of race relations. . . . [t]hat failure must be shared by us all, by every State, by every citizen." He praised Mississippi's citizens for their record of courage in military service to the nation and he ended his speech by calling on them to "preserve both the law and the peace."

As the president completed his talk he was notified that Katzenbach, Meredith, and the three hundred U.S. Marshals with him in a university campus building, the Lyceum, were surrounded by a mob intent on riot and mayhem.[56] Reports of violence filtered in to him, and the president spoke with Barnett on the telephone. "Listen, Governor," he said testily, "somebody's been shot down there already and it's going to get worse. Most of it's happened since the police left and I want them back. Good bye."[57] At midnight, eastern time, Katzenbach told the president that his group was in imminent danger and federal troops had to be brought in to save their lives.

The first federal troops arrived on campus at 2:15 A.M., Mississippi time, as the marshals were running out of tear gas canisters. By dawn, 16,000 federal troops had moved into the area. After the rioting was brought under control the night's damage became evident: over a third of the marshals were injured, twenty-eight by gunfire; two civilians were killed; more than three hundred persons were taken into federal custody. That morning six marshalls escorted James Meredith to class. As order was being restored at the University of Mississippi, Robert Kennedy told an aide, "We're gonna have a hell of a problem about [explaining] why we didn't handle this situation better."[58]

When asked at an October 14, 1962 news conference about the effects of the Oxford riot and the use of federal troops, the president responded, "I don't think that what happened in Oxford, Mississippi has caused a good deal of concern. I think that most people in the South recognize my responsibility to carry out the court order, my Constitutional responsibility."[59] On a live December 17, 1962 television interview show, he remarked, "we sent in troops when it appeared the marshals were going to be overrun. I don't think that anybody who looks at the situation can think that we could possibly do anything else."[60]

John and Robert Kennedy knew that despite their apprehension over public reaction to the administration's handling or mishandling of the Ole Miss situation, JFK's support in the polls actually increased in the aftermath of the crisis. The rally-around-the flag effect took hold of the public as it does in most national crises. Lou Harris, his pollster, informed him, "In key Northern industrial states, sentiment is behind you 2-1/2 to 3–1 on Mississippi." Across almost every group in the nation, including white Protestants (outside of the South), the president's actions drew support. And Harris concluded, "Every Democrat running for major office should put front and center that this country needs firm and resolute leadership such as the President demonstrated in the Mississippi case."[61]

JFK's view of race relations, his own rational approach to problems, and his inherent sense of the importance of constitutional imperatives had ineluctably moved him precisely to the position that he sought to avoid. He was determined not to use federal troops to enforce desegregation at Ole Miss. He had always believed that one of the key lessons of the Little Rock crisis was that federal force should not be used to enforce school desegregation. Yet he ordered the troops in and, to his surprise, the public supported his action.

CONCLUSION

Decision-making at the White House during both of these crises was consistent with the scenario for crisis decision-making: few decision-makers participated in the policy process; decision-making was ad-hoc as each crisis deepened; the alternatives analyzed were few; probing for a resolution was circumscribed—a satisficing solution was sought, with the knowledge that it was clearly not a preferred solution; and the president dominated the end-point decision.

There is little indication of extensive internal White House debate about the wisdom of the federal course of action that was pursued in each case. Eisenhower, despite his public remark that he could not envision the use of federal troops against a state, was direct and abrupt with the resort to federal troops when the desegregation crisis at Little Rock was at hand. He met with Governor Faubus against the advice of his attorney general, but once he came to believe the governor was not trustworthy, all bargaining with the state executive ceased. Presidential assistant Sherman Adams wrote that Eisenhower's use of federal troops at Little Rock was "a Constitutional duty which was the most repugnant to him of all his acts in his eight years in the White House."[62] Yet, the president believed that he had performed his duty as he was bound to do under the Constitution.

Nicholas deB Katzenbach, the deputy attorney general at the scene during the crisis at Ole Miss, recounts, "we had to send the troops in," and he adds, "that was regarded by both President Kennedy and Bobby Kennedy as a great failure."[63] The Kennedys were ever-mindful of what they perceived as Eisenhower's failure at Little Rock. Yet, they could not avoid following the previous administration's path as they were brought into the vortex of the Ole Miss crisis and carried out the actions that were inevitable, if not desirable, constitutional imperatives.

In an insightful set of lectures presented in 1964, Kennedy's assistant attorney general, Burke Marshall, argued the United States was "testing . . . the durability of the federal structure as the conflict [over federal enforcement of civil rights] takes place." By deliberate avoidance of the racial issue, "the system has been protected thus far, since the mid-1870s, by nonrecognition of federally guaranteed rights" for black Americans.[64] In his 1964 study, *Federalism*, William H. Riker argued, "the main beneficiary [of the federal policy process] has been Southern whites, who have been given the freedom to oppress Negroes. . . . " And, he argued, "the judgment to be passed on federalism in the United States is therefore a judgment on the values of segregation and racial oppression."[65] Marshall concluded his talks by arguing, "those who say that civil rights issues cut into the fabric of federalism are correct. They cut most deeply where police power is involved. . . . "[66] That is why each president tried not to make a judgment on civil rights as he dealt with one of the most difficult civil rights crises.

Neither president ever again employed federal troops to resolve a civil rights crisis. Each president's ultimate judgement on federalism was made respectively, if reluctantly, at Little Rock in 1957 and at the University of Mississippi in 1962. The thrust of these judgements flew in the face of a traditional federal reluctance to interfere with state mandated racism. The first Reconstruction ended as the federal troops withdrew from the South. During the second Reconstruction the employment of armed federal force was traumatic to the nation, and it permanently altered the federal-state relationship.[67]

NOTES

1. Nelson W. Polsby, *Political innovation in America* (New Haven, CT: Yale University Press, 1984), pp. 147–59, 168.

2. Polsby, *Political innovation in America*, pp. 161, 165.

3. Charles E. Lindblom, "The Science of muddling through," *Public Administration Review* 19 (Spring 1959): 79–88; Charles E. Lindblom, *The policy-making process* (Englewood Cliffs, NJ: Prentice-Hall, 1980).

4. John W. Kingdon, *Agendas, alternatives, and public policies* (Boston: Little, Brown, 1984), pp. 104, 199.

5. There are a number of accounts of the Little Rock episode that explore these issues more fully than can be done in this chapter. The most extensive study may be found in James C. Duram, *A Moderate among extremists* (Chicago: Nelson-Hall, 1981).

6. The history of this case is superbly presented in Richard Kluger, *Simple justice* (New York: Alfred A. Knopf, 1976).

7. Mark Stern, "Presidential strategies and civil rights: Eisenhower, the early years, 1952–1954," *Presidential Studies Quarterly* 19 (Fall 1989): 769–95; Philip Elman, Oral History, *Harvard Law Review* (February 1987): 834–36; Herbert Brownell, oral history interview by Ed Edwin, January 25, 1967, Columbia University Library, 162.

8. Dwight D. Eisenhower to Walter White, June 29, 1954, President's Personal File, Box 43, Dwight D. Eisenhower Library. Hereafter the Eisenhower Library is cited as DDEL.

9. Dwight D. Eisenhower to Swede Hazlett, October 23, 1954, Ann Whitman File, Name Series, Hazlett, Swede, 1954, DDEL.

10. Dwight D. Eisenhower, *Public Papers of the Presidents of the United States: Dwight D. Eisenhower, 1956* (Washington, DC: U.S. Government Printing Office, 1957), 304–5. Hereafter reference to this source will be *PPP: DDE*, or in the case of president John F. Kennedy, *PPP: JFK*, followed by the appropriate year. On March 9, the president wrote to his attorney general, "Ever since the 'separate but equal' decision they have been the Constitution of the United States." Dwight D. Eisenhower, "Personal and Confidential Memorandum for the Attorney General," March 9, 1956, Ann Whitman Papers, Cabinet Series, Box 6, DDEL.

11. Cabinet Meeting, April 25, 1956, Ann Whitman File, Diary Series, Box 8, DDEL.

12. Dwight D. Eisenhower, telephone call to Herbert Brownell, August 19, 1956, Ann Whitman File, Diary Series, Box 8, DDEL.

13. Dwight D. Eisenhower to Swede Hazlett, July 22, 1957, Ann Whitman File, Name Series, Hazlett, Swede, Box 25, DDEL.

14. After he left the presidency Eisenhower endorsed the decision as morally and legally correct. *New York Times*, October 9, 1963.

15. *New York Times*, October 2, 1955. See also the study done under the auspices of the Anti-Defamation League of B'Nai B'Rith and circulated in mimeographed form: John Howard Griffin and Theodore Freedman, "Field Reports on Segregation in the South, Mansfield, Texas, A Report of the Crisis Situation Resulting from Efforts to Desegregate the School System," (New York: n.d.). Donald W. Jackson graciously provided me with a copy of this report.

16. *PPP: DDE, 1956*, 735, 737.

17. *PPP: DDE, 1956*, 766.

18. *PPP: DDE, 1957*, 546.

19. "Pre-press Conference Notes," September 3, 1957, Ann Whitman File, Press Conference Series, Box 6, DDEL.

20. Dwight D. Eisenhower, *Waging peace* (Garden City, N.Y.: Doubleday, 1965), pp. 164–65; *New York Times*, September 6, 1957, p. 9.

21. *PPP: DDE, 1957*, 673–74.

22. Dwight D. Eisenhower, telephone call to Herbert Brownell, September 11, 1957, President's Personal Files, Diary Series, Box 27, DDEL.

23. Herbert Brownell, interview with author, October 27, 1990, Austin, Texas, p. 2.

24. "Notes Dictated by the President," September 14, 1957, President's Personal Files, Diary Series, Box 9, DDEL.

25. "Notes dictated by the President on October 8, 1957 concerning visit of Governor Orval Faubus . . . on September 14, 1957," Diary Series, President's Personal Files, Box 26, September 1957, Dictation Folder, DDEL.

26. Andy Goodpaster, memorandum to Jim Hagerty, September 19, 1957, Diary Series, President's Personal Files, Box 27, September 1957 Telephone Calls, DDEL.

27. *PPP: DDE, 1957*, 689.

28. These remarks and the following are from "Radio and Television Address to the American People on the Situation in Little Rock. September 24, 1957," *PPP: DDE, 1957*, 689–94.

29. *PPP: DDE, 1957*, 708–9.

30. Herbert Brownell, untitled manuscript of presentation before the Friends of the Supreme Court Historical Society, n.d. Copy in possession of the author.

31. John Kennedy's encounters with the civil rights issue in his prepresidential years, as well as during his campaign and subsequent presidency, are explored by me more extensively in *Calculating visions* (New Brunswick, NJ: Rutgers University Press, 1992), pp. 9–112.

32. Martin Luther King, Jr., oral history interview by Berl I. Bernhard, March 9, 1964, 1, John F. Kennedy Presidential Library. Hereafter the Kennedy Library is referred to as JFKL.

33. Harris Wofford, oral history interview by Berl I. Bernhard, November 29, 1965, 10–11, JFKL.

34. Carl M. Brauer, *John F. Kennedy and the second Reconstruction* (New York: Columbia University Press, 1977), p. 74.

35. Martin Luther King, Jr., oral history interview by Berl I. Bernhard, March 9, 1964, 14, JFKL.

36. Harris Wofford, oral history interview by Larry Hackman, February 3, 1969, 128, Lyndon Baines Johnson Library.

37. Roy Wilkins, oral history interview by Berl I. Bernhard, August 13, 1964, 14, JFKL.

38. Robert F. Kennedy and Burke Marshall, oral history interview by Anthony Lewis, December 4, 1964, II, 5, JFKL.

39. *New York Times*, May 6, 1961.

40. Peter Maas, *Look*, March 28, 1961, pp. 24–26.

41. Quoted in Brauer, *Kennedy and the second Reconstruction*, p. 126.

42. Nicholas deB Katzenbach, "Origin of Kennedy's Civil rights," in Kenneth W. Thompson, ed., *The Kennedy presidency* (Lanham, MD: University of America Press, 1985), p. 52.

43. Nicholas deB Katzenbach, oral history interview by Anthony Lewis, November 29, 1964, 12–13, JFKL; two of the more extensive analyses of this crisis are found in Brauer, *Kennedy and the second Reconstruction*, pp. 180–240, and, Taylor Branch, *Parting the waters: America in the King Years 1954–63* (New York: Simon and Schuster, 1988), pp. 633–72.

44. A chronology of events at Ole Miss during this period may be found in the *New York Times*, October 1, 1961.

45. *New York Times*, September 26, 1962.

46. Victor Navasky, *Kennedy justice* (New York: Atheneum), pp. 209–17.

47. *New York Times*, September 29, 1962.

48. Theodore C. Sorensen, to The President, September 28, 1962, Theodore C. Sorensen Papers, Box 30, JFKL.

49. Arthur M. Schlesinger, Jr., *A thousand days: John F. Kennedy in the White House* (New York: Fawcet Crest, 1967), pp. 862–64.

50. Arthur M. Schlesinger, Jr., *Robert Kennedy and his times* (New York: Ballantine Books, 1978), p. 345.

51. Schlesinger, *Robert Kennedy and his times*, p. 345.

52. Quoted in Brauer, *Kennedy and the second Reconstruction*, pp. 192–93.

53. Theodore Sorenson, *Kennedy* (New York: Harper and Row, 1965), p. 484.

54. *PPP: DDE, 1962*, 726–28.

55. Theodore Sorenson notes: "He [JFK] carefully rewrote this speech to make it clear that the government was merely carrying out the orders of the writ in a case it had not initially brought and was not forcing anything down the throats of Mississippians on its own initiative." See *Kennedy*, p. 484.

56. Walter Lord, *The past that would not die* (New York: Harper and Row, 1965), pp. 180–84.

57. Sorenson, *Kennedy*, p. 486.

58. Audiotape 26a, JFKL.

59. *PPP: JFK, 1962*, 779.

60. *PPP: JFK, 1962*, 893.

61. Lou Harris to John F. Kennedy, October 5, 1962, President's Office Files, Box 105, JFKL.

62. Sherman Adams, *First hand report* (New York: Harper, 1961), p. 355.

63. Katzenbach, "Origins of Kennedy's Civil Rights," p. 52. Schlesinger, in his work *Robert F. Kennedy*, writes, "The call for troops itself was a confession of failure" (p. 348).

64. Burke Marshall, *Federalism and civil rights* (New York: Columbia University Press, 1964), p. 7.

65. William H. Riker, *Federalism* (Boston: Little, Brown, 1964), pp. 152–53.

66. Marshall, *Federalism and civil rights*, pp. 7, 81.

67. Cf. Joseph Lesser, "The course of federalism—An historical overview," in *Federalism: The shifting balance*, ed. J. C. Griffith (Chicago: American Bar Association, 1989), pp. 9–12.

8

John F. Kennedy and the Politics of Civil Rights

————————————— Donald W. Jackson and
James W. Riddlesperger, Jr.

INTRODUCTION

For President John F. Kennedy, civil rights issues were among his most troubling problems as his term began. Success in any policy arena depends on at least three things: how highly a president places the arena on his policy agenda, how he deals with the agenda in government, and how he approaches the subject before the American people. Kennedy's civil rights record offers an instructive case study of presidential leadership in each of these contexts.

President Kennedy had an abstract commitment to civil rights progress, but his first priority was to foreign policy. He wished to pursue civil rights systematically so that he would not have to reorder his priorities. As a result, while Kennedy always advocated civil rights reform, he did not want to lead a civil rights crusade. Instead, civil rights advancement came from pressure by leaders such as the Freedom Riders and Dr. Martin Luther King, Jr., not because Kennedy wished it to rise to the top of the national agenda. Once it came to the forefront, Kennedy sought to lead in his own controlled fashion—for example, by manipulating the March on Washington. Civil rights became a signature policy for the Kennedy administration, not because of his personal commitment, but because of the flow of history, forced on by civil rights activists and unforeseen events.

Presidential leadership comes from the effective use of power. Richard Neustadt (1990: 172) described Kennedy's style as having the following characteristics: "the personal command post, a deliberate reaching down for the details, hard questioning of the alternatives, a drive to protect options from foreclosure by sheer urgency or by ex parte advocacy, and finally a close watch on follow-through." Kennedy's civil rights record presents an opportunity to assess his leadership style and his effectiveness. In civil rights, Kennedy was reluctant to exercise moral leadership early in his term, in part because it might preclude other alternatives. Instead, he pursued a bureaucratic approach to civil rights as long as possible, preferring orderly progress to a conflictual congressional debate that might split his governing coalition on other matters of high priority. When the issue emerged from Pandora's Box, he led by "going public," promoting "himself and his policies in Washington by appealing to the American public for support" (Kernell, 1993: 2). At first, his rhetoric appealed to sensible and simple compliance with the law, but by the time he proposed legislation in 1963, he appealed to public emotions and used passionate pleas for justice through "spectacle" leadership (Miroff, 1990: 289–313).

Many of the most dramatic events of the Civil Rights Era came during the short years of the Kennedy presidency. Beginning with the candidate's phone call to Coretta Scott King near the end of the 1960 presidential campaign, the civil rights era became entangled with John Kennedy's image. During his presidency, the clash between white segregationists in the South and African-American activists came to a head. JFK was integrally involved in the federal government's response to that clash.

Kennedy's personal intervention in dramatic events, such as the freedom rides and the desegregation of the University of Mississippi, constituted the most substantial presidential involvement in civil rights until that time. After his death, his name was invoked so pervasively that the Civil Rights Act of 1964 became part of his legacy. President Lyndon Johnson later recalled: "martyrs have to die for causes. John Kennedy had died. But his 'cause' was not really clear. I had to take the dead man's program and turn it into a martyr's cause" (Kearns, 1976: 185). Such tactics linked Kennedy's name to civil rights, and he has often been viewed as one of the movement's leading lights.

In this chapter, we evaluate the Kennedy record in civil rights by examining documentary evidence in his papers and speeches and assessing interpretations of Kennedy by biographers and civil rights scholars. First we list some working assumptions that come from reading Kennedy materials. Next, we assess the literature on Kennedy, categorizing scholarship on his presidency into three groups: those who see him as a strong proactive leader in the civil rights movement; those who believe he was given a great deal of credit despite a modest commitment to the cause; and those who fall between the two extremes. Third, we assess the documentary record of the Kennedy administration, most carefully regarding major civil rights events of his presidency. Finally, based on the evidence, we assess the civil rights record of JFK in terms of his personal and policy commitments to the cause.

WORKING ASSUMPTIONS

We begin with six working assumptions:

1. From the outset, President Kennedy was committed to advancing civil rights. He saw civil rights as straightforward, with clear and simple constitutional requirements. Segregation violated constitutional and human rights; therefore it should end.

2. Civil rights was troubling to Kennedy because of its implications for other issues, about which Kennedy cared more. JFK was embarrassed that his nation, a leader of the free world, was experiencing problems of racial discrimination and violence.

3. Kennedy addressed civil rights with the executive action of his brother Robert's Justice Department rather than through legislation. He hoped to avoid the confrontation that would result inevitably from public debate. (The strategy changed by the time the 1963 Civil Rights Bill was introduced.)

4. Kennedy wanted to preserve the Democratic coalition, one originally based on support for the New Deal and most threatened by civil rights. In articulating FDR's legacy, Kennedy wished to avoid facing that threat (see Skowronek, 1993). Kennedy wished to preserve the party, but also to assure his own reelection.

5. Kennedy's objectives and strategies were entangled with his brother's. Separating their goals is difficult because "About the most important things, [John Kennedy] was a man of few words—even with those closest to him" (Wofford, 1980: 129).

6. Kennedy's public pursuit of civil rights often came as responses to events he could not control. He would have preferred to attain his objectives quietly, but the events of 1961–1963 forced him into a strong advocacy role in civil rights policy.

THE KENNEDY LITERATURE

One dominant theme in Kennedy literature depicts him as a champion of civil rights, particularly in works written by his associates writing soon after his death (Schlesinger, 1965, 1978; Sorensen, 1965, 1969; Wofford, 1980, Oral Histories; and Marshall, 1964a&b). They emphasize Kennedy's cool approach to politics, but argue that beneath the calm exterior was a leader with a passionate advocacy of civil rights. In reading oral history interviews and books of these associates, the civil rights story takes on an almost biblical tint, with Kennedy as the protagonist and his biographers as the authors of the "gospels," which make up the "testament" of the Kennedy administration. Collectively, these authors predominantly view Kennedy as committed to the civil rights cause from the very beginning of his administration. He was not impassioned at first; during his national candidacy Kennedy seemed to value African Americans chiefly for their voting impact (Sorensen, 1965: 470; Schlesinger, 1978: 287; Wofford, 1980: 129). They argue, though, that he had an unwavering civil rights policy commitment. Sorensen (1965: 471) recalled: "He voted for every civil rights bill coming before him as a Congressman and Senator more as a matter of course than of deep concern." Wofford (1968: 83) described Kennedy as cool about civil rights, but that he thought "discrimination, segregation—you know was wrong, stupid, irrational—denying the right to vote was a scandal."

As candidate and president, Kennedy became more interested in civil rights, as illustrated by two campaign events—the promise to do away with federal housing discrimination with the "stroke of a pen" and a call to Coretta Scott King on the eve of the election. The "stroke of the pen" comment criticized President Eisenhower's lack of commitment to desegregating American public housing. The call to Mrs. King in the waning days of the campaign was seen in retrospect as a brilliant political maneuver. At first, though, it had been a source of controversy. The call, made at the suggestion of Harris Wofford and Sargent Shriver, first drew the ire, then the support, of Robert Kennedy, John's campaign manager.

You see, after the very first reaction—after we called Martin Luther King ['s wife]—was that Bobby Kennedy landed on me like a ton of bricks, and claimed we had lost the election. And who in the hell did I think I was out there in Chicago by myself that screwed the whole election up. . . . within 24 hours, he was leading the pack in the other direction (Shriver, Oral History, 1988: 33).

For Kennedy's men, the phone call coincided with his civil rights advocacy but was justified primarily for its political expedience.

Kennedy's advocates argue that the call was symbolic of Kennedy's empathy with the civil rights movement. Mrs. King was pregnant at the time of the call, and Schlesinger (1965: 74) claims that Kennedy called her at once out of "an instinctive compassion." Kennedy's associates also compare Kennedy's own upbringing and the condition of African Americans. Both Sorensen (1969: 217–18) and Shriver (Oral History, 1988) comment that Kennedy came from an Irish immigrant family that had experienced discrimination in Boston during the lives of Kennedy's grandparents. The analogy is a bit strained, and it says something about the mind-set of JFK's aides that the comparison is made at all. While ethnic slurs had often been directed at the Irish in Boston and elsewhere, they enjoyed success in politics and business, had never been entirely disenfranchised, and Kennedy came from a background of great advantage, not of discrimination.

Kennedy's slow movement is justified by his associates who point out that political constraints limited the president. For example, although Kennedy had promised executive action, most specifically to address housing discrimination, an executive "stroke of the pen" did not come on November 20, 1962. Why? Sorensen (1965: 480–82) argues that Kennedy wished to accomplish other necessary prerequisites first. In order, Sorensen says that Kennedy waited for Robert Weaver, a black, to be confirmed as head of the Housing and Home Finance Agency. Then he waited for a report on housing discrimination from the Civil Rights Commission. Finally, he wanted to wait until after the creation of a cabinet level department of housing. Only after Congress had defeated that proposal did JFK issue the Executive Order. In other words, the delay was justified by Kennedy's aides as a commitment to civil rights rather than ambivalence about the political consequences of executive action.

Even in the area of Justice Department action, some criticized the slow rate of Kennedy's response to civil rights needs. Burke Marshall (1964: 3–4) responds that federalism more than anything else frustrated the administration. The limited accomplishments derived from "the control in state institutions over normally routine decisions affecting the daily lives of all citizens, and the traditional and constitutional reluctance of the federal courts to intrude."

But why did Kennedy wait until 1963 to propose legislation? Schlesinger (1965, 1978) argues that Kennedy's tactical brilliance led him to see that early in his administration the time was not ripe for legislative action. Richard Goodwin (1988: 311), another Kennedy aide, echoes that assessment: Kennedy felt "that a futile crusade 'might look good in the papers,' but would result only in defeat and probably jeopardize the rest of his program." By 1963, he had created an atmosphere that made the passage of a civil rights bill possible. The timing had to do with the increasingly outrageous racial conflict in the South. Sorensen (1965: 470) writes that "Kennedy's convictions on equal rights—like his convictions on all other subjects—were reached gradually, logically and coolly, ultimately involving a dedication of the heart even stronger than that of the mind."

Favorable assessments of Kennedy's civil rights role have also come from scholars, most notably Carl Brauer (1977), who labels Kennedy's civil rights record "a second reconstruction." Brauer (1977: 315–16) points out that some of Kennedy's judicial appointments were not pro–civil rights, and that he was cautious in issuing a housing executive order and other activities, but he suggests that "under Kennedy, civil rights became a focal point of public policy and political debate. Moreover, it was Kennedy's leadership that carried over to the passage of the Civil Rights Act of 1964 and the other civil rights action of the Johnson years." Favorable assessments also come from Kluger (1975: 952), who concluded that Kennedy was the first "president who genuinely committed his administration to broad action taken specifically to improve the position of the Negro," from Barber (1972: 342), who wrote that "in the civil rights struggles, Kennedy took a stand on what he himself had come to believe," and from Gilbert

(1989: 14), who argued that Kennedy served an educational role in civil rights. His "persistence in his support for civil rights in the face of declining levels of public support for his administration is impressive. He was trying to mobilize public sympathy for a major cause and was not deflected from the effort by widespread arguments that he was trying to move too quickly. In short, Kennedy was serving as a national educator on a subject which was unpalatable to much of the nation."

One other favorable account of Kennedy came from Martin Luther King, Jr. King's assessment varies from other observers in that to him, JFK's attitudes transformed during his presidency. King (Oral History, 1964: 2) believed Kennedy "did not have the grasp and the comprehension of the depths and dimensions of the problem" at first but was willing to learn. Even after learning the severity of the problems, however, King (Oral History, 1964: 3) thought Kennedy "long [on] intellectual commitment but that he didn't quite have the emotional commitment." But after the Birmingham incidents of 1963, King (1964: 17) said:

he was coming to see that, on the one hand, the nation did not have—it was not any fixed structure of conservatism, radicalism or anything for that matter, but it was fluid—and that, instead of a fixed trend, there was a wide room for leadership, that the nation was ready to be led to higher heights. And I think out of this you see emerging a new Kennedy who had come to see the moral issues involved in the civil rights struggle and who not only came to see them but was now willing to stand up in a courageous manner for them.

King believed that Kennedy's leadership changed as he discovered the magnitude of the problem rather than as part of a master plan, as Kennedy's aides apparently had seen it.

In contrast to these positive accounts of Kennedy in civil rights, other observers have put a distinctly negative spin on the Kennedy record. Lasky (1963), in his first of several scathing books about Democratic presidents, criticized Kennedy for seeking and accepting the endorsement of southern segregationists during his campaign. While Kennedy told Harlem Democrats that Alabama Governor John Patterson's support was "The greatest cross I have to bear," he never repudiated the endorsement. Such failure came because "Kennedy has always regarded civil rights as strictly a political issue. Rarely has he demonstrated any steadfast interest in the subject. He has never felt the kind of moral struggle which many Southerners feel toward the problem."

Navasky (1971: 96–99) was also critical of the Kennedy civil rights record, focusing primarily on Robert Kennedy and the Justice Department. He argues that the Kennedy's failure to accomplish civil rights progress was due first to the decision of the Kennedys not to "volunteer the FBI for arduous civil rights duty," and second to the fact that the Kennedys and their associates, graduates of "Eastern establishment law schools," thought that "confrontation was to be avoided and mediation rather than coercion was the way to achieve social change. They thought they could reason and negotiate with men like Ross Barnett and George Wallace." Navasky's criticisms castigate the Kennedy's performance in civil rights rather than their abstract commitment.

Henry Fairlie's (1973: 153–54) criticism is more biting. "Just as he did not mention civil rights in his inaugural address, so civil rights was the only significant area of domestic policy in which he did not appoint a task force. . . . In this area, the liberals and the intellectuals were not given the opportunity to set any awkward standards. They were invited where they could not cause any serious trouble."

Similarly, Smith (1980: 166) argues that Kennedy betrayed the trust of his supporters in the 1960 campaign. Early in his administration, "Kennedy failed to issue the order on housing, and he refused to introduce a civil rights bill. His failure to fulfill his solemn promise in these two areas infuriated civil rights leaders." Smith (1980: 171–72) concludes that the lack of civil rights action was "one of Kennedy's saddest mistakes. It was also his most ignoble one. By exploiting a heart-rending problem for his political gain, and by failing then to honor the promise, the President betrayed the Negroes."

In recent years, a middle ground has emerged in the Kennedy literature. Revisionists portray Kennedy as a pragmatist who adopted the civil rights movement as a matter of political expedience and/or necessity. While these authors are not equally favorable in their treatment of the Kennedy administration, they see the emergence of civil rights in similar lights.

Pragmatism is a common theme to the revisionist literature: Kennedy was a moderate tied to a highly pragmatic, rational view of politics and public policy (Stern, 1992: 233).

It may be helpful, before turning to a historical narrative of Kennedy's involvement with civil rights, to set out its central themes. The first is the habit, predominant throughout almost all of Kennedy's Presidency, of defining civil rights in pragmatic terms (Miroff, 1976: 223).

Civil rights was one of those moral dilemmas foreign to Jack's pragmatic cast of mind, as Theodore Hesburgh discovered when he went to the White House to press one of the Civil Rights Commission demands—integration of the Alabama National Guard—and was told by the President that he might have to call up the guard because of tensions in Berlin and therefore couldn't consider such a move (Collier and Horowitz, 1984: 302).

This was a political judgment that a civil rights bill in 1961 or 1962 would divide the country, shatter the Democratic Party, and be rejected by Congress. In my view this reasoning, while morally questionable, was politically unassailable (Bernstein, 1991: 295).

But it seems in retrospect highly likely that the moralistic rhetoric of the June 11 [1963] speech was designed in part for a pragmatic purpose; Jack was wrapping the proposed legislation in the loftiest possible language in hope of securing its passage (Reeves, 1991: 355).

These passages offer a consistent interpretation: that when JFK moved slowly on civil rights, it was because he feared that pushing too hard might jeopardize other items on his agenda. When he pursued civil rights actively, he used the highest of moral rhetoric, but for political reasons more than moral commitment.

Revisionist authors see Kennedy's understanding of civil rights as limited. Instead of having empathy due to his Irish roots as suggested by Sorensen and Shriver, these authors see Kennedy as understanding the issue only in political terms. Richard Reeves (1993: 62), for example, writes that before the presidency, Kennedy had "no particular feelings and great voids of knowledge about the day to day lives and cares and prejudices of his fellow Americans. . . . Kennedy usually knew what he had to know, but the only Negro he had spent time with was his valet for the past fourteen years, George Thomas."

Pragmatism meant that Kennedy wanted to hear the pros and cons of political action, but had little use for people whom he perceived as moral crusaders. Reeves (1991: 336) argues that "the president and his brother, as attorney general, treated those consumed by these [civil rights] principles as objects of scorn." Branch (1988: 587) reports that while Kennedy had spontaneous political discussions with other aides, with civil rights assistant Harris Wofford "he habitually tossed a passing wave and a glancing smile, asking 'are your constituents happy?' "

Because of his approach, President Kennedy hoped that policy changes could proceed in a peaceful and orderly fashion and at the state and local level rather than through federal action. As a result, from the start of his term, JFK sought to have the civil rights crusade proceed cautiously. He was "reluctant to depart from the established custom of federal nonintervention in southern law enforcement, for this tradition served the political needs of a Democratic president anxious to avoid alienating the usually Democratic white South" (Belknap, 1987: x). Parmet (1983: 354) agrees, adding that this reluctance meant that "the President withheld the full power of the Executive Office for too long. There were, as usual, too many reasons for delay."

Kennedy's reluctance is well illustrated by Collier and Horowitz (1984: 302). When discrimination encroached on other policy areas, Kennedy wished to avoid making civil rights a focal point at the expense of the higher priority. Told that African diplomats driving through Maryland on their way to Washington, D.C. "faced segregated dining facilities, Jack summoned White House protocol chief Angier Biddle Duke and said, 'Can't you ask them to fly?' " This story might be relegated to the apocrypha in interpretation, if not in actuality, by Kennedy's defenders, but it shows that because of priorities, civil rights conflicts were to be avoided rather than confronted by the national government.

The president's reluctance to act is largely interpreted by revisionists as a reluctance to use the "bully pulpit" to educate the public on the magnitude of civil rights problems. Unlike Gilbert (1989: 14, see above), a scholar who praises Kennedy's rhetorical leadership, Miroff (1976: 224) finds that JFK:

shied away from publicly discussing the *meaning* of the civil rights struggle. If he accepted (sometimes) his presidential responsibility to act, he never fully appreciated the equally important responsibility to educate. On no other subject was political education so important in the 1960s; on no other subject did Kennedy prove so deficient as an educator.

Eventually the events of the 1960s and the activism of civil rights leaders forced Kennedy to act. Remembering that Kennedy always supported civil rights goals philosophically, and that he had given promises that he would act on those matters, it became mandatory for him to act as the freedom rides and conflicts at the Universities of Mississippi and Alabama began to unfold. Note the following characterizations of Kennedy actions:

The administration tried to cancel the 1963 March on Washington; when they failed, the White House took charge of the arrangements to keep them peaceful (and screened speeches to make sure they were not too militant). The government that tried to stop the march received credit for being its sponsor (Wills, 1981: 209).

the Kennedy Administration had no plans for a major assault on segregated transit and had been prodded into action only by the Freedom Rides (Barnes, 1983: 203).

During several riotous crises ignited by events such as the Freedom Rides and the court-ordered integration of the University of Mississippi, blatant abdication of responsibility by southern officials forced the Kennedy administration to take dramatic and forceful action to keep racist violence from thwarting the exercise of constitutional rights by blacks and their supporters (Belknap, 1987: xi).

Birmingham convinced John and Robert Kennedy as well as Burke Marshall that they must ask Congress for a comprehensive civil rights law (Bernstein, 1991: 95).

Rather than the leader of a second "reconstruction," these revisionists see JFK as someone forced to react on behalf of a movement led by activists over whom he had no control. His strong responses, coming in the forms of first calling out the National Guard and second, proposing the Civil Rights Act of 1963, came not because he thought them moral responses, but rather because they had become politically expedient. Reeves (1991: 338) quotes Father Theodore Hesburgh as supporting this interpretation: "political expediency was a very strong force in [Kennedy's] whole Administration." Miroff (1976: 269) agrees, concluding that Kennedy granted civil rights his full attention "only when it imposed itself . . . with an intensity too great to be ignored."

Finally, the revisionists give Kennedy credit for an abstract policy commitment to civil rights, but in contrast to his advocates, they argue that the policy commitment had little to do with moral outrage and that morality was not the primary cause for action. Miroff (1976: 270) argues that the "legend" that portrayed Kennedy as an engaged and sensitive proponent of racial justice "bore slight resemblance to the actual history of his Presidency." Similarly, Branch (1988: 918) concludes that Kennedy "acquired the Lincolnesque mantle of a unifying crusader who had bled against the thorn of race. Honest biographers found it impossible to trace an engaged personality in proportion to the honor." Some revisionists are characterized as favorable to JFK and others as negative, but they consistently see Kennedy as a major actor in civil rights policy, occasionally responding with vigor. They also see Kennedy as primarily a cunning political strategist, taking advantage of opportunity, rather than as the moral leader of the Civil Rights Movement. Protagonists instead were black activists who would not let the issue die and white segregationists who opposed reasonable progress on all occasions.

THE KENNEDY CIVIL RIGHTS RECORD

In this section, we assess the Kennedy administration record chronologically by the major civil rights events of his administration. Using files in the Kennedy Library near Boston and public statements of the president, in addition to accounts of the events from those who were there, we assess which of the schools of thought concerning Kennedy has greater weight. We conclude that the interpretations by revisionist scholars come closer to the reality of the Kennedy record than do the accounts by his advocates. The events reviewed are familiar to students of recent American history and together they constitute the civil rights "parables" of the Kennedy administration.

By all accounts, Kennedy had only passing interest in civil rights politics before running for president. Sorensen (1965: 17) writes that in his prepresidential days, Kennedy "knew and cared relatively little about the problems of civil rights and civil liberties." On the most important issue that confronted Kennedy while in Congress, the Civil Rights Act of 1957,

Kennedy acted pragmatically. In the abstract sense, he was committed to a strong civil rights measure, advocating the strongest section of the bill, which would have granted the Justice Department strong enforcement powers. That section was omitted from the bill by Senate vote. The most controversial section of the bill, which gave those accused of violating the Civil Rights Act the right to have a jury trial (which in the South might have severely limited the impact of the bill), was one that the strongest advocates of civil rights opposed. Kennedy supported the amendment after determining that the provision would probably not have much impact and that the bill could not pass without it (Burns, 1959: 204).

During the 1960 campaign, Kennedy did two things which attracted great attention: he argued that the executive powers of the president could outlaw discrimination in federally subsidized housing and in businesses that held government contracts "with the stroke of a pen," and he made the phone call to Coretta Scott King on the eve of the election. Both have been cited as illustrations of the Kennedy commitment to civil rights, and yet each has a pragmatic turn. The "stroke of a pen" comment has an interesting history of its own. Goodwin (1988: 133) suggests that he wrote it for delivery in a campaign speech, and that Kennedy delivered the line "without the slightest hint of doubt or equivocation." Wofford (Oral History, November 29, 1965) remembers that he had used the phase in his own speeches and that Kennedy adopted it in one of the debates with Richard Nixon. Whatever the origin of the phrase, it became an albatross for Kennedy by 1962. Civil rights activists were beginning to exert constant pressure, encouraging their supporters to send JFK a pen, since his apparently was dry (Branch, 1988: 586–87). Pens came to the White House by the thousands. Kennedy was concerned that the timing was wrong and that an executive order might delay other items on his legislative agenda. It led him to query in frustration, "Who the hell wrote that?" (Goodwin, 1988: 133). While Kennedy had a commitment to act, he did not want to be forced to act before he thought it tactically advantageous.

The phone call to Coretta King also needs interpretation. No record exists that Kennedy ever explained his motivation for the call. Stern (1989a: 813; 1992: 34) argues that the call was not a planned-out, strategic move by the candidate. Instead, it was planned by Harris Wofford and Sargent Shriver to be done on the spur of the moment. They wanted the candidate to call her both because they were concerned and because they believed that neither the candidate nor the rest of the campaign staff understood the black voters' intensity and depth of concern with the issue. Perhaps Martin Luther King, Jr. (Oral History, 1964: 11–12) summarized it best in saying that "there are moments in history . . . that what is morally right is politically expedient, politically sound. And I would like to feel—I really feel this—that he made the call because he was concerned. He had come to know me as a person. . . . At the same time, I think he naturally had political considerations in mind."

Kennedy wished to deal with civil rights quickly and quietly, so that it might not interfere with other priorities. In August 1960, he asked Harris Wofford (Oral History, 1965: 7), "Now in five minutes, tick off the things a President ought to do to clean up this goddamn civil rights mess." Once elected, Kennedy wished to develop a political strategy to deal with the civil right issues. He had Harris Wofford prepare a memo outlining a plan. Wofford's (Prepresidential Files, Box 1071, Wofford File Memo, JFKL) thirty-one-page memo proposed "little or no legislation this year aside from the extension of the Civil Rights Commission, and a large measure of executive action. You have the power to do more than you will be able to do on this problem in one year. If you make this a year full of executive action you can overcome the disappointment of Negroes and civil rights groups, although they will holler for a while." This important memo shows that even among the strongest administration advocates of civil rights reform there was a feeling that pushing too fast on legislation might limit the effectiveness of Kennedy's overall program. Instead, it recommended that the president take a personal interest in executive action. The record shows that while a great deal of executive action occurred, it was largely done by Kennedy's subordinates, mostly in the Justice Department, and was done as quietly as could be, in as conciliatory a manner as possible. Kennedy himself seems largely to have remained detached from executive action, at least in the beginning.

He did personally intervene in some cases. On Inauguration Day, Kennedy himself noticed that the honor guards in the parade were all white and moved to ensure that the various military branches were desegregating, both in the honor guard setting and in their admissions to the service academies (Branch, 1988: 400). Another exception was JFK's letter to General U.S. Grant III on the eve of the one hundreth anniversary of the beginning of the Civil War at Fort Sumter, South Carolina. Grant chaired the National Civil War Commission and had scheduled the centennial event at a segregated hotel which would not house Negro delegates. Kennedy wrote to Grant urging him "to take action which would assure that the arrangements . . . meet the standards set for us by the Constitution and by our moral conscience" (RFK Papers, General Correspondence, Box 66, White House Memoranda Folder, JFKL). When Grant failed to move from segregated facilities, Kennedy mustered enough votes to move the opening banquet to a Naval base, which itself turned out to be segregated. The embarrassing case was soon forgotten because of the Bay of Pigs invasion, which occurred five days later (Branch, 1988: 401).

In the Justice Department, there were symbolic acts and legal actions. Robert Kennedy resigned from the Metropolitan Club because of its racial policies, prompting journalist Carl Rowan to write to RFK that his action marked a "marvelous move for a nation that for so long has desperately needed this kind of moral leadership at your level" (RFK Files, General Correspondence, Box 9, Civil Rights 8–11/61 Folder, JFKL). And Robert Kennedy, concerned about the scarcity of black attorneys at Justice, wrote a letter to deans of many law schools asking them to identify "qualified Negro attorneys of your acquaintance who might be interested in coming to the Department" so that he might "break down the barrier" of race (RFK Files, General Correspondence, Box 9, Civil Rights 1–6/61 Folder, JFKL).

In legal action, Burke Marshall took charge of civil rights policy in the Justice Department. His year-end reports show extensive activity. In voting rights, the Kennedy administration prosecuted six voting discrimination suits held over from the Eisenhower years and filed twelve more in its first year. The administration also attempted to lessen employment discrimination, especially in the federal government. In school desegregation, Marshall argued that Justice moved "with vigor to protect the integrity of the court orders, to preserve the due administration of justice and to encourage and assist local officials and community leaders who are effective in promoting peaceful desegregation of the schools" (Burke Marshall Papers, Box 16, Year End Report Files, JFKL). The report also mentions Justice Department activities regarding the freedom rides.

Meanwhile, as the Kennedy administration pursued low-profile tactics, civil rights advocates began to be critical of the administration's pace. The National Committee against Discrimination in Housing noted in September of 1961 that it had been "thirteen months since he promised that the new Democratic administration would act and eight months since he took office," but still there was no executive order concerning housing (White House Central Files, Box 371, Human Rights, Folder 9/26–10/31/61, JFKL). Wofford began to be frustrated that Kennedy would not meet with black leaders such as the leaders of the Student Nonviolent Coordinating Committee (SNCC), arguing that "it would be better for the President to see them for ten or fifteen minutes than to wait until they launch fasts in jail or encampments outside the White House asking to see him" (Memo, Wofford to O'Donnell, White House Central Files, Box 358, Folder 5/11–11/15/61, JFKL).

The first important civil rights activity of Kennedy's presidency came in the form of the freedom rides in May of 1961. On April 26, 1961, James Farmer, the leader of the freedom ride movement, wrote to JFK that the rides were an expression "of our duty to affirm our principles by asserting our rights. With the survival of democracy at stake, there is an imperative, immediate need for acts of self-determination" (White House Central Files, Human Rights, Box 374, Folder 4/24/61–3/21/63, JFKL). Although Kennedy tried to postpone the rides so they would not interfere with his upcoming meeting with French President Charles de Gaulle and Soviet leader Nikita Khrushchev (Schlesinger, 1978: 295), the administration supported the riders, asserting for the nation the rights of citizens to travel on integrated transportation. Kennedy called out the National Guard, obtained a federal court order enjoining segregationists from interfering with interstate bus travel, and issued a statement calling for the restoration of order in Alabama (Miroff, 1976: 234). When pushed, the Kennedys were willing to bring the full power of the national government to bear in these affairs.

But the rhetoric of the president and the attorney general did not embrace the movement. Kennedy (Kennedy Presidential Press Conferences, 1978: 124) expressed the feeling that "there's no question of the legal rights of the freedom travelers—Freedom riders, to move in interstate commerce," indicating that he would use federal power to insure that right if necessary. Rather than making the moral argument about human rights, he said "the basic question is not the Freedom Riders. The basic question is that anyone who moves in interstate commerce should be able to do so freely." Instead of embracing the movement, Kennedy saw the freedom rides as a simple question of legality. Robert Kennedy was concerned about violence and called for a cooling-off period before the Freedom Riders continued (Belknap, 1987: 87; Schlesinger, 1978: 299). The motive for such sentiment could be either humanitarian in nature or a concern that the rides were embarrassing his brother on the eve of his talks with Khrushchev and de Gaulle. When Kennedy called off federal forces, thus allowing the arrest of the Freedom Riders in Jackson, it appeared that he had at least tacitly allowed their arrest for acts that by federal law were clearly legal (Schlesinger, 1978: 299). At the very least, RFK's actions indicated a misinterpretation and underestimation of the determination of the Freedom Riders and showed an administration more interested in image than in action.

The fall of 1962 brought another major conflict when James Meredith attempted to register as a student at the University of Mississippi. Again, there was no question about enforcing Meredith's legal rights. The attorney general organized the federal enforcement effort and communicated with segregationist Governor Ross Barnett. The many conversations between RFK and the governor illustrate the Kennedy approach to civil rights policy. At first, they wished to address the problem as if it were simply a legal affair, rather than a moral issue. President Kennedy stated as much in his address to the nation on September 30: "Even among law abiding men few laws are universally loved, but they are uniformly respected and not resisted. Americans are free, in short, to disagree with the law but not disobey it" (Public Papers of the President, 1962: 727). Only when it became obvious that the governor would not cooperate did the Justice Department use all of the weapons in its arsenal. Asked to comment on the administration's pursuit of Meredith's registration, President

Kennedy responded that while costly, failure to act on behalf of Meredith "would have been far more expensive." Again, however, JFK did not emphasize the racial nature of the issue, but justified the federal action by saying:

This country, of course, cannot survive if the United States Government and the executive branch do not carry out the decisions of the court. It might be a decision in this case which some people may not agree with. The next time it might be another matter, and this government would unravel very fast. So there's no question in my mind that the United States executive branch had to take the action that it did (Kennedy Presidential Press Conferences, 1978: 429).

This quote is revealing both for what it says and what it leaves unsaid. First, Kennedy seems to want to make the issue one of federalism rather than equal protection, making it more abstract and less emotional. Second, he seems to disavow the actions of his Justice Department that had brought action in the federal courts to produce the orders he felt must be carried out. Finally, he indicates that some people might disagree with the orders, but does not indicate whether he thought theirs was a valid position. This may have been an attempt to maintain some sympathy for southern Democrats who Kennedy wanted to keep in his coalition. Still, JFK at least contemplated reprisals that might force Mississippi to be more reasonable in the future. In Burke Marshall's file are three folders labeled "Stick it to Mississippi." They contain listings of federal contracts and defense procurements to use as ammunition against the state should a confrontation occur again (Marshall Files, Box 20, JFKL).

In 1963, perhaps the most dramatic of civil rights events came with violent confrontations between civil rights activists, led by Dr. Martin Luther King, Jr. and segregationists, led by police head "Bull" Connor, in Birmingham, Alabama. In early May, civil rights marchers were arrested and others were beaten. The administration sympathized with the movement and acted strongly to help keep the situation from spinning out of control. Again, however, the president seemed to define the incidents in Birmingham to limit the national government commitment to keeping the peace. While there was negotiation between Robert Kennedy and Dr. King about the timing of the marches, and while the Justice Department sent Burke Marshall to Birmingham to try to mediate between civil rights marchers and white leaders, the federal government's intervention did not go any further. President Kennedy stated that "There isn't any federal statute that was involved in the last few days in Birmingham, Ala." (Kennedy Presidential Press Conferences, 1978: 498). Again, the president apparently wished to limit his role as a leader in the move for civil rights, using the issue of federalism as a convenient crutch.

Birmingham, however, was seen by Martin Luther King and others as a critical changing point. In a sense, they felt that Kennedy was "born again" to the movement. That seemingly new commitment coincided with the major civil rights event of the summer of 1963—the March on Washington. And its confirmation came in a switch in tactics by the Kennedy administration—moving from an executive strategy to a legislative one with the introduction in 1963 of an Omnibus Civil Rights Bill. As events unfolded, Kennedy's rhetorical style also changed. In a June 11 speech, rather than defining the struggle in legal terms, Kennedy said "We are confronted primarily with a moral issue. It is as old as the Scriptures and as clear as the American Constitution . . . " (Public Papers of the President, 1963: 469). And his message to Congress pushing the passage of his Civil Rights Bill contained some of the most emotional appeals of his presidency:

I ask you to look into your hearts—not in search of charity, for the Negro neither needs nor wants condescension—but for one plain, proud, and priceless quality that unites us as Americans: a sense of justice. In this year of the Emancipation Centennial, justice requires us to insure the blessings of liberty for all Americans and their posterity—not merely for reasons of economic efficiency, world diplomacy and domestic tranquility—but, above all, because it is right" (Public Papers of the President, 1963: 494).

Yet these changes did not make Kennedy a complete convert to the cause. He still wanted to exercise control over the flow of the issue. In a meeting with civil rights leaders before the March on Washington, Kennedy expressed the hope that the March could be called off (Miroff, 1976: 260). While movement leaders saw the March as a way to mobilize support for the civil rights bill, Kennedy feared that the March might cause a "white backlash" that would jeopardize its passage. Again, Kennedy's pragmatic approach reveals a lack of empathy for the depth of feeling among the black leadership or that civil rights leaders wished to be involved in legislative strategy. It would have been ironic had the leaders of the civil rights movement left such a dramatic legislative battle and policy leadership of the issue to an almost entirely white legislature and executive. When the March occurred, it was with the assistance of the administration and resulted in Martin Luther King's famous "I have a dream" speech. Even then, however, the administration was instrumental in censoring speeches that would have been excessively critical of its leadership (Miroff, 1976: 264–65). This manipulation can be interpreted either as "damage control" by the administration or as a strategy to make the March a sign of unity between the president and the Civil Rights Movement. In any case, Kennedy wished to orchestrate the March, much as he wished to control the legislative agenda.

With regard to the civil rights measure itself, how is Kennedy to be judged? The 1963 Civil Rights bill was, as might be expected, criticized from both the left and the right. Critics of the left wanted to toughen the bill, while Kennedy wished to pursue a more moderate bill because he thought such a measure would be more easily passed (Miroff, 1976: 261). While the bill was not passed in Kennedy's lifetime, he had finally warmed to the legislative battle. When the bill was at last proposed, Kennedy pursued it with vengeance. The attorney general was deeply involved in the legislative process, with many memos in his files discussing tactics designed to attain passage (RFK Papers, General Correspondence, Box 11, Civil Rights Legislation 7/63 File, JFKL). Similarly, in the president's legislative files are a number of memos regarding what his personal role should be. One memo, from Secretary of the Senate Robert Baker, suggested particular tactics of President Kennedy's that had been effective in other contexts (President's Legislative Files, Box 53, June 1963 Folder, JFKL).

ASSESSING KENNEDY'S ROLE

In assessing Kennedy, both in terms of his personal and presidential commitment to civil rights, several generalizations can be made. First, Kennedy eventually had a strong policy commitment to civil rights. He made civil rights pledges during the 1960 campaign and he never seriously wavered when confronted with civil rights conflict. His understanding of the racial politics of the South might have been lacking, but in terms of his own policy preference, Kennedy advocated civil rights reform.

It is equally clear that at least for the first two years of his presidency, civil rights was not an issue of primary importance to Kennedy. While his principal civil rights policy advisor, Harris Wofford, recommended that Kennedy pursue an executive strategy early in his administration, Kennedy was seemingly happy to leave the issue to routine administration rather than presidential leadership. During this period the president was involved in civil rights, but his involvement was apparently always a reaction to events forced by the Civil Rights Movement rather than one precipitated by any presidential initiative. And when he made public statements, they involved straightforward pronouncements concerning keeping the peace and following the law rather than broad-sweeping moral pronouncements about the inherent moral issues involved. While Kennedy was interested in exercising the full amount of presidential power in the arena of foreign policy, using his charismatic personality to its fullest, he always seemed a little more restrained in pursuit of civil rights. Neustadt (1990: 175) attributes his reserved approach to civil rights to the fact that "he had a distaste for preaching, really for the preachiness of politics, backed by genuine mistrust of mass emotion as a tool in politics." In contrast, recalling the Kennedy era, the late Supreme Court Justice Thurgood Marshall (Oral History, 1964: 6, emphasis added) attributed Kennedy's style to a relative reluctance to carry the torch of civil rights policy. He said that "at any time that it would be necessary for the federal arm of the government to move, specifically the executive arm, that I was convinced that the President was determined to use the full force of his office, whenever it became necessary. But *not* until it became necessary."

Once Kennedy decided on a legislative strategy, he pursued that initiative vigorously. By his third year in office, whether through being forced into a leadership position by southern segregationist leaders or by having seen the moral nature of the civil rights policy arena, Kennedy had warmed to the issue. He appeared willing to talk of the issue in moral terms, and he also became personally involved in the legislative battle (Bradlee, 1975). This is indicative of an issue moving to the top of a president's agenda, especially when it is combined with, as Kernell (1993) writes, a strategy of "going public." But even then, Kennedy never let himself fully embrace the spirit of the civil rights movement. Both in his attempt to control the nature of the March on Washington and in his introduction of a moderate civil rights bill, he seemed more interested in legislative attainment than in the total realization of civil rights.

A major problem in interpreting the Kennedy record is that while the key events are well known, misperceptions often both preceded and followed these events and misperceptions sometimes have led to misinterpretations. A case in point concerns James Meredith's application to the University of Mississippi. Brauer (1988: 120) writes the following to explain the application:

Kennedy's [inaugural] speech moved a generation. Years later it was still being cited, by many who were young when they heard it, as a turning point in their lives. For some, its immediate impact was very tangible. The day after he gave it, James H. Meredith, a black twenty-eight-year-old air force veteran, decided to seek admission to the all-white University of Mississippi.

In fact, while the application was filed on the day after the inauguration, it was the strong Democratic civil rights plank (known as the Bowles platform) at the 1960 National Convention that persuaded Meredith to act rather than the Inaugural Address.

The election of President Kennedy provided the proper atmosphere for the development of such a situation. The strongest point in our favor was the civil rights platform which Kennedy had insisted on at the Democratic convention. Since the election was one of the closest in the history of the United States and the Negro vote had been widely reported as being the deciding factor, the new Democratic administration was on the spot and would be forced to act if put under pressure (Meredith, 1966: 51).

In his book, Meredith makes no reference to the Inaugural Address.

More interestingly, Meredith's belief that John Kennedy backed the strong plank is probably wrong. At the convention, Kennedy's support of the strong plank may have been caused by both John and Robert Kennedy's inattention to its details. Branch (1988: 319) reports that Robert Kennedy told campaign workers to support the strongest proposed plank and speculates that:

Having been unable thus far to get Kennedy to even read the civil rights plank, [Harris] Wofford feared that perhaps he [Robert Kennedy] did not realize what he had just done. Or perhaps he had made a calculated decision that supporting the plank would help hold Northern delegates against the threat of Lyndon Johnson. Or perhaps Kennedy had given the order simply because its brevity was worth more at the moment than all the political benefits he could imagine from more complicated alternatives.

According to Harris Wofford (1980: 52), Robert Kennedy supported the plank simply because he had not considered it enough to know it was stronger than John Kennedy would have preferred.

Bob Kennedy talked with me in general about the platform and concluded that our delegates should be asked to support a strong civil rights plank, but had not taken the time to listen to details and I had not expected him to go very far in his support. Instead of checking further, Bob stood on a chair in Suite 8315 on the morning the Platform Committee was to decide, and as part of his daily briefing told the large assembly of Kennedy workers to support the full Bowles draft.

Others have argued that Robert Kennedy's support of the strong plank was quite deliberate. Whichever version is correct, John Kennedy did not support the Bowles plank, which Wofford (1980: 52) describes as "a maximal position," because, as Sorensen (1965: 157) wrote, it "promised, in Kennedy's private view, too many antagonistic specifics that could not be fulfilled, raising too many unwarranted hopes and unnecessary fears."

To add one more misinterpretation, consider the assessment of the Kennedy operation from the standpoint of Theodore White (1961: 157), in his now classic interpretation of the 1960 election. He recalled that "Control as exercised from 8315 was precise, taut, disciplined—yet as casual as that of a veteran combat army, blooded in battle, which has learned to know its component parts and recognizes the full reach of its skills and courage."

Following this maze of perceptions and interpretations reminds the observer of the conflicting understandings that often attach to such "parables." Brauer believes Meredith acted on the inspiration of Kennedy's Inaugural Address, which he did not. Meredith sees President Kennedy as supporting the strong civil rights plank, which he did not. Branch argues that the support was perhaps based on political calculations, which it probably was not. Nor was it a result of careful planning, as White infers. Kennedy favored a more modest plank. The unanswered question that remains is, would Meredith have applied to the University of Mississippi had President Kennedy really known what he was doing?

When we began this review, we wished to gain a glimpse at the personal leadership style and feelings of JFK in civil rights. One thing that emerges from our reading is that Kennedy really did have an informal operating style, with a relatively sparse paper trail concerning his tactics or thoughts. Greenstein (1982) found a "hidden hand" in Eisenhower's leadership by analyzing documents in his presidential library. With Kennedy, one can barely find his fingerprints in his papers. Most of what we know about JFK comes in the form of letters or memos to the president rather than any record of his personal reaction. Even his aides have had to make assumptions about Kennedy's personal commitment to the civil rights cause. He never really let on what his feelings were, even to close associates. In a real sense, JFK was rather an enigmatic leader in the arena of civil rights. His close personal friends Kenneth O'Donnell and Dave Powers (1970) wrote an affectionate memoir concerning Kennedy's life, lamenting that with his untimely passing, "Johnny, We Hardly Knew Ye." In a real sense, this characterization seems appropriate for assessing Kennedy's own personal commitment to civil rights.

On balance, the Kennedy record seems quite consistent with the revisionist interpretation. He deserves credit for his exercise of leadership in civil rights, but his leadership was largely of a reactive sort, with events constantly being forced upon him by civil rights activists. Only when the legislative game came into play during the summer of 1963 did Kennedy's role approximate that of a protagonist. Kennedy pushed civil rights further than any president previously had, but barring some unforeseen revelations about his personal convictions on civil rights, we may never know the depth or intensity of his own views.

9

Decentralizing Fair Housing Enforcement During the Reagan Presidency

—————— CHARLES M. LAMB AND JIM TWOMBLY

Theories of federalism have contributed to the denial of civil rights throughout the course of American history. Most notably, federalism provided the theoretical justification for the states' rights doctrine. Advocates of states' rights during the nineteenth century included passionate pro-slavery forces. Then, in the twentieth century, the doctrine of states' rights inspired widespread evasion, delay, and noncompliance by southern governments concerning the rights of African Americans.[1] This was especially true in the area of school desegregation (*e.g.*, Peltason, 1971). The civil rights legislation of the 1960s sought to remedy some of these problems. By placing civil rights squarely on the national agenda, that legislation endowed the federal government with broad new authority to root out racial discrimination at the state and local levels (*e.g.*, Graham, 1990).

Ironically, a generation later, state and local governments had assumed, in effect, the lead position in a federal-state-local partnership for implementing federal fair housing policy. During the 1980s, state and local civil rights agencies combined, received, and conciliated far more housing discrimination complaints than ever before under the Fair Housing Act of 1968, commonly known as Title VIII. Collectively they also provided more total monetary relief for Title VIII complaints than ever before. Meanwhile, the Department of Housing and Urban Development (HUD) became less vital in carrying out these responsibilities (Lamb, 1992).

The prominent part played by state and local governments in federal fair housing enforcement in the 1980s was largely the making of the Reagan administration and President Reagan's "New Federalism" (*e.g.*, Conlan, 1988; Eisinger and Gormley, 1988; Nathan, 1989). New Federalism was political shorthand for governmental decentralization in domestic policy generally. Reagan, a longtime critic of federal involvement in various areas of social policy, believed that federal spending and federal regulation should be cut back sharply. At the same time, he felt the functions of state and local governments should be strengthened, and they should be given additional responsibilities.[2] In the realm of fair housing, this meant that state and local agencies would be given much more federal financial and technical assistance to develop the institutional capacity to receive, investigate, and conciliate most fair housing complaints filed under the Fair Housing Act.

In this chapter, we explore how New Federalism manifested itself in the implementation of fair housing policy during the Reagan administration. As a reflection of Reagan's New Federalism, we examine HUD's Fair Housing Assistance Program (FHAP) and the extent to which state and local governments increasingly shouldered fair housing enforcement responsibilities during the 1980s. The origins of FHAP preceded Reagan, but it flowered during his presidency, strongly encouraging state and local civil rights agencies to play a vigorous role in implementing the Fair Housing Act. After looking at FHAP and its rapid growth during the Reagan years, we rely on data provided by HUD to analyze changes in the volume of Title VIII complaints handled by state and local entities from 1977 through 1988. We expect to find significant changes in the volume of complaint processing at the state and local levels during these years because of FHAP. We then discuss some implications of these findings and suggest the need for further research and the direction it should take.

FAIR HOUSING AND SUBSTANTIAL EQUIVALENCY

Housing discrimination and segregation are salient, formidable, persistent issues in the United States (e.g., Farley and Frey, 1994; Massey and Denton, 1993; Turner, Struyk, and Yinger, 1991). To combat discrimination, and secondarily to reduce residential segregation, the Fair Housing Act was passed in 1968 after four years of spirited debate and stout political opposition (Graham, 1990: ch. 10). That law prohibits discrimination on the grounds of race, color, religion, sex, and national origin in the sale, rental, and financing of housing, and in the performance of brokerage services (e.g., Kushner, 1983; Schwemm, 1991).[3] Persons who believe they have been illegally discriminated against are afforded two options for pursuing relief under the 1968 legislation: either file a housing discrimination complaint with HUD or file a private lawsuit in federal or state court.[4]

Section 810(c) of the Fair Housing Act is crucial to an understanding of FHAP. It requires that HUD allow state and local civil rights agencies to have the first opportunity to handle Title VIII housing discrimination complaints, if those agencies have "substantial equivalency" status.[5] Substantial equivalency means, first of all, that a state or local agency has been recognized by HUD as having legal authority equal to that provided in Title VIII, at the federal level, to receive, investigate, and conciliate housing discrimination complaints. Second, it means that a state or local entity must, in fact, have the administrative capacity to enforce its laws in a substantially equivalent manner (U.S. Department of Housing and Urban Development, 1988: 28–29; Wallace, Holshouser, Lane, and Williams, 1985: 27–33).

A political compromise, struck during the passage of the Fair Housing Act, was responsible for the substantial equivalency requirement and the more general notion that state and local agencies should shoulder a share of the burden of dealing with housing discrimination complaints filed under Title VIII. That compromise was clearly designed to diminish the federal role in Title VIII enforcement (Schwemm, 1991: ch. 24, 3–4; Wallace, Holshouser, Lane, and Williams, 1985: 10–11). Viewed from this perspective, Title VIII's substantial equivalency requirement was a means of ensuring that the federal government would not dominate the implementation of fair housing policy. Seen from another perspective, however, it was a means whereby the federal government could seek to influence state and local governments to pass stronger fair housing laws.

Whichever perspective one embraces, clearly HUD played the dominant role in Title VIII enforcement during the 1970s, with a limited number of state and local governments taking an active part. Three factors seem to account for this. To begin with, most state and local agencies were not certified as substantially equivalent by HUD because they did not provide the same rights and remedies as Title VIII, or they did not possess the administrative capacity to carry out their laws effectively. Federal law, even though bestowing very limited powers on HUD to enforce Title VIII, did broadly prohibit housing discrimination and create formal enforcement mechanisms under Title VIII. This was not always true of state and local civil rights laws. Second, even where state and local agencies had an equally broad and tough antidiscrimination policy with which to work, and equivalent enforcement mechanisms, there was still a good chance that they would have small budgets and staffs. Third, related to this, since there were no federal financial incentives provided for state and local entities to take on Title VIII enforcement activities, many of these agencies had little desire to help with that troublesome job.

Figure 9.1 indicates the extent to which HUD shouldered the lion's share of Title VIII work during the late 1970s. HUD received over 12,000 housing discrimination complaints between 1977 and 1980, handling over 93 percent of them during those four fiscal years. Certified state and local civil rights agencies typically received only a trickle of referrals from HUD. But a striking change is apparent after that. With the continued growth of Title VIII complaints after Reagan's election, greater emphasis was placed on FHAP by the administration. A resulting surge occurred in

Figure 9.1
Cases Handled, Fiscal Years 1977–1988

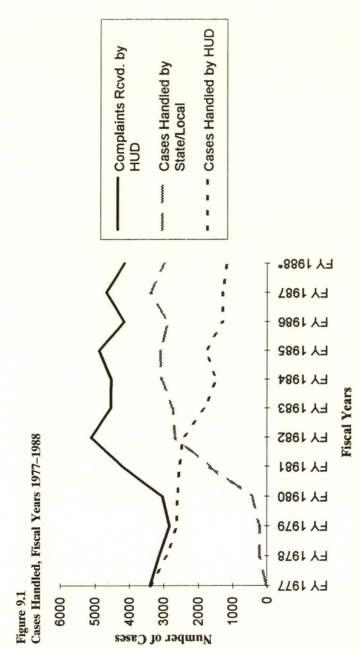

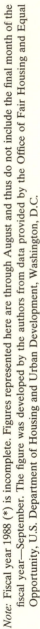

Fiscal Years

Note: Fiscal year 1988 (*) is incomplete. Figures represented here are through August and thus do not include the final month of the fiscal year—September. The figure was developed by the authors from data provided by the Office of Fair Housing and Equal Opportunity, U.S. Department of Housing and Urban Development, Washington, D.C.

the number of substantially equivalent agencies eligible for FHAP financial assistance, as discussed in the next section, and therefore a dramatic increase is seen in Figure 9.1 in the volume of Title VIII complaints handled by state and local agencies.

THE ORIGINS AND DEVELOPMENT OF FHAP

The Fair Housing Assistance Program was designed to realize a more significant Title VIII enforcement role for state and local governments. For well over a decade now, FHAP has provided federal financial and technical assistance to substantially equivalent civil rights agencies at the state and local levels to process housing discrimination complaints, to train state and local personnel in administering fair housing programs, and to carry out special projects (e.g., Wallace, Holshouser, Lane, and Williams, 1985).

Yet FHAP is of relatively recent vintage and never formally existed as a budget-line program in the 1970s. While HUD was assigned legal responsibilities concerning substantial equivalency matters at the time the Fair Housing Act went into effect, these matters were handled for over a decade at HUD headquarters without a formal program providing financial assistance to state and local agencies.[6] In 1974, and again in 1979, the U.S. Commission on Civil Rights recommended that a program like FHAP be established to dispense federal financial aid to substantially equivalent state and local agencies to process Title VIII complaints (1974: 349; 1979: 234).

Congress first appropriated FHAP funds for fiscal year 1980, the final year of the Carter administration, officially signalling the inauguration of the Fair Housing Assistance Program as it is known today. Of that $3.7 million, roughly half was earmarked to assist state and local agencies in processing housing discrimination complaints. The remainder of the first FHAP budget was designated for personnel training, technical assistance, information systems, or innovative projects. Both competitive and non-competitive grants were available.[7] Criteria for receiving FHAP assistance were initially published by HUD in May 1980, and finalized in July 1980. To be eligible for funding, state and local agencies were required to have substantial equivalency status and to sign a memorandum of understanding on the procedures to be used in referring and processing Title VIII complaints (*Housing and Development Reporter* 7: 713, 806, 1089; 8: 144, 910).

Only after FHAP financial incentives became available did state and local governments overcome inertia, and political opposition in many instances, to come up to federal fair housing standards. Given the possibility of FHAP financing, state and local governments demonstrated an immediate interest in Title VIII enforcement, with some state legislatures moving quickly to pass more stringent housing discrimination laws in the 1980s to qualify for funding (U.S. Department of Housing and Urban Development, 1988: 29).

While FHAP was initially funded in the final year of the Carter presidency, the program grew markedly during the Reagan years and was continued under the Bush and Clinton administrations (e.g., U.S. Department of Housing and Urban Development, 1992a: 20). At the time that President Reagan took office, however, little solid evidence indicated that state and local agencies could and would process Title VIII complaints effectively and efficiently. Substantially equivalent agencies had experienced only limited success before FHAP.[8] If the past performance of these state and local entities was a sign of things to come, FHAP's future probably would not be bright.

Despite this, the Reagan administration found the idea of decentralizing fair housing enforcement to be very attractive, and the basic notion underlying FHAP was quite compatible with Reagan's New Federalism. For if state and local governments were to take on additional Title VIII responsibilities, their institutional capacities would have to be upgraded significantly, and that was an explicit goal of FHAP. The Reagan administration therefore decided to support FHAP wholeheartedly, and HUD highlighted the program throughout Reagan's eight years in office.[9]

The administration's objective, it seems, was to refer as many discrimination complaints as possible to the state and local levels (Schwemm, 1989: 292). In contrast, HUD career officials seemed to view FHAP "as the only mechanism by which HUD could obtain funds for strengthening the Title VIII enforcement effort" (Wallace, Holshouser, Lane, and Williams, 1985: 13). According to one HUD report released toward the end of the Reagan period, "previous Administrations had relatively little success in developing the localities' potential," but during the Reagan administration "HUD moved aggressively to increase State and local authority and responsibility for Fair Housing, and the result was dramatic" (U.S. Department of Housing and Urban Development, 1989: 78).

Figure 9.2 graphically represents just how dramatic it was![10] The number of state and local jurisdictions eligible to receive FHAP funding more than doubled during the first term of the Reagan presidency. Singling out this fact in a 1984 speech, Reagan sounded pleased with the accomplishment (*Public Papers of the Presidents*, 1984: 501). As shown in Table 9.1, by the end of 1988 a total of 112 agencies were eligible for FHAP financial assistance, compared to 38 in 1980. All told, during the Reagan presidency, the number of state agencies eligible for FHAP funds rose by 33 percent, and the number of local agencies soared by 591 percent, for a total increase of 195 percent. That process continued during the Bush administration, so that at one time no less than 122 state and local governments were certified (U.S. Commission on Civil Rights, 1992).

Figure 9.2
Number of FHAP-Eligible Jurisdictions

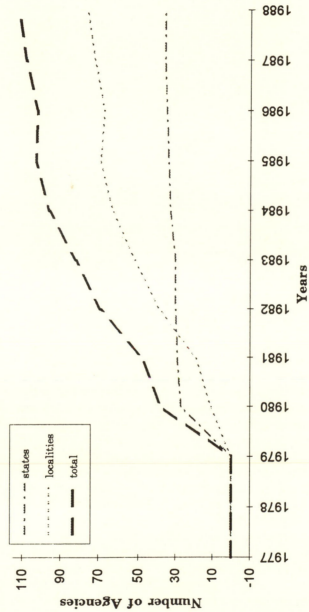

states _._ _.._ .._

localities ....

total

Number of Agencies

Years

Table 9.1
Jurisdictions Eligible for FHAP Funding

Year	States	Localities	Total
1977	0	0	0
1978	0	0	0
1979	0	0	0
1980	27	11	38
1981	29	19	48
1982	30	39	69
1983	30	52	82
1984	33	63	96
1985	34	69	103
1986	35	67	102
1987	36	72	108
1988	36	76	112

Note: The last reported number of jurisdictions having substantially equivalent laws, as reported in the *Federal Register* for each year, is the source of the data from 1980–1988. Even though some states and localities were granted substantially equivalent status prior to 1980, there was no FHAP program or funds available to them, and those years are coded as 0. (See note 10.)

Apart from FHAP funds to strengthen state and local handling of fair housing complaints, and financial assistance to augment the size of staffs for carrying out this function, FHAP also supplied monetary support for over one hundred specialized projects during the Reagan years. These projects ranged from fair housing education and testing to the creation of fair housing data systems (U.S. Department of Housing and Urban Development, 1988: 29). State and local agencies received $5.85 million in FHAP outlays in 1984 (*e.g.*, U.S. Department of Commerce, Bureau of the Census, 1984: 10, table 2), and that figure rose to over $7.63 million in 1988. As a result, by the end of the Reagan period state and local agencies were assigning 20 percent of their total staffs, and 16 percent of their total budgets, to housing discrimination matters (U.S. Commission on Civil Rights, 1992: 7).

The Reagan administration eventually invested, in terms of actual FHAP outlays, nearly $38 million to mobilize state and local enforcement of federal fair housing policy between 1981 and 1988 (see Table 9.2), despite its attempts to control new federal spending.[11] That trend carried over to the Bush administration (*e.g.*, U.S. Department of Housing and Urban Development, 1991: 4). According to HUD (1992b: 9), $7.5 million was obligated under FHAP for fiscal year 1991, for example. By contrast, only $3.7 million

Table 9.2
Budget Authority and Outlays for FHAP Funding (in millions of dollars)

Year	Budget Authority	Budget Outlays
1977	0	0
1978	0	0
1979	0	0
1980	3.700	na
1981	5.700	0.723
1982	5.016	2.360
1983	5.700	4.634
1984	4.700	5.854
1985	6.700	5.462
1986	6.341	5.439
1987	6.341	5.752
1988	4.800	7.639

Note: Except for 1983 outlays, all budget data are taken from the *Budget of the United States Government* for each year. 1983 outlay data is taken from a 1983 Census Bureau report entitled *Federal Expenditures by State for Fiscal Year 1983.* The outlay figure for 1980 was not available at time of publication.

of FHAP funds had been authorized in the final year of the Carter presidency (Wallace, Holshouser, Lane, and Williams, 1985: 13).

The growth and evolution of FHAP was "the most obvious change" in fair housing implementation during the Reagan presidency, according to HUD General Counsel John Knapp. In light of increased FHAP funding, not only was there a marked rise in the percentage of complaints handled at the state and local levels during the Reagan years, but the decentralization of the complaint process was said to make it far more accessible to the average complainant. HUD mainly handled fair housing complaints in its regional offices. That awkward process could now be averted, as complainants could go directly to a local or state human rights office with a claim of discrimination. Knapp contended that in the 1980s rapid gains were made in the effectiveness and efficiency with which housing discrimination complaints were processed. This progress, he said, was directly due to FHAP (U.S. House of Representatives, 1987: 73–74).

Decentralization was seemingly foremost in the minds of Reagan administration officials. Their principal goal was to secure active state and local involvement in the implementation of national civil rights policy. By 1987, administration officials believed that state and local governments had largely replaced HUD as the dominant force in the field of federal fair housing enforcement, and it is certainly true that HUD's role in Title VIII enforcement diminished substantially during the Reagan years (Lamb, 1992; Twombly and Lamb, 1992).

DATA AND METHOD

Our general hypothesis is that Reagan's New Federalism agenda had an impact in the arena of fair housing enforcement. Specifically, we hypothesize that as the FHAP program grew, the level of responsibility for processing complaints by state and local entities would also grow. Data were collected to control for a number of factors, the relevance of which has been indicated by prior research (Twombly and Lamb, 1992). We examine the twelve-year period of the Carter and Reagan administrations in order to set up an interrupted time series design to test the difference in policy implementation across the two administrations.

We have obtained computerized records of all complaints filed with HUD under Title VIII. From this database we were able to extract two measures of the level of state involvement in the enforcement process. The first measure is a simple count of the number of cases turned over to state and local agencies by HUD each quarter. The second is calculated by dividing the number of state and local cases by the total number of Title VIII complaints filed each quarter, thus providing a rough probability measure.[12]

A very simple approach to testing our hypothesis is to conduct a difference in means test for each dependent measure. The results of that test are reported in Table 9.3. Notice that the test provides a significant result for the simple count of cases and for the difference between the means of the probability measure before and after the implementation of Reagan's New Federalism via FHAP.

This test leaves much unexplained, however, and does not control for other factors. Certainly the role of the legislature should be taken into account, as should environmental considerations like the number of rental units available and the relative strength of the president. As shown in our earlier research, the "liberalness" of the appropriate subcommittees in the Senate, as measured by the annual mean ADA score of the committee members, is included in the model as a measure of legislative influence on HUD behavior. This is in keeping with a vast literature on the control exerted by the legislature on government agencies (for a review see Moe, 1987).

We postulated in our earlier work that contextual variables, such as economic performance, would have a constraining effect on HUD behavior (Twombly and Lamb, 1992). We suggested that as the economy provided more units of rental housing, HUD would enforce the Fair Housing Act less vigorously. We hinted at two possible explanations for this rela-

Table 9.3
Difference in Means Test (significant result in **bold** & df = 45)

Variable	Pre-New Federalism			Post-New Federalism			Difference in Means
	N	Mean	Std Dev	N	Mean	Std Dev	t-value
Number of State Cases	16	60.6875	53.828	31	433.871	253.106	**-5.80**
Probability of State Case	16	0.0753	0.062	31	0.4894	0.171	**-9.36**

Note: "State Case" here refers to cases turned over to state **and** local agencies by HUD. The results here differ from earlier published results (Lamb and Twombly 1993) due to an error in the data for the earlier analysis that was undetected until this revision.

tionship. First, with more units of housing available, it was less likely that complaints would be filed with HUD. Second, HUD officials could see a market with a housing surplus as providing a private sector alternative remedy to individual complaints of discrimination.

To keep this analysis as uncomplicated as possible, New Federalism is measured by a dichotomous variable which is equal to 0 prior to the beginning of Reagan's term and 1 thereafter. Naturally, without any other factor measuring characteristics of the president or the presidency, this variable would be measuring a simple change in administration and as such group together a number of factors (*e.g.*, political agenda, strength, presidential coattails in Congress, etc.). We include the Gallup Poll measure of presidential popularity to control for the relative and fluctuating strength of the president. In doing so, we multiply Carter's popularity by zero and Reagan's by one. This drops out the confounding effect of Carter's popularity and allows us to examine the ability of Reagan to implement his agenda at any time during his administration.

We measure FHAP growth in two ways. First, a quarter-by-quarter counter is included in the models in order to measure the possible growing impact of FHAP. There is a problem with using this measure throughout the Reagan presidency. Examination of the data indicated the possibility of a difference in implementation from Reagan's first term to his second. A difference in means test revealed a possible lame-duck effect, where FHAP's effect on HUD output is negative.[13] Given this finding, we removed the "growth counter" (set it equal to 0) after Reagan's first term. Second, we used the number of jurisdictions eligible to receive FHAP assistance as an alternative measure of growth. This alternative measure of growth was, naturally, correlated with both the quarter-by-quarter counter and the dichotomous variable used in the prior model. As a result we did not include the two measures in the same model.

Lacking a sufficient number of observations to develop an adequate model using autoregressive integrated moving average (ARIMA) techniques (McCleary and Hay, 1980), we performed a rather straightforward ordinary least squares (OLS) analysis and attempted to correct for violations of the basic OLS assumptions caused by the use of time series data. The first analysis revealed the possible presence of two problems: multicollinearity and autocorrelation. To correct for multicollinearity, the affected variables were differenced and run again in an OLS model to check for possible autocorrelated error terms. The Durbin-Watson test indicated positive autocorrelation was present. A first-order autoregressive model corrected this problem.

RESULTS OF ANALYSIS

Despite the methodological difficulties, in the initial analysis our measure for New Federalism was significant in both models—the number of state cases and the probability of state cases (see Table 9.4). This finding held up through all corrections made for multicollinearity and autocorrelation. In addition, Reagan's strength, as measured by his public approval rating, had a significant impact on the scope of HUD enforcement. One might expect that our measure of strength—Reagan's popularity—would be positively correlated with the number of state cases and the probability that a case would be turned over to the states. It should be noted, however, that our measure is differenced to correct for multicollinearity and as such reflects quarterly changes in popularity and should eliminate any underlying time dependent covariation. Since presidential popularity generally declines during a president's term, it would be reasonable to expect that a program initiated when a president first assumes office (and has a higher approval rating) would gain its own momentum. As such, it would be negatively correlated with the president's generally declining popularity.

We also tested to see if there was growth in the number of cases handled by the states between 1980 and 1988. Again, to measure this effect we created a quarter-by-quarter counter variable to see if, as time passed, the number of cases referred by HUD increased. As indicated earlier, this measure was problematic, forcing us to code the growth as 0 in Reagan's second term. This eliminated the possible lame-duck effect. Thus, we performed two tests—one where the effects of the counter were removed in the second term, and another where each term had a separate counter. Table 9.5, not surprisingly, reports a significant result for both shift in arena and growth in the program during Reagan's first term.[14]

Table 9.6 reports results which further support our assertion of the growing role of state and local governments in implementing the Fair Housing Act. Clearly, as the number of FHAP program fund recipients increases, so does both the number and probability of a state or local case. None of the results of this analysis contradicts any of our previous findings.

In short, our results support the general hypothesis that the decentralization efforts of the Reagan administration led to increased responsibility for state and local entities in the processing of Title VIII complaints. The coefficients for all three variables used to measure the growth in FHAP (the New Federalism dummy variable, the counter, and the number of FHAP jurisdications) were significant and in the anticipated direction. Each had a positive impact on the number of state and local cases and on the probability that a case would be handled by a state or local agency. Further, Reagan's strength, as measured by his popularity, had a significant negative relationship with the dependent measures.

DISCUSSION AND CONCLUSIONS

The Fair Housing Act of 1968 assigns the primary responsibility for its implementation to HUD. For over a decade HUD carried out that duty overwhelmingly on its own. The agency was widely criticized for its weak

Table 9.4
Results of Regression Analysis—Simple Shift Resulting from New Federalism (with an AR1 component)
(Results significant at the 0.05 level or better in **bold** & N=47)

Variable	Number of State Cases			Probability of a State Case		
	Coefficient	Std Err	t-ratio	Coefficient	Std Err	t-ratio
Intercept	367.8315	310.59	1.184	-0.1508	0.1837	-0.821
Rental Vacancies	104.2401	65.93	1.581	-0.0492	0.0431	-1.140
Senate ADA	-6.2992	6.38	-0.987	0.0050	0.0038	1.327
Popularity	**-6.9838**	**3.08**	**-2.270**	**-0.0049**	**0.0020**	**-2.474**
New Federalism	**325.5645**	**102.41**	**3.179**	**0.4302**	**0.0597**	**7.212**
R²	0.3142			0.6049		

Note: The R² reported here is the **regression R²** reported by the SAS Proc Autoreg procedure, which is a measure of the goodness of fit of the transformed model. SAS also reports a **total R²**, which is a measure of the accuracy with which the next value beyond the supplied data could be predicted.

Table 9.5
Results of Regression Analysis—Simple Shift Plus Growth in Program (with an AR1 component)
(Results significant at the 0.05 level or better in **bold**) N=47

Variable	Number of State Cases			Probability of a State Case		
	Coefficient	Std Err	t-ratio	Coefficient	Std Err	t-ratio
Intercept	-58.7261	184.502	-0.318	-0.3632	0.128	-2.842
Rental Vacancies	67.0894	71.453	0.939	-0.0668	0.049	-1.349
Senate ADA	1.7437	3.809	0.458	0.0091	0.003	3.454
Popularity	**-6.6642**	**2.637**	**-2.528**	**-0.0046**	**0.002**	**-2.538**
New Federalism	**217.9766**	**56.577**	**3.853**	**0.3590**	**0.039**	**9.162**
FHAP-Grow	**18.1322**	**3.071**	**5.905**	**0.0092**	**0.002**	**4.336**
R²	0.6632			0.7888		

Note: The R² reported here is the **regression R²** reported by the SAS Proc Autoreg procedure, which is a measure of the goodness of fit of the transformed model. SAS also reports a **total R²**, which is a measure of the accuracy with which the next value beyond the supplied data could be predicted.

141

Table 9.6
Results of Regression Analysis—Growth in FHAP Recipients (with an AR1 component)
(Results significant at the 0.05 level or better in **bold**) N=47

Variable	Number of State Cases				Probability of a State Case		
	Coefficient	Std Err	t-ratio		Coefficient	Std Err	t-ratio
Intercept	446.958	396.20	1.128		0.237	0.1924	1.232
Rental Vacancies	80.739	65.88	1.226		-0.015	0.0255	-0.576
Senate ADA	-6.939	8.40	-0.826		-0.002	0.0039	-0.621
Popularity	**-5.324**	**2.97**	**-1.791**		**-0.003**	**0.0012**	**-2.892**
FHAP-Recipients	**2.842**	**1.42**	**2.001**		**0.004**	**0.0009**	**4.000**
R^2	0.6180				0.8903		

Note: The R^2 reported here is the **regression R^2** reported by the SAS Proc Autoreg procedure, which is a measure of the goodness of fit of the transformed model. SAS also reports a **total R^2**, which is a measure of the accuracy with which the next value beyond the supplied data could be predicted.

enforcement performance, although much of the problem was due to the fact that HUD was given no real enforcement powers in Title VIII. Viewed in this bureaucratic context, President Reagan's New Federalism presented the prospect of a new direction in fair housing enforcement.

New Federalism was driven by the theory that state and local governments should take on more responsibilities vis-à-vis the federal bureaucracy. Given Reagan's championing of governmental decentralization, as well as statements by administration officials, it seems that in the realm of fair housing policy, the Fair Housing Assistance Program was New Federalism at work. FHAP, although initiated before Reagan's election in 1980, was well suited for the Reagan agenda of governmental decentralization, and during his administration it matured and thrived.

Indeed, under the Reagan administration and FHAP, the principal enforcers of equal housing opportunity became state and local civil rights agencies, whose activities were simply monitored by HUD. By the end of the Reagan era, a marked change had therefore emerged in federal fair housing policy: while retaining its formal responsibility as the lead federal agency in implementing Title VIII, HUD had in fact delegated most enforcement duties and procedures to FHAP agencies at the state and local levels.

Specifically, with regard to this dramatic change in fair housing enforcement, our research indicates a conscious effort, beginning in the Carter administration and greatly accelerated during the Reagan presidency, to shift enforcement responsibility to state and local entities. This effort grew throughout the Reagan years, and some evidence suggests that it continued during the first half of the Bush administration. Unlike many other federal mandates on localities, FHAP provided sufficient financial inducement to encourage state and local governments to participate, thereby becoming agents of the federal government in fair housing enforcement. In a sense, the regulatees became the regulators! This rare development distinguishes fair housing enforcement from enforcement in most other areas of civil rights.

We would emphasize a few general points in light of these findings. First, this change may or may not be a positive development for federal fair housing implementation. Granted, state and local governments are assigned a legally-mandated position in the Title VIII implementation process, and they are certainly capable of making a useful enforcement contribution (e.g., James and Crowe, 1985; U.S. Commission on Civil Rights, 1992). Yet the implications of this decentralization in fair housing implementation must be carefully scrutinized.

Not only have some state and local governments traditionally been suspect at rooting out racial discrimination, and lax about regulatory enforcement in general, but the Fair Housing Act specifically designates HUD as the lead agency in its implementation. Remember that, under the legislation, state and local entities are to play a role in federal fair housing enforcement only if they pass laws providing rights and remedies substantially equivalent to Title VIII, and only if they possess the administrative capacity to enforce those laws. Additionally, despite the flaws in HUD's enforcement record, that agency has developed a great deal of enforcement expertise through the years—experience that should not be lost in an implementation process that is far from simple or easy.

Further research may indicate that the policy consequences of this decentralization are notewothy. General implementation research tells us that, depending on the local political environment, original legislative intentions may be subverted (Scholz and Wei, 1986; Scholz, Twombly, and Headrick, 1991). In this case, the policy goal of equal housing opportunity could be subverted.

For example, in the rush to expand the number of substantially equivalent organizations during the Reagan years, some state and local agencies were certified for FHAP assistance that should not have been. According to Robert Schwemm (1989: 292), a leading expert on fair housing law, the Reagan administration "too quickly abandoned federal enforcement . . . by certifying some state and local agencies who were not, in fact, providing substantially equivalent rights and remedies." Beyond that, Massey and Denton (1993: 197) indicate that Title VIII implementation has sometimes involved substantially equivalent state and local agencies that were poorly managed and funded, and which had "little interest in enforcement."

Although perhaps not widespread problems, they do raise suspicions and questions. Ultimately we want to know if the stated objectives of Title VIII were achieved to a greater extent under FHAP than when HUD was the primary operational enforcer of the Fair Housing Act. While HUD's enforcement record has been weak in many respects, it remains an open question whether FHAP agencies performed the overall fair housing enforcement role more effectively and efficiently during most of the 1980s, and whether FHAP agencies provided the proper level of relief for complainants who experienced unlawful discrimination. If some state and local entities were certified as being substantially equivalent when in fact they were not, or if some substantially equivalent agencies had little real interest in fair housing implementation, it may be that Title VIII enforcement remained ineffectual during the 1980s. It may also be that meager relief persisted, even while these agencies received FHAP funds.

We plan to address some of these questions as part of our ongoing research into HUD's behavior and performance over the past twenty or so years. It appears, based on our work thus far, that the Reagan administration may have been successful at reducing the levels of relief (a measure of stringency of enforcement) granted by HUD (Twombly and Lamb, 1992). Future research should investigate the correlation between levels of relief and state or local enforcement, thereby allowing us to determine if the effect of FHAP was to decrease the overall stringency of enforcement. Since many states and localities tend to be more conservative than federal agencies in their approach to regulatory stringency, especially in some areas of civil rights, it is possible that by transferring enforcement responsibility to the states, Reagan may have increased the overall number of housing discrimination cases handled by them but reduced the level of relief granted. Only further research can help us with this question.

Not surprisingly, this last question raises others for consideration. Is FHAP-type decentralization the best cure for HUD's feeble record in fair housing enforcement? Or is the FHAP model of decentralization a good partial cure—yet one that was taken too far during the Reagan years? Should we assume that greater decentralization of fair housing implementation (including enforcement by virtually all fifty states and most cities of any size) will necessarily improve on HUD's past record in enforcement and provision of appropriate remedies? If so, under what circumstances does decentralization experience diminishing returns in fair housing implementation? Given the decentralized nature of the current system, at what point is HUD no longer meeting its statutory responsibilities as the lead agency in federal fair housing enforcement? Should "lead agency" primarily mean simply providing financial assistance to state and local governments (*e.g.*, U.S. House of Representatives, 1987: 84)? Under what circumstances should or must HUD reassert its leadershp role vis-à-vis state and local entities?

Additionally, in a system where federal enforcement responsibility is often delegated to agents (*e.g.*, states and localities), is there sufficient oversight by federal "principals"? Given this problem of agency, would enforcement benefit from a reorganized HUD, from the lead role being played by another existing agency, or from the creation of a new federal agency, where less day-to-day responsibility is delegated to agents? This is particularly a problem with agents whose inclination or ability to implement the will of the principal is disputable (see Moe, 1987, for a discussion of the principal-agent model). Answers to these questions can only be provided by objective and accurate analysis of HUD's past performance on the one hand, and how well states and localities have ensured fair housing rights and provided remedies on the other.

NOTES

We wish to thank our research and teaching assistants, Joanne Coury and Lisa Dalfonso, for their help in the early stages of this project. Additionally, Frank Zinni provided a number of beneficial suggestions regarding the analysis. Don Henning, of the Office of the Dean of the Faculty of Social Sciences, SUNY at Buffalo, was most helpful in getting the data into a readable format. Yet, of course, the authors are responsible for any mistakes in the analysis and interpretation.

1. Numerous Supreme Court decisions indicate how the civil rights of racial minorities were abridged by state and local governments during the twentieth century. See, for example, *Brown v. Board of Education* (1954); *Gomillion v. Lightfoot* (1960); *Hills v. Gautreaux* (1976); *Keyes v. School District No. 1, Denver* (1973); *Reitman v. Mulkey* (1967); *Shelley v. Kraemer* (1948); *Swann v. Charlotte-Mecklenburg Board of Education* (1971).

2. Reagan's views on American federalism, and how it should be reformed, were revealed in various public statements, especially during his first two years in office. See, for example, his February 18, 1981, speech on economic recovery before a joint session of Congress and his 1982 State of the Union address (*Public Papers of the Presidents* 1981: 108–15; 1982: 72–79).

3. The Fair Housing Act contains three major exemptions. One is single-family homes that are sold or rented, without the the assistance of a real estate agent and without the use of discriminatory advertising, by someone owning or receiving income from up to three such dwellings. Another is the so-called Mrs. Murphy's boarding house exemption—housing designed for up to four families within which the owner also resides. The final exemption pertains to housing owned by private clubs and religious organizations.

4. Title VIII was amended by the Fair Housing Amendments Act of 1988 to cover family status and the handicapped, and to expand the enforcement powers of HUD (see Schwemm, 1991). The implementation of the 1988 amendments is beyond the time frame of this study.

5. Section 810(c) of the Fair Housing Act declares that "Whenever a State or local fair housing law provides rights and remedies for alleged discriminatory housing practices which are substantially equivalent to the rights and remedies provided in [Title VIII], the Secretary shall notify the appropriate State or local agency of any complaint filed under this title which appears to constitute a violation of such State or local fair housing law . . . " State and local agencies with substantial equivalency status were given thirty days to resolve complaints before HUD would take any action.

6. In its two comprehensive fair housing enforcement studies of the 1970s, the U.S. Commission on Civil Rights (1974: 42; 1979: 32) reported that HUD's "central office" was responsible for reviewing and evaluating state and local laws to ascertain whether the relevant state and local agencies were entitled to substantial equivalency status. Precisely what the Commission meant by "central office" is unclear, although it was probably referring to the Office of Civil Rights Compliance and Enforcement at HUD headquarters, since that was its source for interviews on the topic. The Commission noted that HUD did provide technical assistance, but no financial assistance, to substantially equivalent agencies in 1974 and 1979, and that Congress had turned down HUD's requests for such financial assistance. The Commission recommended that HUD should again request funds from Congress to assist state and local agencies in processing Title VIII complaints (1974: 349; 1979: 234). Other sources also indicate that FHAP did not formally exist during the 1970s. There is no reference to FHAP in HUD's annual reports, or in the *Housing and Development Reporter*, before 1980. In its 1980 annual report, HUD mentiond its "new Fair Housing Assistance program" (1981: 17), and the January 1980 issue of the *Housing and Development Reporter* made its first reference to FHAP (7: 713).

7. For details on FHAP's competitive and noncompetitive grants, see, for example, *Housing and Development Reporter* 14: 297–98 (August 25, 1986). In 1989, HUD discontinued the competitive grant component of FHAP, which was deemed to be ineffective. See *Housing and Development Reporter* 17: 29 (May 29, 1989).

8. Just 694 complaints were referred by HUD to the state and local levels in fiscal year 1976, for example, and less than two-thirds of them were closed. Nor did state and local agencies have an impressive track record in conciliating complaints. For fiscal years 1973–1976, a mere 14 percent of the complaints referred by HUD were successfully conciliated by state and local entities. During the Carter administration, slightly more than half of all state and local referrals were withdrawn by HUD because investigations were not commenced within thirty days. This simply added to the total amount of time taken to investigate and conciliate a fair housing complaint (U.S. Commission on Civil Rights, 1979: 33).

9. The concept was quite similar to that later employed in the 1982 Job Training Partnership Act (JTPA) to replace the controversial CETA program. JTPA made use of state and local mechanisms, but in combination with private sector organizations, to replace the cumbersome bureaucracy created by CETA.

10. A few points should be underscored regarding the data presented in Figure 9.2 and Table 9.1 and then used in the analysis. These data indicate the number of state and local jurisdictions eligible to receive FHAP funds between 1977 and 1988. Since Congress did not fund FHAP until fiscal year 1980, obviously no FHAP agencies existed before that year. Consequently, although various state and local entities were recognized by HUD in the 1970s as having substantially equivalent fair housing laws, they are coded as 0 and are not apparent in Figure 9.2 and Table 9.1. The annual data shown for the number of jurisdictions eligible for FHAP funding were collected from the *Federal Register*. Specifically, it is the last reported number of state and local jurisdictions recognized each year as having laws substantially equivalent to Title VIII.

11. An earlier version of this study cited $36 million (Lamb and Twombly, 1993: 591), but we have since found new data to indicate the amount reported here ($38 million). We feel the new source, *The Budget of the United States Government*, is more accurate and reliable than the HUD figure cited earlier.

12. The following analysis is based on computerized data provided by HUD. It should be noted that one quarter in particular, the fourth quarter of 1984, appears to have fewer cases than surrounding quarters and seems not to agree with HUD activity reported elsewhere. As a check on the reliability of the overall data set, the models reported below were also run without the fourth quarter of 1984, and the results were fairly consistent. The most substantive change was that our growth measure was no longer significant in the probability model.

13. This was especially the case for the raw number of cases handled by state and local agencies. In Reagan's first term, the mean number of cases handled was over 610 per quarter. In the second term, the figure dropped to just over 172 cases handled by state and local agencies per quarter (the t-ratio for the difference was 3.53 with degrees of freedom equal to 38 and thus significant at the .05 level or better).

14. The second test mentioned above is not reported here. While mixed, the results are generally supportive of the notion that there was a distinct difference between the two terms. The model for number of cases had no significant coeffi-

cients, but the probability model showed results consistent with our hypotheses. It should also be noted that the inclusion of the counter variable reduced the problem of autocorrelation. Concerning the number of state and local cases, the Durbin-Watson test indicated no autocorrelation. In the probability model, it was inconclusive, and thus we report uncorrected OLS models.

10

Modeling Presidential Influence in the Civil Rights Policymaking Processs

————————————————— STEVEN A. SHULL AND
DENNIS W. GLEIBER

INTRODUCTION

Civil rights has been salient in U.S. public policy for presidents and other actors, particularly since World War II. Broad policy areas, such as economic policy and national security matters, no longer involve much discretion for modern presidents. Domestic issue areas like civil rights often allow greater latitude, and the president is a prominent catalyst for such policy programs. The president's interaction with other policymaking actors is important, but what the president chooses to do or not do is largely up to him. Presidents play a crucial role in shaping civil rights policy because major and lasting changes ultimately depend on presidential support. Thus, presidents can exert leadership or influence throughout the civil rights policymaking process. This chapter seeks more adequately to model and to estimate the magnitude of that influence.

Good theoretical reasons exist for studying presidential influence in civil rights. Foreign, economic, and domestic policy may be too general to identify patterns of presidential influence and behavior. Further, the literature suggests that such public policies are often interrelated as opposed to being unique (LeLoup and Shull, 1979; Sigelman, 1979). Social welfare would be a good issue area for analysis, but it seems closely tied to economic policy. Civil rights, on the other hand, is more independent, allowing for more presidential discretion and greater variation in the frequency of government activities.[1]

Civil rights has been a visible and important issue area in American politics, gaining greater and more continuous prominence in the last two generations. Despite its highly emotional content, civil rights has varied in salience over time. This results from more continuing and compelling crises in economic and foreign policy areas. Economic issues, the business cycle, or the election cycle are less likely to contaminate civil rights policymaking because of its more direct concern with procedures than specific content.

Civil rights policy has evolved rapidly during the postwar period, but documenting such change is not our goal here. Rather, we examine presidential influence in the civil rights policy process in order to observe the nature and magnitude of presidential influence in civil rights because of its high profile, public salience, and the locus of the president in each of the stages of policymaking. Although often submerged throughout American history, civil rights issues have never been far from the surface. Certainly in the modern era, civil rights has emerged as a prominent public policy concern (Walker, 1977; Converse, 1964; Carmines and Stimson, 1980, 1989).

Associated with its increasing salience, civil rights attitudes are important in shaping mass belief systems (Carmines and Stimson, 1980: 10). Race in particular has contributed to heightened issue consistency and a greater structure of political beliefs today than Converse (1964) found earlier. Race is now increasingly important in differentiating political candidates and parties (Carmines and Stimson, 1989; Edsall and Edsall, 1991). This pervasiveness of civil rights for the mass public in the post-Vietnam era should be reflected in the behavior of our government, presidents, and public policies. Indeed, civil rights received renewed interest on the governmental and presidential agendas during the 1980s after several years of lesser attention.

Civil rights policy exists in a highly charged atmosphere. Other institutions and officials have played leadership roles (Rodgers and Bullock, 1972), but presidents are strategically placed in the political structure to play a central role in moving civil rights issues through the several stages of the policymaking process. Although research has shown that civil rights may not be the most important domestic policy area for recent presidents (Clausen, 1973; Kessel, 1974; LeLoup and Shull, 1979), they are likely to be involved. Historically, groups and individuals other than presidents had much to do with placing civil rights issues on the national policy agenda. Yet, the president's position at the apex of the only truly national constituency means that his interest in this or any policy area facilitates the move to higher levels of the government's agenda (Redford, 1969: 107–23). Although the president's ability to control policy now is more constrained than before the 1970s (Rockman, 1984: 168, 176), presidents can take the lead for substantial change in civil rights. Illustrative is President Reagan's influence over the U.S. Civil Rights Commission through the appointment process.

Presidents influence civil rights from agenda setting through implementation. Although previous literature suggests that the president's influence generally wanes as the policy process unfolds, the president is chief executive and thus has authority to influence even the implementation of policy (Hargrove, 1974: 230; Redford, 1969: 124) and, particularly, civil rights. Presidential influence is the conversion of preferences and resources into activities necessary for government outputs (see Figure 10.1). The level of government activity necessary for this conversion depends on presidential commitment and political resources available. These resources can be used to explain activities across the policymaking process, and those relationships represent the several aspects of presidential influence in civil rights policymaking.

This chapter progresses in three steps in order to show presidential influence in civil rights policymaking. First, we specify activities by presidents and other actors that are representative of government action at the several stages in the policymaking process. The extant literature often posits such stages but does not provide variables that reflect or measure them (Jones, 1984; Ripley and Franklin, 1986). Second, we examine the differences in presidential influence in the policy process across administrations using a set of dummy variables for the seven presidents, Eisenhower through Reagan. The third step provides a theoretical interpretation of the observed differences between administrations. We offer an alternative to Neustadt's (1980) theory of presidential power. We examine the concept of presidential power measured as the conversion of preferences into activities, not a simple attribute. We include resources similar to those identified by Neustadt and consider their variable (direct and conditional) effects across the civil rights policy process.

The relational view of presidential power implies that presidential preferences are converted into government activities capable of changing policy. Politically relevant resources are often a direct element in that conversion process and often the condition necessary for the conversion of the influenced actor. Therefore, preferences and resources should work together directly and conditionally to produce varying levels of activity, which are necessary antecedents to policy change. It is the structure and magnitude of this relationship of the conversion of preferences and resources into policymaking activity that we use as the first approximation of the nature and degree of presidential influence. We believe that activities at each stage of policymaking should be explained by both preferences and resources. A conditional model offers the best theoretical specification of this process, estimated using interactive terms. Examining an empirically identified and validated issue area like civil rights (*e.g.* Clausen, 1973; Kessel, 1974; LeLoup and Shull, 1979) should facilitate a more satisfying explanation of presidential influence in policymaking.

Figure 10.1
A Conditional Model of Presidential Political Influence (CONCEPTS and indicators)

PREFERENCES ⎯⎯⎯⎯> PERSUASION ⎯⎯⎯⎯⎯⎯> influence ⎯⎯⎯> ACTIVITY

Statements

Liberalism
Extremism

⎯⎯⎯⎯ RESOURCES ⎯⎯⎯⎯

Public Prestige
Partisan Strength in Congress

Statements = agenda setting
Positions = formulation/modifications
Legislative Success of the President = adoption
Executive Orders = adoption/implementation
CRD cases closed = implementation

CONCEPTUALIZATION AND MEASUREMENT

This research requires simultaneous examination of two broad concepts: policy process and presidential influence. By policy process we mean the conversion of ideas into governmental outputs, consisting of four sequential stages: agenda setting, formulation-modification, adoption, and implementation. These stages are taken from the traditional policy literature (see, for example, Jones, 1984; Anderson, 1990), although authors use different terms to label the same functional components of the process. Particular government activities represent each of the various policy stages. The functional nature of the several stages precludes rigid definition and measurement (Lindblom, 1980; Sabatier and Jenkins-Smith, 1993). Although we expect to see a temporal ordering to the process, our surrogate measures are not necessarily conceptually limited to particular stages. Despite such limits on content validity, our measures provide a first step toward operationalizing this model of governing.

Agenda setting is the initial stage of policymaking where problems are identified for government action. We use presidential policy statements to measure agenda setting on the assumption that presidential assertiveness in civil rights can focus attention and trigger action by others. Going public (Kernell, 1986) is an important impetus for later policy decisions. Policy statements are specific policy preferences or recommendations contained in the president's public communications.[2] Increasingly the literature uses public communications to tap agenda setting (Light, 1982; Ragsdale, 1984; Shull, 1983).

Policy statements also provide a measure of Neustadt's (1980) concept of persuasion. While we often think of the mass public as the target of presidential statements, elite audiences are also direct or indirect targets of public statements.[3] In this way going public is at least one indicator of the frequency, though not the quality of, or skill at, presidential persuasion.

Formulation involves tangible proposals or actions rather than merely making statements. It includes information gathering, screening and weighing of alternatives, and the development of a preferred choice. Our measure for the formulation stage is the number of presidential positions on civil rights votes in Congress. The content of such votes is assumed to be determined largely by Congress, but presidents often respond to many such prospective votes in an effort to modify content or outcome.[4] The frequency of legislative positions focuses on the degree of presidential involvement and bargaining in policymaking prior to adoption.

Adoption refers to approval or legitimation of proposals or initiatives. The percentage of the above positions that Congress approves represents the legislative success of the president (LSP) in the adoption stage. Congressional Quarterly, Inc. collects these two measures and, despite problems, the literature uses them widely (Edwards, 1989; Pritchard, 1983; Rivers and Rose, 1985; Bond and Fleisher, 1984; Shull, 1983).

We have included another measure of policy adoption by presidents independent of legislative action. The president may issue executive orders in reaction to *not* obtaining his way with Congress (Nathan, 1983). Of course, executive orders may also be implemented when the president is executing legislative mandates.[5]

Implementation refers to the execution or carrying out of policies and is largely under the purview of the permanent bureaucracy. However, as chief executive, the president is ultimately responsible for policy implementation. We use the number of civil and criminal cases closed by the Civil Rights Division (CRD) of the Department of Justice as one indicator of bureaucratic implementation. Department of Justice activities are chosen because it is a political department close to the president, described by Cronin (1980) as part of the "inner cabinet." Cases closed measures government outputs and can carry the full range of implementation from out of court settlements to final judicial decisions. While administrative agencies operate somewhat independently from presidents, we believe that Halpern (1985: 151) is correct that presidents influence even the implementation of civil rights policy. Although presidents may have less influence at this stage of the process, they must try if they are to obtain compliance with their wishes (Rodgers and Bullock, 1972; Ripley and Franklin, 1986). Bureaucrats may indeed respond to presidential preferences, especially in an agency like the CRD.

To model presidential influence in the policy process requires measures of government outputs, or the activities from which outputs follow, and their antecedent conditions. Influence is the conversion of preference into outputs. This conversion depends on (1) power resources: popular support and partisan strength in Congress, and (2) persuasion. Our database includes measures of all these concepts for the period from 1953 to 1985. Neustadt (1980) states that the power of the president results from his persuasive ability, his public prestige, and his professional reputation. Many scholars have tried to operationalize this model of power (Tatlovich and Daynes, 1979; Edwards, 1976, 1977; Cronin, 1980: 130; Thomas, 1977: 170). We model influence as the capacity of presidential views and resources to account for the frequency of government activities in the development of civil rights policy.

INFLUENCE OF INDIVIDUAL PRESIDENTS

In this section we examine differences of influence between administrations across the stages of the policy process (see Table 10.1). Using dummy variable regression analysis, we describe each president's behavior relative to that of Eisenhower. We estimate a separate equation for each of the

Table 10.1
The Influence of Individual Presidents on the Policy Process[a]

President	AGENDA SETTING Presidential Statements	FORMULATION MODIFICATION Legislative Positions	ADOPTION IMPLEM. Legislative Success of pres.	ADOPTION Executive Order	IMPLEMENTATION CRD Cases Closed
Reagan	13.9	.05	24.4	2.0	-10.5
Carter	23.6	1.0	46.9	2.1	29.0
Ford	8.6	-.80	-15.6	-.38	11.9
Nixon	9.2	4.7	38.3	-.09	-47.4
Johnson	26.1	20.1	80.0	.23	17.7
Kennedy	13.1	.25	6.7	.63	97.8
Eisenhower (constant)	4.9	.75	15.6	.38	141.5
R^2	.45	.43	.42	.46	.43
p	.01	.02	.02	.01	.05
adj R^2	.33	.30	.29	.34	.26
N = 33 (implementation = 28)					

a. Cell entries are Bs. Although Bs are not normally comparable, Bs for dummy variables are on the same metric and therefore are comparable.

five dependent phenomena representing the stages of the policy process. Using year as the unit of analysis, the data include administrations from Eisenhower through Reagan. The population N for each equation is 33, except for the implementation stage. For that equation the data begin in 1958 with the creation of the Civil Rights Division and the N is 28.

Agenda Setting

Civil rights rhetoric became more frequent and important during the Kennedy administration. The number of civil rights statements was up nearly 200 percent from the Eisenhower level. The increasing salience of civil rights continues to be observed in the additional increase during the Johnson administration. However, once Nixon takes office the frequency of statements declines by 50 percent, remaining at that level during the Ford presidency. Under Carter, statements increase again almost to the Johnson level and subsequently drop off again. Thus, Johnson and Carter make by far the most statements, although Kennedy and Reagan had moderate levels. Eisenhower made the fewest civil rights statements.

Unless the president is responding to some unspecified systematic set of critical events, there is evidence of some individual presidential discretion in agenda setting. The explanatory power of the equation (R^2 = .45, p of F = .01)[6] indicates the strength of these individual differences. The significance of all coefficients, except those for Eisenhower and Ford, indicate important individual differences as well. With a Durbin-Watson level of 1.93, serial correlation is no problem for estimation. The equation underestimates the number of statements in 1964 and 1980, and overestimates statements in 1967 and 1977. Control for these outliers makes no difference in the substantive interpretation of the president's involvement in the agenda-setting stage.

Formulation

In policy formulation, both Eisenhower and Kennedy took less than one position per year. Surprisingly, like Eisenhower, Reagan took few positions. Ford took by the far the fewest; he actually took no position on a civil rights vote during his two-and-one-half years in office. Johnson had by far the most positions, but Nixon took the next largest number. Indeed, these two presidents are the only two producing significant individual president effects.

This equation explained 43 percent of the variance and was significant at the .02 level. 1964 was again an outlier and in this equation the only extreme one. Other Johnson years (1965–1967) were also outliers. The Durbin-Watson statistic of 2.09 suggests no autocorrelation. We discuss the reestimation of these first two equations without 1964 at the end of this section.

Adoption

Recall that in this analysis, adoption has two operational dimensions: legislative and executive. With respect to the legislative, presidents vary considerably in their legislative success. Eisenhower's success was just 16% while Kennedy's was 23%. Ford had no success since he took no positions. Johnson's support was by far the highest at 95%, while Carter at 60% and Nixon at 55% were also fairly successful. Yet Johnson's level of success is significantly different. The variance explained in this equation was 42%, significant at the .02 level (see Table 10.1). There are no extreme outliers and no problem with auto-correlation, although the D/W statistic is in the indeterminant range.

Concerning the executive dimension of adoption, only Carter and Reagan issued many civil rights executive orders, and then only about 2.0 per year. All the other coefficients were not significantly different from zero. The equation produced an R^2 of .46, significant at the .01 level. The distribution is approximately normal, with no extreme outliers, nor is there any indication of autocorrelation for this equation.

Implementation

Although the equation for CRD cases closed describes a statistically significant relationship with presidential administration ($R^2 = .43$), there is no statistical evidence distinguishing one administration other than the absolute magnitudes of the partial regression coefficients. None of the individual president coefficients were significant and only one (Kennedy $p = .06$) approaches the conventional acceptance level. During the Eisenhower administration, the number of cases closed per year averages about 141. This frequency increases to nearly 240 per year during the Kennedy administration. Thereafter, the number of cases goes back down to about 160 for Johnson and below 100 per year for Nixon. It increases again, reaching the Johnson level during the Carter administration, but remains around 130 cases closed per year for Reagan's presidency.

Reestimations for Agenda Setting and Formulation

Recall that we observe large residuals for 1964 in the first two equations. By removing that year and reestimating the equation, we retain 32 cases for agenda setting and formulation. Reestimation without 1964 increases the R^2 for agenda setting to .59, significant at the .001 level. Coefficients for all presidents are significant (p's LT .05) for Ford and Eisenhower.

The explanatory power for the formulation equation increases to .50 R^2, significant at the .01 level. The Johnson and Nixon dummy variables remain significant, where Johnson took ten times the number of positions as Nixon, whose civil rights positions returned to the level of Eisenhower years. Again, there was no problem with autocorrelation, but the equation overestimates 1968, while underestimating 1967.

The analysis to this point demonstrates that presidential influence in civil rights policymaking differs across stages of the policy process and from one administration to another. It does not provide us with a theoretically interesting description of those differences. In the next section we begin to examine the nature and sources of presidential influence by introducing measures of presidential preferences and political resources. In this way we test our conceptualization of presidential power.

PREFERENCE-RESOURCES MODEL
OF PRESIDENTIAL INFLUENCE

Presidential preferences may be related to partisanship but are likely to have greater variance than party identification of the president. They are also independent of other aspects of party, like partisan control of Congress. We use two measures of the president's preferences: his position on congressional roll call votes favored by the liberal organization known as the Americans for Democratic Action (called liberalism), and intensity of preference, measured as the absolute value of the ADA score folded at the midpoint of the scale. Together, these two measures, *ideological liberalism* and *intensity*, should tap different aspects of the personal preference[7] of the president, which we treat as an exogenous explanatory factor.

To date, empirical research has not provided an explanation of presidential preferences including its components: personal ideology, national constituency interests, and special group demands. Our decision to use these measures results from the theoretical importance of preference in a model of influence and the lack of general theory to more completely conceptualize aspects of presidential preferences. Liberalism and intensity (or extremism) have the distinct advantage of tapping the substance, political complexity, and variable magnitude of a president's personal political preferences. Focusing on these two aspects of preference recognizes the many cross-pressures the president must confront when engaged in policymaking.[8] Using generalized liberalism as the basis of the measures reflects the conventional view that general liberalism should constrain more specific civil rights liberalism.

We provide several indicators of presidential *power resources*. *Public support* in Gallup polls is a mass-based resource measuring popular prestige. We use the average score per year on the familiar question: In general, how is (*president's name*) handling his job as president? We agree with Neustadt (1980: 65) that popular prestige may be more complex than the attitude tapped by the Gallup question, but popular approval is clearly a component of popular prestige. Despite his warning, empirical studies using the Gallup score suggest its construct validity (Edwards, 1989: ch. 6; Bond and Fleisher, 1990: ch. 7) and appropriateness for this application.

Without an adequate measure of professional reputation in the literature, our approach is to use an alternative conceptualization of politically relevant, elite-based resources that taps the president's role as leader of his party. We use the president's partisan strength in Congress (PSC—mean percentage of the president's partisans in the House and the Senate) as an elite-based indicator of presidential power resources. Prior studies have found party strength in Congress to be important in determining the legislative success of the president (LSP) (Bond and Fleisher, 1990; Rivers and Rose, 1985). As an indicator of such power resources, it should also be related to activities at other stages of policymaking because of the many party elites with whom the president must interact and contend in the system of checks and balances.

Unlike some interpreters of Neustadt (Sperlich, 1975) we conclude that these mass- and elite-based resources condition the president's ability to influence civil rights policymaking. Personal resources, like skill and persuasion are also important. We use the preference-resource model to explain presidential statements taken as a measure of agenda setting, the first stage in the policy process. We also use statements as a measure of the personal-based resource and mediating variable persuasion. Although we often think of the mass public as the target of presidential communications, elite audiences are also direct or indirect targets of public statements. Neustadt (1980) asserts that persuasion is the most important component of such influence. If so, it should be a better explanation of civil rights policymaking than either partisan strength or public prestige.

ANALYSIS

We begin our analysis by presenting five path models of presidential influence, one for each stage in the policy process. Next we modify each model to include significant conditional factors that more adequately describe the roles of presidential resources and preferences in policymaking. Model 1 in Table 10.2 shows that the frequency of the president's statements on civil rights can be predicted from his liberalism and the extremism of his ideology. Presidential resources do not add to the explanatory power in model 2. Presidents are guided in part by their political preferences in agenda setting. This stage of policymaking is marked by presidential discretion and significant independence from other actors (*e.g.*, the public and political party) in the system.

The remainder of Table 10.2 presents evidence of the impact of per-

Table 10.2
Path Models of Presidential Political Influence[a]

	AGENDA SETTING	FORMULATION-MODIFICATION	ADOPTION	ADOPTION-IMPLEM.	IMPLEMENTATON
	Presidential Statements	Legislative Positions	Legislative Success of pres.	Executive Orders	CRD Cases Closed
Model 1					
Preference (Liberalism)	.38*	.38*	.29	.09	.28
Preference (Extremism)	.37*	.27	.24	.30	.52*
R^2	.31	.23	.15	.09	.37
p	.00	.02	.09	.25	.00
adj R^2	.26	.18	.09	.02	.33
Model 2					
Preference (Liberalism)	.33	.70*	.07	.80	.40
Preference (Extremism)	.31	.45*	.11	.02	.54*
Public Prestige	-.11	.13	-.13	-.12	.00
Partisan Strength Congress	.11	-.45	.32	.94*	-.15
R^2	.33	.30	.19	.32	.38

p	.03	.04	.20	.03	.01
adj R²	.23	.19	.08	.22	.29

Model 3

Preference (Liberalism)	.47*	-.08	-.91	.28
Preference (Extremism)	.22*	-.03	-.13	.45
Public Prestige	.12	-.08	-.08	.04
Partisan Strength Congress	-.53	.32	.90	-.19
Persuasion (Statements)	.70	.45	.35	.36
R²	.63	.23	.40	.47
p	.00	.10	.01	.00
adj R²	.56	.20	.29	.36

N = 32

a. cell entries represent standardized path coefficients

* represents significant coefficients (p > .05)

161

sonal-based resources and construct validation for our operationalization of persuasion using presidential statements. The addition of the independent variable persuasion in model 3 significantly increases explanatory power an average of 8 percent across the subsequent aspects of the policy process. The greatest increase associated with persuasion is observed in formulation ($sR^2 = .13$), where statements is the most important factor (beta = .70).[9]

Although statements as persuasion provides the least increase in explanatory power for legislative success of the president in civil rights, it is nonetheless the most important variable (beta = .45) in the model. Issuing civil rights executive orders is only moderately well explained, but there is a role for persuasion here as well. The results for bureaucratic activity also support our decision to remodel presidential influence by adding measures of presidential preference and persuasion to traditional measures of power resources.

CONDITIONAL MODEL

We believe that presidential power is not adequately described by direct effects estimated using a simple additive model. Instead we hypothesize that the magnitude of influence (congruence of preference with actions and outcomes) varies with the level and combination of political resources available. Therefore we have estimated multiple regression equations including the statistically significant variables from preferences, resources, and the interactions that carry information about the conditional impact of resources on the conversion of preferences. We retain variables that display a significant increase in explanatory power based on increases in squared multiple semipartial correlation coefficient associated with the inclusion of respective interactive terms (Cohen and Cohen, 1983: chs. 3 and 8). The results of that analysis are reported in Table 10.3.

Table 10.3 describes a more complex and variable structure for explaining presidential activity in the civil rights policy process than that presented thus far in the literature. The addition of interactive terms to estimate the nature and magnitude of the hypothesized conditional relationships (especially those of resources on the impact of presidential preferences) provides significantly greater explanatory power. In each stage of the civil rights policy process the adj R^2 for the conditional model is increased by 16 to 29 percent compared to the path models in Table 10.2. The adjusted coefficients of determination are used here to discount the variance being explained that is simply an artifact of introducing additional interaction terms carrying the conditional relationships. These results for government activity in civil rights policymaking are quite strong.

Of equal importance is the lack of a pattern in the models for measures of the stages of the policy process. Executive orders are best explained by this conditional model of presidential influence. The importance of the president's preferences are variable, as is the usefulness of his arsenal of power resources. The nature of presidential influence becomes more obvious by reorganizing the coefficients from Table 10.3 into the equations reported in Table 10.4.

Some aspect of preference is included in each model of presidential influence in the civil rights policy process except for legislative success. This suggests that while the president plays a role in legislative adoption, his preferences are not directly related to the level of activity and his level of success. Legislative success as a measure of adoption suggests no direct influence for the president. These findings suggest that when Neustadt and others theorize about presidential power, they may be considering only legislative adoption. Adoption is the only model that involves only the three forms of presidential resources and includes a significant interaction combining prestige and partisan strength (PSC) suggested by Neustadt. It should also be noted that preferences are antecedent conditions of the indicator statements. Therefore, even legislative success is a function (although indirectly) of presidential preferences.

Looking first at agenda setting (using civil rights statements as a dependent variable), popular presidents are less likely to speak out. However, popular prestige conditions the willingness of intense presidents to make statements. In later stages of the policy process, persuasion (also measured by public statements) is found to play a significant role. When that is the case, it should be remembered that the president's willingness to speak out publicly is variably related to aspects of preference as indicated above.

The variability of presidential influence across the stages of the process is striking. We have shown elsewhere (Gleiber and Shull, 1992) for all policy, not just civil rights, that only position-taking is affected by both aspects of preference. However, it is only liberalism (and not intensity) that increases position-taking on civil rights legislation. Liberal presidents have less active civil rights divisions, while extremism has a decreasing effect as public support increases. Conservative presidents are more likely than liberal ones to issue executive orders. This finding exemplifies Nathan's (1983) notion that conservative presidents use administrative actions to bypass Congress.

The conventional wisdom and the theoretical role assigned by Neustadt to popular prestige as a presidential resource find considerable empirical support in this analysis. Popular prestige is included in each of our models. However, popular prestige does not display the consistent positive effects that the theory suggests. For example, a president must have majority popular support before the intensity of his preferences can begin to increase his willingness to speak out publicly. Prestige also decreases the willingness of extreme presidents to take positions. Popular prestige plays

Table 10.3
Presidential Influence: The Impact of Preference on Activities Conditioned by Resources and Persuasion

	AGENDA SETTING	FORMULATION-MODIFICATION	ADOPTION	ADOPTION-IMPLEM.	IMPLEMENTATION
	Presidential Statements	Legislative Positions	Legislative Success of President	Executive Orders	CRD Cases Closed
Intercept	101.90	-16.43	-56.55	-5.77	86.75
Preference (Liberalism)			.31	-.03	-4.07
Preference (Extremism)			-1.42		
Public Prestige	-2.56	.31	-1.31	.05	-3.74
Partisan strength Cong.		-.25	2.75	.10	
Persuasion (Statements)		-1.10	-36.55	.19	1.44
L X PP					
L X PSC					
E X PP	.05	-.03			1.66
PSC X PP				.04	
ST X PP				.59	-.03
ST X PSC			.03	.87	-.00

ST X PP X PSC

						-.01
Rsq	.45	.89	.51	.52	.63	
p	.08	.00	.00	.02	.00	
adj Rsq	.39	.85	.39	.42	.58	
Increase in Rsq	.12	.26	.28	.12	.16	

N = 32

na = not applicable

ni = No significant increase in Rsq

Ideology (Liberalism) (L)

Ideology (Extremism) (E)

Public Prestige (PP)

Partisan strength in Congress (PSC)

Persuasion (Statements) (ST)

Table 10.4
Contextual Effects of Presidential Preferences and Political Resources on Stages of the Policy Process

Government activities in the civil rights policy process.

	Intercept	PREFERENCES		Popular Prestige	POWER RESOURCES		DOJ$_{\text{eff}}$
		Ideology (Liberalism)	Ideology (Extremism)		Partisan strength in Congress	Persuasion (Statements)	
Statements	101.90		(0.0 + .05(PP))	-2.56			
Positions	-16.43	.13	(-1.42 - .03(PPI))	+.31	.25 (-1.10)	+.03 (PSCI)	
LSP	-56.55			-1.31	+2.75 (-36.55 + .59 (PP) + .87(PSC) -.01(PPXPSCI))		
ExOrd	-5.77	-.03		+.05	+.10 (.19 -.002(PPI))		
CRD Cases	86.75	(-4.07 + 10(PP))		-3.74			.06

a conditional role in explaining each of the activities used as measures of the president's involvement in the civil rights policy process. However, the particular role of popular prestige is variable, conditioning intensity and liberalness of preference and also the resource persuasion.

Partisan strength in Congress (PSC) is included in the models of position-taking, legislative success, and executive orders. While this may be a result of the congressional basis of the indicator used, it also shows variable impact for this form of presidential resources. Unlike prestige, partisan strength appears to have a more consistent positive effect when it plays a role in influence. The one exception is the negative coefficient in the positions model. Yet, persuasion is more effective on the president's own partisans in Congress.

A few additional results deserve mention. There is a very weak counterintuitive and negative effect of prestige with PSC on persuasion. This appears to be a simple discounting of the additive impact of the conditional effects of the resources on persuasion. Also, there is no preference term in the model of legislative success of the president. Both of the power resources are included in the model, and the impact of persuasion is considerable in civil rights. Also of interest is the conditional relationship of the power resources for executive orders. Popular prestige is an important conditional variable, especially as it effects the impact of persuasion. Finally, only ideological preference and public prestige contribute to the explanation of activity in the civil rights division.

The theoretical models for each stage of the policy process show greater explanatory power than the atheoretical models using just presidential administration. When presidential dummy variables are added to the theoretical models, there is no further increase in explanatory power. Therefore we conclude that our conceptualization of presidential influence is adequately specified, accounting for the systematic variance in presidential influence with regard to these forms of government activity.

CONCLUSIONS

Considerable complexity and variability in explanations of presidential influence exist in the stages of civil rights policymaking. Persuasion and partisan strength were important throughout the policymaking process, but popular prestige was a ubiquitous conditional variable. These strong empirical results for civil rights suggest that issue content may well be important to the nature of the policy process, the behavior of particular actors in that process and, particularly, for presidential influence in policymaking. Thus, our analysis reveals a potential nexus between policy process and policy content (see also Shull, 1993).

Conditional models of policy process activities have much greater explanatory power than simple additive models, indicative of the contextual/

conditional nature of power resources and their use. This should not be surprising since the nature of government activity in the policy process is such that the primary theoretical linkages are not expected to be simple resource exchanges but rather persuasion in the conceptual sense developed by Neustadt. In such a context, power resources should facilitate the congruence of preference and activity, not be directly transformed into policy activity or success.

These findings suggest several directions that would enhance our knowledge of presidential influence in policymaking. First, preferences affect policymaking, but are conditioned by the individual-based power resource persuasion. Our measures of preference are based on general liberalism only; we did not have independent direct measures of civil rights liberalism or intensity. Thus, future research could seek to operationalize presidential preferences more explicitly by including a more direct measure of presidential civil rights preferences (degree of support in policy statements rather than merely number of policy statements). Also needed is a better measure of the president's professional reputation than has been offered heretofore, allowing a fuller test of Neustadt.[10]

This look at the nature of presidential influence in civil rights policymaking suggests that substantive content should be returned to a more prominent place in the policy literature. In our study, government activities in civil rights revealed considerable variability across policy stages. It is a unique and discretionary policy area. Dramatic changes in salience in civil rights over the past two generations also suggest substantial variance in policymaking roles and behavior. This suggests that even great contextual complexity may be involved in presidential influence. Social welfare or other policy areas should be compared in future research on presidential influence in the policymaking process. Indeed, one might also compare civil rights and/or social welfare with all policymaking generally to make certain that individual policy areas maintain their individual importance in conditioning the nature of the process.[11]

The policymaking process creates a venue for presidential influence. Surely presidents like Johnson and Reagan made a difference, not only in setting the agenda but throughout the civil rights policymaking process (Shull, 1989). Presidential influence observed here was not greater at earlier stages in the process as expected; rather the president's greatest influence was in policy implementation where presidents have often criticized an overly intrusive, independent bureaucracy. Still, presidents play a role at each policymaking stage and, thus, the president-policy linkage deserves much greater empirical attention than it has received heretofore.

NOTES

1. By our definition civil rights refers to government protection for groups, while liberties provide constitutional protection for individuals against govern-

ment. Unlike liberties, rights are not inalienable but government bestows them. Although most civil rights issues concern racial equality, other minorities (Hispanics, Native Americans, women, the aged, and the disabled) are also included in the analysis.

2. A policy statement is any substantive expression of philosophy, attitude, or opinion about issues and is an indicator of changing presidential attention. For an expression to qualify as a policy statement, the president must explicitly encourage, propose, support, or oppose specific actions or behavior and may refer to past, present, or future policy. We located many statements by the presidents under consideration that met these criteria. Some speeches contain many policy statements and others none.

3. This measure is not an indicator of the elusive, private aspects of persuasion.

4. Presidents take positions in public statements and statements have both agenda-setting and formulation functions. In either case, statements are persuasion. It is important to note that our measure of statements includes only public communications, and these are multifunctional. Public communications are often described as directed toward the mass public, yet clearly most public addresses are designed to influence government actors too. Presidents respond to many congressional votes but do so selectively. In fact, position-taking is a special case of statements.

5. To date, scholars have not differentiated the function of the thousands of executive orders. When this is accomplished, the adoption-implementation distinction can be more carefully researched. Nearly all of the forty civil rights orders examined seem to be adoption. Although executive orders may not measure presidential activity in only one stage of the policy process, they constitute a significant component of discretionary activity worthy of independent consideration.

6. Throughout this section we discuss the R^2 as a description of the dispersion in the joint frequency distribution. Adjusted R^2 is also reported in Table 10.1 for those who feel that the R^2 may be artificially inflated by the number of independent variables necessary to represent the qualitative concept presidential administration. Of course the adj R^2s are slightly smaller, but the relative magnitudes are the same because the number of IVs is the same from one equation to another. None of the adj R^2s are so small as to suggest no relationship.

7. The correlation between liberalism and intensity is $r = .08$, ns).

8. Substantively and empirically the president's party carries much of the same information as ideological preference and the two measures are highly correlated ($r = .88$). Therefore, to avoid theoretical redundancy and multicollinearity, we do not include president's party as a separate variable.

9. The use of the same empirical indicator to measure two different concepts is unusual. We recognize that agenda setting and persuasion are conceptually and functionally similar, and perhaps incapable of being distinguished even with detailed content analysis of all presidential statements.

10. We believe that Lockerbee and Borelli (1989) offer a promising first look at professional reputation. We have begun a similar but time-consuming data collection project (based upon editorial endorsement of the president from the *New York Times* Index) that we hope to incorporate in future research.

11. Variations of this model with general policy may be seen in Gleiber and Shull, 1992.

Bibliography

Adams, S. (1961). *First hand report*. New York: Harper.

Alexander v. Holmes County, 396 U.S. 19 (1969).

Alyeska Pipeline Service Co. v. Wilderness Society, 421 U.S. 240 (1975).

Amaker, N. C. (1988). *Civil rights and the Reagan administration*. Washington, DC: The Urban Institute Press.

Anderson, J. E. (1990). *Public policy making: An introduction*. Boston: Houghton Mifflin.

Armstrong, W. M. (1974). *The Gilded Age letters of E.L. Godkin*. Albany: State University of New York Press.

Asher, H. B. (1992). *Presidential elections & American politics*. 5th ed. Belmont, CA: Brooks/Cole Publishing.

Ayers, E. L. (1992). *The promise of the new south: Life after Reconstruction*. New York: Oxford University Press.

Barber, J. D. (1992). *The presidential character: Predicting performance in the White House*. 4th ed. Englewood Cliffs, NJ: Prentice-Hall.

Barber, J. D. (1972). *The presidential character: Predicting performance in the White House*. Englewood Cliff, NJ: Prentice-Hall.

Bardach, E., and R. A. Kagan. (1982). *Going by the book: The problem of regulatory unreasonableness*. Philadelphia: Temple University Press.

Barnes, C. A. (1983). *Journey from Jim Crow: The desegregation of southern transit*. New York: Columbia University Press.

Baungartner, F., and B. Jones. (1992). *Agendas and instability in American politics*. Chicago: University of Chicago Press.

Beck, N. (1982). "Parties, administrations, and American macroeconomic outcomes." *American Political Science Review* 76: 83–93.

Behr, R. L., and S. Iyengar. (1985). "Television news, real-world cues, and changes in the public agenda." *Public Opinion Quarterly* 49: 38–57.

Belknap, M. R. (1987). *Federal law and southern order: Racial violence and con-*

stitutional conflict in the post-Brown South. Athens: University of Georgia Press.

Berman, L. (1988). "Lyndon Johnson: Paths chosen and opportunities lost." In F. I. Greenstein (ed.), *Leadership in the modern presidency.* Cambridge: Harvard University Press, pp. 134–63.

Bernstein, I. (1991). *Promises kept: John F. Kennedy's new frontier.* New York: Oxford University Press.

Blumenstyk, G. (1991). "Justice dept. affirms federal backing for black colleges." *Chronicle of Higher Education* (October 16): A41, A44.

Bob Jones University v. United States, 461 U.S. 474 (1983).

Bobo, L., and J. R. Kluegel. (1991). "Modern American prejudice: Stereotypes, social distance, and perceptions of discrimination toward Blacks, Hispanics, and Asians." Paper presented at the Annual Meetings of the American Sociological Association, Cincinnati, Ohio, August 23–27, 1991.

Bond, J. R., and R. Fleisher. (1990). *The president in the legislative arena.* Chicago: University of Chicago Press.

Bond, J. R., and R. Fleisher. (1984). "Presidential popularity and congressional voting." *Western Political Quarterly* 37: 291–306.

Bond, J. R., and R. Fleisher (1980). "The limits of presidential popularity as a source of influence in the U.S. House." *Legislative Studies Quarterly* 5: 69–78.

Brace, P., and B. Hinckley. (1992). *Follow the leader.* New York: Basic Books.

Bradlee, B. C. (1975). *Conversations with Kennedy.* New York: W.W. Norton.

Branch, T. (1988). *Parting the waters: America in the King years 1954–63.* New York: Simon and Schuster.

Brauer, C. M. (1988). "John F. Kennedy: The endurance of inspirational leadership." In F. I. Greenstein (ed.), *Leadership in the modern presidency.* Cambridge: Harvard University Press.

Brauer, C. M. (1977). *John F. Kennedy and the second reconstruction.* New York: Columbia University Press.

Brown v. Board of Education, 347 U.S. 483 (1954); 349 U.S. 494 (1955).

Brownell, H. (1990). Interview with M. Stern. Austin, Texas, October 27.

Brownell, H. (1967). Oral History. Columbia University Library, New York.

Bullock, C. S., III, and C. M. Lamb (eds.). (1984). *Implementation of civil rights policy.* Monterey, CA: Brooks/Cole.

Bullock, C. S., III, and K. I. Butler (1985). "Voting rights." In T. Yarbrough (ed.), *The Reagan administration and human rights.* New York: Praeger, pp. 29–54.

Bureau of National Literature, Inc. (1897). *A compilation of the messages of the presidents.* XVII. New York.

Burns, J. M. (1959). *John Kennedy: A political profile.* New York: Harcourt, Brace.

Caplan, L. (1988). *The tenth justice: The Solicitor General and the rule of law.* New York: Vintage Books.

Carmines, E. G., and J. A. Stimson. (1989). *Issue evolution: Race and the transformation of American politics.* Princeton, NJ: Princeton University Press.

Carmines, E. G., and J. A. Stimson. (1980). "The faces of issue voting." *American Political Science Review* 74: 78–91.

Cavalli, C. D. (1992). "Presidential activity in the legislative arena." Paper presented at the Annual Meeting of the Southern Political Science Association, Atlanta, GA.

Chavez, L., and M. Green, (1984). "A defense of the Reagan Administration's civil rights policies." *New Perspectives* (Summer): 34.

City of Lockhart v. United States, 460 U.S. 125 (1983).

City of Mobile v. Bolden, 447 U.S. 55 (1980).

City of Port Arthur v. United States, 459 U.S. 159 (1982).

Clausen, A. R. (1973). *How congressmen decide: A policy focus.* New York: St. Martin's Press.

Cohen, J., and P. Cohen. (1983). *Applied multiple regression correlation analysis for the behavioral sciences.* 2d. ed. Hillsdale, NJ: Lawrence Earlbaum Assoc., Inc.

Cole v. Young, 351 U.S. 536 (1956).

Collier, P., and D. Horowitz. (1984). *The Kennedys: An American drama.* New York: Summit Books.

Columbus Board of Education v. Penick, 443 U.S. 499 (1979).

Congress and the nation. (1969). Vol. 2. Washington, DC: Congressional Quarterly.

Congressional Quarterly Almanac 1965. Washington, DC: Congressional Quarterly, Inc.

Congressional Quarterly Almanac 1964. Washington, DC: Congressional Quarterly, Inc.

Congressional Quarterly Almanac 1957. Washington, DC: Congressional Quarterly, Inc.

Congressional Quarterly Almanac 1956. Washington, DC: Congressional Quarterly, Inc.

Conlan, T. (1988). *New federalism: Intergovernmental reform from Nixon to Reagan.* Washington, DC: Brookings Institution.

Converse, P. E. (1964). "Nature of belief systems in mass publics." In D. Apter (ed.), *Ideology and discontent.* New York: Free Press.

Cooper, J., and G. Bombardier. (1968). "Presidential leadership and party success." *Journal of Politics* 30: 1012–27.

Cooper v. Aaron, 358 U.S. 1 (1958).

Cronin, T. E. (1980). *State of the presidency.* 2nd ed. Boston: Little, Brown and Co.

Cross, T. (1984). *The Black power imperative: Racial inequality and the politics of nonviolence.* New York: Faulker.

Dayton Board of Education v. Brinkman, 443 U.S. 516 (1979).

Denton, R. E., Jr. (1982). *Symbolic dimension of the American presidency.* Prospect Heights, IL: Waveland Press.

Downs, A. (1972). "Up and down with ecology: The issue-attention cycle." *The Public Interest* 28: 38–50.

Du Bois, W.E.B. (1986). *Writings.* New York: The Library of America.

Duram, J. C. (1981). *A moderate among extremists.* Chicago: Nelson-Hall.

Durden, R. F. (1954). "The prostrate state revisited: James S. Pike and South Carolina reconstruction." *Journal of Negro History*, 39, no. 2: 87–110.

Edelman, M. (1964). *The symbolic uses of politics.* Urbana, IL: University of Illinois Press.

Edsall, T. B., and M. D. Edsall. (1991). *Chain reaction: The impact of race, rights, and taxes on American politics*. New York: W.W. Norton & Co.

Edwards, G. C., III. (1989). *At the margins*. New Haven, CT: Yale University Press.

Edwards, G. C., III. (1983). *The public presidency: The pursuit of popular support*. New York: St. Martin's Press.

Edwards, G. C., III. (1980). *Presidential influence in Congress*. San Francisco: W.H. Freeman and Co.

Edwards, G. C., III. (1977). "Presidential influence in the Senate: presidential prestige as a source of presidential power." *American Politics Quarterly*. 5: 481–500.

Edwards, G. C., III. (1976). "Presidential influence in the House: Presidential prestige as a source of presidential power." *American Political Science Review*. 70: 101–13.

E.E.O.C. v. Arabian American Oil, 499 U.S. 254 (1991).

Eisenger, P. K., and W. Gormley (1988). "The Midwest response." In P. K. Eisinger and W. Gormley (eds.), *The Midwest response to the New Federalism*. Madison: University of Wisconsin Press, pp. 3–17.

Eisenhower, D. D. (1965). *Waging Peace, 1956–1961*. New York: Doubleday.

Elder, C., and R. G. Cobb. (1983). *Political use of symbols*. New York: Longman, Inc.

Elman, P. (1987). "The solicitor general's office, Justice Frankfurter, and civil rights litigation, 1946–1960: An oral history." *Harvard Law Review* 100: 817–52.

Eyestone, R. (1978). *From social issues to public policy*. New York: John Wiley.

Fairlie, H. (1973). *The Kennedy promise: The politics of expectation*. Garden City, NY: Doubleday & Co.

Farley, R., and W. Frey. (1994). "Changes in the Segregation of Whites from Blacks during the 1980s: Small steps toward a more integrated society." *American Sociological Review* 59: 23–45.

Firefighters Local No. 1784 v. Stotts, 467 U.S. 561 (1984).

Fishel J. (1985). *Presidents & promises: From campaign pledge to presidential performance*. Washington, DC: CQ Press.

Fisher, A. B. (1985). "Businessmen Like to Hire by the Numbers." *Fortune* (September 16): 27.

Fleisher, R., and J. R. Bond. (1992). "Assessing presidential support in the House II: Lessons from George Bush." *American Journal of Political Science* 36: 525–41.

Fleisher, R., and J. R. Bond. (1983). "Assessing presidential support in the house: Lessons from Reagan and Carter." *Journal of Politics* 45: 745–58.

Fordice, United States v., 112 S.Ct. 2727 (1992).

Franklin, J. H. (1989). *Race and history: Selected essays 1938–1988*. Baton Rouge: Lousiana State University Press.

Funkhouser, G. R. (1973). "The issues of the sixties: An exploratory study in the dynamics of public opinion." *Public Opinion Quarterly* 37: 62–75.

Gallup Opinion Index, The. (1980, report no. 1982). Princeton, NJ: Gallup International.

Gallup Poll: Public Opinion, 1935–1971. (1972). 3 vols. New York: Random House.

Gilbert, R. E. (1989). "Moral leadership in civil rights: An evaluation of John F. Kennedy." *Political Communication and Persuasion* 6: 1–19.

Glazer, N. (1975). *Affirmative discrimination: Ethnic inequality and public policy.* New York: Basic Books.

Gleiber, D. W., and S. A. Shull. (1992). "Presidential influence in policy making." *Western Political Quarterly* 45: 441–67.

Goldstein, B. L. (1984). "The historical case for goals and timetables." *New Perspectives* 16 (Summer): 20.

Gomillion v. Lightfoot, 364 U.S. 339 (1960).

Goodwin, D. K. (1991). *Lyndon Johnson and the American dream.* New York: St. Martin's Press.

Goodwin, R. N. (1988). *Remembering America: A voice from the sixties.* Boston: Little, Brown.

Graham, H. D. (1990). *The civil rights era: Origins and development of national policy.* New York: Oxford University Press.

Green v. County School Board, 391 U.S. 430 (1968).

Greenhouse, L. (1992a). "An administration shift over retroactive laws." *New York Times* (April 17): A18.

Greenhouse, L. (1992b). "Changed path for court? new balance is held by 3 cautious justices." *New York Times* (June 26): A1, A16.

Greenstein, F. I. (1988). "Dwight D. Eisenhower: Leadership theorist in the White House." In F. I. Greenstein (ed.), *Leadership in the modern presidency.* Cambridge: Harvard University Press, pp. 76–107.

Greenstein, F. I. (1982). *The hidden-hand presidency: Eisenhower as leader.* New York: Basic Books.

Griffin v. Board of Education, 375 U.S. 391 (1964).

Griggs v. Duke Power Co., 401 U.S. 424 (1971).

Grossman, J. B. (1969). "A model for judicial policy analysis: The Supreme Court and the sit-in cases." In J. Grossmand and J. Tanenhaus (eds.), *Frontiers of Judicial Research.* New York: John Wiley, pp. 405–58.

Grove City College v. Bell, 465 U.S. 555 (1984).

Halpern, S. C. (1985). "Title VI enforcement." In T. Yarbrough (ed.), *The Reagan administration and human rights.* New York: Praeger.

Hamm v. City of Rock Hill, 379 U.S. 306 (1964).

Hargrove, E. C. (1974). *Power of the modern presidency.* New York: Alfred A. Knopf.

Heart of Atlanta Motel v. United States, 371 U.S. 241 (1964).

Henderson, P. G. (1988). *Managing the presidency: The Eisenhower legacy—from Kennedy to Reagan.* Boulder, CO: Westview Press.

Hills v. Gautreaux, 425 U.S. 284 (1976).

Holden, M., Jr. (Forthcoming). "Race and constitutional change in the 20th century: The role of the executive." In J. F. Franklin and G. R. McNeil (eds.), *African Americans and the living constitution.* Washington, DC: Smithsonian Institution Press.

Housing and Development Reporter (1979–89). Washington, DC: Bureau of National Affairs.

Huckfeldt, R., and C. W. Kohfeld. (1989). *Race and the decline of class in America.* Urbana, IL: University of Illinois Press.

Iyengar, S., and D. R. Kinder. (1987). *News that matters: Television and American opinion*. Chicago: University of Chicago Press.

Jackson, D. W., and J. W. Riddlesperger, Jr. (1993). "The Eisenhower Administration and the 1957 Civil Rights Act." In S. A. Warshaw (ed.), *Reexamining the Eisenhower presidency*. Westport, CT: Greenwood Press, pp. 85–101.

James, F. J., and E. G. Crowe. (1985). "Stronger administrative enforcement of federal fair housing laws? Lessons from the states." *Journal of Intergroup Relations* 13: 124–48.

Jaschik, S. (1991). "Justice department challenges states' practice of giving more money to black colleges." *Chronicle of Higher Education* (July 10): A1, A22.

Jaynes, G. D., and W. James, Jr. (eds.). (1989). *A common destiny: Blacks and American society*. Washington, DC: National Academy Press.

Johnson, D. B. (1978). *National party platforms, 1840–1976*. Urbana, IL: University of Illinois Press.

Jones, A. J., Jr. (1992). "Kinder, gentler? George Bush and civil rights." In R. J. Barilleaux and M. E. Stuckey (eds.), *Leadership and the Bush presidency: Prudence or drift in an era of change?* Westport, CT: Praeger, pp. 177–90.

Jones, C. O. (1984). *An introduction to the study of public policy*. 3rd ed. Monterey, CA: Brooks/Cole Publishing Company.

Katzenbach, N. (1964). Oral History. John F. Kennedy Library. Boston, Massachusetts.

Kearns, D. (1976). *Lyndon Johnson and the American dream*. New York: Harper and Row.

Kennedy, J. F. Papers. John F. Kennedy Library. Boston, Massachusetts.

Kennedy, J. F. (1961–1963). *Public papers of the president*. Washington DC: U.S. Government Printing Office.

Kennedy, R. F. Papers. John F. Kennedy Library. Boston, Massachusetts.

Kennedy presidential press conferences, The. (1978). New York: Earl M. Coleman Enterprises, Inc.

Kernell, S. (1993). *Going public: New strategies for presidential leadership*. 2nd ed. Washington, DC: CQ Press.

Kernell, S. (1986). *Going public: New strategies for presidential leadership*. Washington, DC: CQ Press.

Kessel, J. H. (1984). *Presidential parties*. Homewood, IL: Dorsey Press.

Kessel, J. H. (1977). "The seasons of presidential politics." *Social Science Quarterly* 58: 418–35.

Kessel, J. H. (1974). "Parameters of presidential politics." *Social Science Quarterly* 55: 8–24.

Keyes v. School District No. 1, Denver, 413 U.S. 189 (1973).

King, G., and L. Ragsdale. (1988). *The elusive executive: Discovering statistical patterns in the presidency*. Washington, DC: Congressional Quarterly, Inc.

King, M. L., Jr. (1964). Oral History. John F. Kennedy Library. Boston, Massachusetts.

Kingdon, J. W. (1984). *Agendas, alternatives and public policies*. Boston: Little, Brown.

Kingdon, J. W. (1973). *Congressmen's voting decisions*. New York: Harper and Row.

Kluger, R. (1975). *Simple justice: The history of Brown v. Board of Education and black America's struggle for equality*. New York: Alfred A. Knopf.

Kushner, J. A. (1983). *Fair housing: Discrimination in real estate, community development and revitalization*. Colorado Springs, CO: Shepard's/McGraw-Hill.

Lamb, C. M. (1992). "Fair housing implementation from Nixon to Reagan." Working Paper No. 11. Madison, WI: Robert M. La Follette Institute of Public Affairs, University of Wisconsin-Madison.

Lamb, C. M. (1991). "Fair housing implementation from Nixon to Reagan." Paper presented to the Annual Meeting of the American Political Science Association.

Lamb, C. M., and J. Twombly. (1993). "Taking the local: The Reagan administration, new federalism, and fair housing implementation." *Policy Studies Journal* 21: 589–98.

Lasky, V. (1963). *JFK: The man and the myth*. New York: MacMillan.

Lawson, S. F. (1991). *Running for freedom: Civil rights and black politics in America since 1941*. Philadelphia: Temple University Press.

Leadership Conference on Civil Rights. (1982). *Without justice*: A report on the conduct of the Justice Department in civil rights in 1981–1982. Washington, D.C.

LeLoup, L. T., and S. A. Shull. (1993). *Congress and the president: The policy connection*. Belmont, CA: Wadsworth Publishing Co.

LeLoup, L. T., and S. A. Shull. (1979). "Congress versus the executive: The 'two presidencies' reconsidered." *Social Science Quarterly* 59: 704–19.

Lesser, J. (1989). "The course of federalism—An historical overview." In J. C. Griffith (ed.), *Federalism: The shifting balance*. Chicago: American Bar Association.

Leuchtenburg, W. E. (1991). "The conversion of Harry Truman." *American Heritage* 42: 55–68.

Light, P. C. (1982). *The president's agenda: Domestic policy choice from Kennedy to Carter*. Baltimore: Johns Hopkins University Press.

Lindblom, C. (1980). *The policy making process*. 2d ed. Englewood Cliffs, NJ: Prentice-Hall.

Lindblom, C. E. (1959). "The science of muddling through." *Public Administration Review* 19 (Spring): 79–88.

Link, W. A. (1992). *The paradox of southern progressivism: 1800–1930*. Chapel Hill: University of North Carolina Press.

Lisio, D. J. (1985). *Hoover, Blacks, and Lily-Whites: A study of southern strategies*. Chapel Hill: University of North Carolina Press.

Lockerbee, B., and S. A. Borelli. (1989). "Getting inside the beltway: Perceptions of presidential skill and success in congress." *British Journal of Political Science* 19: 97–106.

Lorance v. AT&T Technologies, 109 S.Ct. 2261 (1989).

Lord, W. (1965). *The past that would not die*. New York: Harper and Row.

Mackenzie, G. C. (1981). *The politics of presidential appointments*. New York: Free Press.

MacKuen, M. (1981). "Social communication and the mass policy agenda." In M. Mackuen and S. Coombs (eds.), *More than news: Media power in public affairs*. Beverly Hills, CA: Sage, pp. 19–44.

Marshall, B. (1964a). *Federalism and civil rights*. New York: Columbia University Press.

Marshall, B. (1964b). Oral History. John F. Kennedy Library. Boston, Massachusetts.

Marshall, B. Papers. John F. Kennedy Library. Boston, Massachusetts.

Marshall, T. Oral History. John F. Kennedy Library. Boston, Massachusetts.

Martin v. Wilks, 490 U.S. 755 (1989).

Massey, D. S., and N. A. Denton. (1993). *American apartheid: Segregation and the making of the underclass*. Cambridge: Harvard University Press.

Mayhew, D. R. (1966). *Party loyalty among congressmen*. Cambridge: Harvard University Press.

McAdam, D. (1982). *Political process and the development of Black insurgency, 1930–1970*. Chicago: University of Chicago Press.

McAuliffe, M. S. (1981). "Commentary: Eisenhower, the president." *Journal of American History* 68: 625–32.

McCleary, R., and R. A. Hay, Jr. (1980). *Applied time series analysis for the social sciences*. Beverly Hills, CA: Sage.

McClosky, H., and J. Zaller (1984). *The American ethos: Public attitudes toward capitalism and democracy*. Cambridge: Harvard University Press.

McLaurin v. Oklahoma Board of Regents, 339 U.S. 637 (1950).

Mendoza, United States v., 464 U.S. 154 (1984).

Meredith, James. (1966). *Three years in Mississippi*. Bloomington: Indiana University Press.

Milliken v. Bradley, 418 U.S. 717 (1974); 433 U.S. 467 (1977).

Miroff, B. (1990). "The presidency and the public: Leadership as spectacle." In M. Nelson (ed.), *The presidency and the political system*. 2nd ed. Washington, DC: CQ Press, pp. 271–92.

Miroff, B. (1976). *Pragmatic illusions: The presidential politics of John F. Kennedy*. New York: David McKay Co.

Moe, T. M. (1987). "An assessment of the positive theory of legislative dominance." *Legislative Studies Quarterly* 12: 475–520.

Morgan, R. P. (1970). *The president and civil rights: policy-making by executive order*. New York: St. Martin's Press.

Murphy, W. F., and J. Tanenhaus (1990). "Publicity, public opinion, and the court." *Northwestern University Law Review* 84: 983–1023.

Nathan, R. P. (1989). "The role of the states in American federalism." In C. E. Van Horn (ed.), *The State of the States*. Washington, DC: Congressional Quarterly Press, pp. 15–32.

Nathan, R. P. (1983). *The administrative presidency*. 2nd ed. New York: John Wiley and Sons.

Navasky, V. (1971). *Kennedy justice*. New York: Atheneum.

Neustadt, R. E. (1990). *Presidential power and the modern presidents*. New York: Free Press.

Neustadt, R. E. (1980). *Presidential power*. 3rd ed. New York: John Wiley and Sons.

Neustadt, R. E. (1976). *Presidential power: The politics of leadership with reflections on Johnson and Nixon.* New York: John Wiley and Sons.

Neustadt, R. E. (1960). *Presidential power.* New York: John Wiley and Sons.

Noble, K. B. (1986a). "Employers are split on affirmative action goals." *New York Times* (March 3): 13.

Noble, K. B. (1986b). "Hiring goals: A big-vs.-small business split." *New York Times* (March 3): 1.

Northwest Airlines v. Transport Workers Union, 451 U.S. 77 (1981).

Orfield, G. M. (1975). *Congressional power: Congress and social change.* New York: Harcourt, Brace, Jovanovich.

Page, B. I., and M. P. Petracca. (1983). *The American presidency.* New York: McGraw-Hill.

Parmet, H. S. (1983). *JFK: The presidency of John F. Kennedy.* New York: The Dial Press.

Patterson v. McLean Credit Union, 491 U.S. 164 (1989).

Pear, R. (1986a). "Dispute on policy on jobs continues." *New York Times* (January 30): 9.

Pear, R. (1986b). "Justice department says court undermines job equality rule." *New York Times* (May 23): 1.

Pear, R. (1985a). "Rewriting nation's civil rights policy." *New York Times* (October 7): 10.

Pear, R. (1985b). "Rules to enforce voting rights due." *New York Times* (September 2).

Peltason, J. W. (1971). *Fifty-eight lonely men: Southern federal judges and school desegregation.* Urbana, IL: University of Illinois Press.

Perry, H. L. (1991). "Pluralist theory & national black politics in the United States." *Polity* 23: 549–65.

Peterson, M. A. (1990). *Legislating together: The White House and Capitol Hill from Eisenhower to Reagan.* Cambridge: Harvard University Press.

"Plan to end minority hiring goals called 'uncontrollable.' " (1985). *San Francisco Chronicle,* (August 16): 18.

Polsby, N. W. (1984). *Political innovation in America.* New Haven, CT: Yale University Press.

Poole, K. T. (1981). "Dimensions of interest group evaluations of the U.S. Senate, 1969–1978." *American Journal of Political Science* 25: 49–67.

Powledge, F. (1991). *Free at last? The civil rights movement and the people who made it.* Boston: Little, Brown.

Price Waterhouse v. Hopkins, 490 U.S. 228 (1989).

Pritchard, A. (1983). "Presidents do influence voting in the U.S. Congress," *Legislative Studies Quarterly* 8: 691–712.

Public papers of the presidents of the United States: George Bush. (1989–1993). Washington, DC: U.S. Government Printing Office.

Public papers of the presidents of the United States: Ronald Reagan. (1981–1989). Washington, DC: U.S. Government Printing Office.

Public papers of the presidents of the United States: James E. Carter. (1977–1981). Washington, DC: U.S. Government Printing Office.

Public papers of the presidents of the United States: Gerald R. Ford. (1974–1977). Washington, DC: U.S. Government Printing Office.

Public papers of the presidents of the United States: Richard M. Nixon. (1969–1974). Washington, DC: U.S. Government Printing Office.

Public papers of the presidents of the United States: Lyndon B. Johnson. (1963–1969). Washington, DC: U.S. Government Printing Office.

Public papers of the presidents of the United States: John F. Kennedy. (1961–1963). Washington, DC: U.S. Government Printing Office.

Public papers of the presidents of the United States: Dwight D. Eisenhower. (1953–1961). Washington, DC: U.S. Government Printing Office.

Ragsdale, L. (1984). "Politics of presidential speechmaking, 1949–80." *American Political Science Review* 78: 971–84.

Redford, E. S. (1969). *Democracy in the administrative state*. New York: Oxford University Press.

Reeves, R. (1993). *President Kennedy: Profile of power*. New York: Simon and Schuster.

Reeves, T. C. (1991). *A question of character: A life of John F. Kennedy*. New York: Free Press.

Reitman v. Mulkey, 387 U.S. 369 (1967).

Ricci, D. M. (1984). *The tragedy of political science: Politics, scholarship and democracy*. New Haven, CT: Yale University Press.

Riker, W. H. (1964). *Federalism*. Boston: Little, Brown.

Ripley, R. B., and G. A. Franklin. (1986). *Bureaucracy and policy implementation*. 2nd ed. Homewood, IL: Dorsey Press.

Rivers, D., and N. L. Rose. (1985). "Passing the president's program: Public opinion and presidential influence in congress." *American Journal of Political Science* 29: 183–96.

Rockman, B. A. (1984). *The leadership question*. New York: Praeger.

Rodgers, H. R., and C. S. Bullock, III. (1972). *Law and social change*. New York: McGraw-Hill.

Sabatier, P., and H. Jenkins-Smith. (1993). *Policy change and learning*. Boulder, CO: Westview Press.

Salokar, R. M. (1992). "Gay rights in Florida: Privacy, interest groups and politics." Paper presented at the Annual Meeting of the American Political Science Association.

Schlesinger, A. M., Jr. (1978). *Robert Kennedy and his times*. Boston: Houghton Mifflin; New York: Ballantine Books.

Schlesinger, A. M., Jr. (1965, 1967). *A thousand days: John F. Kennedy in the White House*. Boston: Houghton Mifflin; New York: Fawcett Crest.

Schlesinger, R., and E. Israel. (1966). *The State of the Union Messages of the Presidents: 1905–1966*. Vol. III. New York: Chelsea House.

Scholz, J. T., and F. Wei. (1986). "Regulatory enforcement in a federalist system." *American Political Science Review* 80: 1249–70.

Scholz, J. T., J. Twombly, and B. Headrick. (1991). "Street level political controls over federal bureaucracy." *American Political Science Review* 85: 829–50.

Schuman, H., C. Steeh, and L. Bobo. (1985). *Racial attitudes in America: Trends and interpretations*. Cambridge: Harvard University Press.

Schwarz, J. E., and B. Fenmore. (1977). "Presidential election results and congressional roll call behavior: The cases of 1964, 1968, and 1972." *Legislative Studies Quarterly* 2: 409–22.

Schwemm, R. G. (1991). *Housing discrimination law and litigation.* New York: Clark Boardman Callaghan.

Schwemm, R. G. (1989). "Federal fair housing enforcement: A critique of the Reagan administration's record and recommendations for the future." In R. C. Govan and W. L. Taylor (eds.), *One nation indivisible: The civil rights challenge for the 1990s.* Washington, DC: Citizens' Commission on Civil Rights, pp. 268–303.

Scigliano, R. (1971). *The supreme court and the presidency.* New York: Free Press.

Shelley v. Kraemer, 334 U.S. 1 (1948).

Shenon, Philip. (1985). "Meese sees racism in goals on hiring." *New York Times* (September 18).

Shriver, S. (1988.) Oral History Interview. "Kennedy's call to King." John F. Kennedy Library, Boston, Massachusetts.

Shull, S. A. (1993). *A kinder, gentler racism? The Reagan-Bush civil rights legacy.* Armonk, NY: M. E. Sharpe, Inc.

Shull, S. A. (1989). *The president and civil rights policy: leadership and change.* Westport, CT: Greenwood Press.

Shull, S. A. (1983). *Domestic policy formation: presidential-congressional partnership?* Westport, CT: Greenwood Press.

Sigelman, L. (1979). "Reassessing the 'two presidencies' thesis." *Journal of Politics* 41: 1195–1205.

Skowronek, S. (1993). *The politics presidents make.* Cambridge: Harvard University Press.

Skowronek, S. (1990). "Presidential leadership in political time." In M. Nelson (ed.), *The presidency and the political system.* 3rd ed. Washington, DC: Congressional Quarterly Press.

Smith, M. E. (1980). *John F. Kennedy's 13 great mistakes in the White House.* Smithtown, NY: Suffolk House.

Smith, R. M. (1993). "Beyond Tocqueville, Myrdal, and Hartz: The multiple traditions in America." *The American Political Science Review* 87: 549–66.

Smith v. Allwright, 321 U.S. 649 (1944).

Sorensen, T. C. (1969). *The Kennedy legacy.* New York: MacMillan.

Sorensen, T. C. (1965). *Kennedy.* New York: Harper and Row.

Sorensen, T. C. Papers. John F. Kennedy Library, Boston, Massachusetts.

Southern, D. (1987). *Gunner Mydral and black-white relations: The use and abuse of an American dilemma.* Baton Rouge: Louisiana State University Press.

Sperlich, P. W. (1975). "Bargaining and overload: An essay on presidential power." In A. Wildavsky (ed.), *Perspectives on the presidency.* Boston: Little, Brown and Co., pp. 406–30.

Stampp, K. M. (1965). *The era of reconstruction, 1865–1877.* New York: Vintage Books.

Steel, L. (1968). "Nine men in black who think white." *New York Times Magazine* (October 13): 56 ff.

Stern, M. (1992). *Calculating visions: Kennedy, Johnson and civil rights.* New Brunswick, NJ: Rutgers University Press.

Stern, M. (1989a). "John F. Kennedy and civil rights: From congress to the presidency." *Presidential Studies Quarterly* 19: 797–823.

Stern, M. (1989b). "Presidential strategies and civil rights: Eisenhower, the early years, 1952–1954." *Presidential Studies Quarterly* 19 (Fall): 769–95.

Sundquist, J. L. (1981). *Decline and resurgence of Congress.* Washington, DC: Brookings Institution.

Sundquist, J. L. (1968). *Politics and policy: The Eisenhower, Kennedy, and Johnson years.* Washington, DC: Brookings Institution.

Swann v. Charlotte-Mecklenburg Board of Education, 402 U.S. 1 (1971).

Sweatt v. Painter, 339 U.S. 629 (1950).

Tatlovich, R., and B. Daynes. (1979). "Towards a paradigm to explain presidential power." *Presidential Studies Quarterly* 9: 428–40.

Teamsters v. United States, 431 U.S. 324 (1977).

Thomas, N. C. (1977). "Studying the presidency: Where do we go from here?" *Presidential Studies Quarterly* 7: 169–75.

Thompson, K. W., ed. (1985). *The Kennedy presidency.* Lanham, MD: University of America Press.

Thornburg v. Gingles, 478 U.S. 30 (1986).

Tulis, J. K. (1990). "The interpretable presidency." In M. Nelson (ed.), *The presidency and the political system.* 3rd ed. Washington, DC: Congressional Quarterly Press.

Turner, M. A., R. J. Struyk, and J. Yinger. (1991). *Housing discrimination study: Synthesis.* Washington, DC: Department of Housing and Urban Development, Office of Policy Development and Research.

Twombly, J., and C. M. Lamb. (1992). "Fair housing implementation from Carter to Reagan." Paper presented at the American Political Science Association Convention, Chicago, September 4.

U.S. Bureau of the Census. (1962). *Congressional district data book, 1962.* Washington, DC: U.S. Government Printing Office.

U.S. Commission on Civil Rights. (1992). *Prospects and impact of losing state and local agencies from the federal fair housing system.* Washington, DC: U.S. Government Printing Office.

U.S. Commission on Civil Rights. (1979). *The federal fair housing enforcement effort.* Washington, DC: U.S. Government Printing Office.

U.S. Commission on Civil Rights. (1974). *The federal civil rights enforcement effort—1974: To provide for fair housing.* Washington, DC: U.S. Government Printing Office.

U.S. Department of Commerce, Bureau of the Census. (1984). *Federal expenditures by state for fiscal year 1983.* Washington, DC: U.S. Government Printing Office.

U.S. Department of Housing and Urban Development. (1992a). *1991 annual report.* Washington, DC: U.S. Government Printing Office.

U.S. Department of Housing and Urban Development. (1992b). *Profile of HUD.* Washington, DC: Department of Housing and Urban Development, Office of Management and Planning.

U.S. Department of Housing and Urban Development. (1991). *The state of fair housing.* Washington, DC: U.S. Government Printing Office.

U.S. Department of Housing and Urban Development. (1989). *New directions in housing and urban policy.* Washington, DC: U.S. Government Printing Office.

U.S. Department of Housing and Urban Development. (1988). *Fair housing—The law in perspective.* Washington, DC: U.S. Government Printing Office.

U.S. Department of Housing and Urban Development. (1981). *1980 annual report.* Washington, DC: U.S. Government Printing Office.

U.S. House of Representatives, Subcommittee on Civil and Constitutional Rights. (1987). *Hearings on the fair housing amendments act.* 99th Cong., 2d sess. Washington, DC: U.S. Government Printing Office.

U.S. Office of Management and Budget. (1977–1989). *Budget of the United States government.* Washington, DC: U.S. Government Printing Office.

Vose, C. E. (1959). *Caucasians only: The Supreme Court, the NAACP, and the restrictive covenant cases.* Berkeley: University of California Press.

Walker, J. L. (1977). "Setting the agenda in the U.S. Senate: A theory of problem selection." *British Journal of Political Science* 47: 596–617.

Wallace, J. E., W. L. Holshouser, T. S. Lane, and J. Williams. (1985). *The fair housing assistance program evaluation.* Washington, DC: U.S. Department of Housing and Urban Development, Office of Policy Development and Research.

Wards Cove Packing Co. v. Atonio, 490 U.S. 642 (1989).

Warth v. Seldin, 422 U.S. 490 (1975).

Wasby, S. L. (1982). *Vote dilution, minority voting rights, and the courts.* Washington, DC: Joint Center for Political Studies.

Wasby, S. L. (1970). *The impact of the United States Supreme Court.* Homewood, IL: The Dorsey Press.

Wasby, S. L., A. A. D'Amato, and R. M. Metrailer. (1977). *Desegregation from Brown to Alexander: An exploration of Supreme Court strategies.* Carbondale, IL: Southern Illinois University Press.

Washington v. Seattle School District No. 1, 458 U.S. 457 (1982).

Wayne, S. J. (1982). "Expectations of the president." In D. Graber (ed.), *The president and the public.* Philadelphia: Institute for the Study of Human Affairs, pp. 17–38.

Wayne, S. J. (1978). *The legislative presidency.* New York: Harper and Row.

Weiss, N. J. (1983). *Farewell to the party of Lincoln: Black politics in the age of FDR.* Princeton, NJ: Princeton University Press.

West Virginia University Hospitals v. Casey, 499 U.S. 83 (1991).

White, Lee. Papers. John F. Kennedy Library. Boston, Massachusetts.

White, T. H. (1961). *The making of the president 1960.* New York: Atheneum.

Whitman, A. Diary Series. Dwight D. Eisenhower Library. Abilene, Kansas.

Whitman, A. Name Series. Dwight D. Eisenhower Library. Abilene, Kansas.

Whitman, A. Press Conference Series. Dwight D. Eisenhower Library. Abilene, Kansas.

Wiecek, W. M. (1989). "Civil rights and equality." In L. W. Levy, K. L. Karst, and D. J. Mahoney. *Civil rights and equality: Selections of the American Constitution.* New York: MacMillan Publishing Company.

Wilkins, R. (1964). Oral History. John F. Kennedy Library. Boston, Massachusetts.

Wills, G. (1981). *The Kennedy imprisonment: A meditation on power.* Boston: Little, Brown.

Wofford, H. (1980). *Of Kennedys and kings: Making sense of the 1960s.* New York: Farrar, Straus, Giroux.

Wofford, H. (1965, 1968). Oral History. John F. Kennedy Library. Boston, Massachusetts.

Wofford, Harris. Papers. John F. Kennedy Library. Boston, Massachusetts.

Wolk, A. (1971). *The presidency and black civil rights: Eisenhower to Nixon.* Rutherford, NJ: Fairleigh Dickinson Press.

Wood, B. D. (1990). "Does politics make a difference at the EEOC?" *American Journal of Political Science* 34: 503–30.

Wood, B. D., and R. W. Waterman. (1991). "The Dynamics of political control of the bureaucracy." *American Political Science Review* 85: 801–28.

Wright, G. C., Jr. (1976). "Linear models for evaluating conditional relationships." *American Journal of Political Science* 20: 349–73.

Wygant v. Jackson Board of Education, 476 U.S. 267 (1986).

Zangrando, R.L. (1980). *The NAACP crusade against lynching, 1909–1950.* Philadelphia: Temple University Press.

Index

About the Contributors

RONALD E. BROWN is an Associate Professor of Political Science at Wayne State University. His major interests include the study of the influence of race and religion on African American political life. He is currently working on a co-edited book entitled *Black Political Participation*. Professor Brown has co-authored articles in the *American Political Science Review* and the *National Review of Political Science*.

JEFFREY E. COHEN is an Associate Professor of Political Science at the University of Kansas, specializing in American politics and public policy. He is the author of two books, *The Politics of the U.S. Cabinet: Representation in the Executive Branch, 1789–1984* and *The Politics of Telecommunications Regulation: The States and the Divestiture of AT&T*. He has also published numerous articles in leading political science journals, including the *American Political Science Review* and the *American Journal of Political Science*.

ROBERT R. DETLEFSEN is Director of Research and Education at the Center for Individual Rights in Washington, D.C. He has been a Postdoctoral Fellow in the Program on Constitutional Government at Harvard University, and has taught at the University of California, Berkeley. He is the author of *Civil Rights Under Reagan*, and his articles and reviews have been published in scholarly journals and in *The New Republic*. His current research interests include constitutional interpretation and administrative law.

DENNIS W. GLEIBER is an Associate Professor of Political Science at the University of New Orleans. He has published articles in, among others, *American Political Science Review, American Journal of Political Science, American Politics Quarterly, Western Political Quarterly, Legislative Politics Quarterly,* and *Scandinavian Political Studies.* His interests include methodology and formal and positive theory.

DONALD W. JACKSON is the Herman Brown Professor of Political Science at Texas Christian University. He practiced law in Dallas, Texas from 1962 to 1968 and served in 1974–1975 as a Judicial Fellow at the Supreme Court of the United States. His published research on American presidents and civil rights policy includes articles on Presidents Eisenhower and Kennedy (with James W. Riddlesperger, Jr.). His most recent major works include *Even the Children of Strangers: Equality Under the U.S. Constitution* and *Comparative Judicial Review and Public Policy* (co-edited with C. Neal Tate, Greenwood Press, 1992). In addition to his continuing research on American presidents, he is presently researching the formative years of the European Court of Human Rights.

JAMES D. KING is an Associate Professor on the Political Science faculty at the University of Wyoming. His research focuses on American political institutions, with particular emphasis on presidential staffing and electoral politics. The products of this research have appeared in *Presidential Studies Quarterly, Journal of Politics, Social Science Quarterly, Western Political Quarterly,* and other scholarly journals.

CHARLES M. LAMB is an Associate Professor of Political Science at the State University of New York at Buffalo, where he teaches courses in public law and public policy. He has co-edited four volumes, including *Implementation of Civil Rights Policy* with Charles S. Bullock III. Currently he is working on a book on federal fair housing policy from the New Deal through the Clinton administration.

JAMES W. RIDDLESPERGER, JR. is an Associate Professor of Political Science at Texas Christian University. His research focuses on American politics, with a particular emphasis on the presidency. His articles have appeared in, among others, the following journals: *Journal of Politics, Policy Studies Journal, Social Science Quarterly, Social Science Journal, Presidential Studies Quarterly, Legislative Studies Quarterly,* and *Judicature.*

ALBERT C. RINGELSTEIN is an Adjunct Assistant Professor of Government at the University of New Orleans. He is the author of several articles, appearing in such journals as *Western Political Quarterly, Social Science Journal,* and *Congress and the Presidency.* His teaching interests are in American political institutions and behavior.

STEVEN A. SHULL is a Research Professor of Political Science at the University of New Orleans. He is the author or editor of eleven books and dozens of articles in scholarly journals. His most recently published books are *A Kinder, Gentler Racism?* and *Congress and the President.* He was a Fulbright Senior Scholar in Hong Kong, and received his university's Career Achievement Award for Excellence in Research.

MARK STERN is Professor of Political Science and Vice President for Academic Affairs at Shepherd College in Shepherdstown, West Virginia. He is author of over two dozen articles in scholarly journals. His most recently published book is entitled *Calculating Visions: Kennedy, Johnson, and Civil Rights.*

JIM TWOMBLY is an Assistant Professor of Political Science at the State University of New York at Buffalo. He has published articles in such publications as the *American Political Science Review.* His current research interests include determinants of bureaucratic behavior with emphasis on OSHA and HUD, regulation as symbolic politics, and the voting behavior of political parties in Congress.

STEPHEN L. WASBY is a professor of political science at the State University of New York at Albany. He is the author of *The Supreme Court in the Federal Judicial System* (4th ed.) and co-author of *Desegregation from Brown to Alexander: An Exploration of Supreme Court Strategies*, as well as a number of articles on civil rights litigation by interest groups— which is one of his continuing major research interests.

Policy Studies Organization publications issued with Greenwood Press/Quorum Books

Using Theory to Improve Program and Policy Evaluations
Huey-tysh Chen and Peter H. Rossi, editors

Comparative Judicial Review and Public Policy
Donald W. Jackson and C. Neal Tate, editors

Moving the Earth: Cooperative Federalism and Implementation of the Surface Mining Act
Uday Desai, editor

Professional Developments in Policy Studies
Stuart Nagel

International Agricultural Trade and Market Development in the 1990s
John W. Helmuth and Don F. Hadwiger, editors

Comparative Studies of Local Economic Development: Problems in Policy Implementation
Peter B. Meyer, editor

Ownership, Control, and the Future of Housing Policy
R. Allen Hays, editor

Public Administration in China
Miriam K. Mills and Stuart S. Nagel, editors

Public Policy in China
Stuart S. Nagel and Miriam K. Mills, editors

Minority Group Influence: Agenda Setting, Formulation, and Public Policy
Paula D. McClain, editor

Problems and Prospects for Nuclear Waste Disposal Policy
Eric B. Herzik and Alvin H. Mushkatel, editors

American Indian Policy
Lyman H. Legters and Fremont J. Lyden, editors

ISBN 0-313-29624-3

EAN

9 780313 296246

HARDCOVER BAR CODE